RECYCLING
ADVANCED
ENGLISH
REVISED EDITION

CLARE WEST

GEORGIAN PRESS

Georgian Press (Jersey) Limited
Pirouet House
Union Street
St Helier
Jersey JE4 8ZQ
Channel Islands

www.georgianpress.co.uk

First published by Georgian Press (Jersey) Limited 1995
Reprinted six times
This revised edition first published 2002
Reprinted 2004, 2005, 2007

ISBN 978-1-873630-58-7 (with removable key)

Produced by AMR Design Limited (www.amrdesign.com)
Drawings by Martyn Ford

Printed in Egypt by International Printing House

CONTENTS

SECTION 3   VOCABULARY

SECTION 4   WORD STUDY

SECTION 5   WRITING

The Key begins on page 241 of the With Key edition.

INTRODUCTION

Recycling Advanced English is for students at advanced level who wish to improve their general English and/or prepare for the Cambridge Certificate in Advanced English (CAE) or the revised Certificate of Proficiency in English (CPE). It can be used to supplement any coursebook at this level, and is suitable for use in the classroom, for homework, or (in the case of the With Key edition) for self-study.

The book aims to provide:

- coverage of the five main areas of difficulty at advanced level – grammar, phrasal verbs, vocabulary, word study and writing
- concise, clearly-presented explanations
- extensive practice of each point covered
- a strong element of recycling
- a user-friendly, attractive layout, so that the material is accessible and a pleasure to use
- a variety of exercise types which are not exam-specific
- examples of all the CAE and revised CPE task-types for Papers 2 and 3
- an appendix of useful reference material.

Recycling Advanced English is divided into five distinct sections:

Section 1 GRAMMAR (25 units)

This large section aims to cover all the major grammatical points at advanced level, with practice and revision exercises for consolidation.

Section 2 PHRASAL VERBS (15 units)

In this section, phrasal verbs are grouped according to their particle, and there is also a focus on three-part phrasal verbs and phrasal verbs as nouns, with extensive practice in varying formats.

Section 3 VOCABULARY (22 units)

Here there are texts and tasks presenting and practising vocabulary from key topics which regularly occur in advanced classwork and examination syllabuses.

Section 4 WORD STUDY (17 units)

This section attempts to get beneath the surface of the language and to delve deeper into the linguistic areas which cause difficulties for the advanced learner, such as idioms, false friends, humour and collocations.

RECYCLING UNITS are an important element in Sections 1 – 4, providing consolidation of each block of preceding units. It is therefore advisable to use the Recycling units in the order in which they appear.

Section 5 WRITING (11 units)

This section offers guidance on a number of different writing tasks and styles, with appropriate phrases to learn, as well as practice exercises. All the types of composition required for CAE and revised CPE are covered, with model answers in the Appendix. There is also a unit of tips on writing, and additional writing tasks for extra practice.

The APPENDIX provides additional grammar reference material and model answers for writing tasks.

The Revised Edition

The book has been revised and expanded for a number of reasons: to update some of the material, to incorporate the valuable suggestions sent in by readers, and to bring the tasks in line with the revisions to the CAE and CPE syllabuses. Much of the book remains essentially the same as its predecessor, but there are minor alterations to almost all units, and major changes to many of the tasks, especially those in the Recycling units. There are five completely new units.

New material includes:

- a page on **Discourse markers** in Unit 12 of the Grammar section
- two new units in the Vocabulary section – **E-mail and the internet** and **UK government**
- three new units in the Word Study section – **Humour, puns and jokes, Collocations** and **New language**
- additions to the Writing section to cover all **CAE** and **revised CPE task types**.

I would like to thank all the people who have offered their comments and suggestions. Whether you are using this book for exam preparation, or purely to improve your English at advanced level, I hope you will enjoy **Recycling Advanced English** and find that it motivates you and helps you to make progress.

Clare West, 2002

Articles and uncountables

No article is used when generalising (with plural, abstract and uncountable nouns) but **the** or **a/an** is used when talking about particular examples. The definite article **the** is used when it is clear which noun we mean, whereas the indefinite article **a/an** is used when a noun is referred to for the first time.

Singular countable nouns must always have an article (or possessive), except in the following cases: prepositions with *home, school, college, university, church, work, class, hospital, prison, bed, sea, breakfast, lunch, supper, dinner.*

Note also:
* *at night, on foot, by car/bus/tube* etc. (means of transport), *to/in/from town* (when referring to the town we live in, a local large town or the capital), *go to sleep* and *go home*

Notice the difference between *She's in prison* (she's a prisoner) and *She's in the prison* (she either works there or is visiting).

The article is also omitted in certain double expressions:
* *from top to bottom, on land and sea, hand in hand, face to face*

The indefinite article **a/an** is normally used to indicate someone's profession:
* *He wants to train as a psychotherapist.*

A Complete the sentences by putting *the, a/an* or no article (–) into the spaces.

1 You remember my sister Jane? ____ one who has always been afraid of ____ spiders?

2 She's been studying ____ architecture at ____ university for ____ last three years.

3 At ____ moment she's researching into ____ work of Le Corbusier. Don't you know him? He's ____ well-known French architect.

4 She's pretty busy in ____ daytime, but she finds she's at ____ bit of ____ loose end at night, so ____ last year she joined ____ film club.

5 ____ club members can watch ____ films at ____ very low prices, in ____ disused warehouse on ____ other side of ____ town.

6 So when she gets home from ____ college, she usually goes straight over there by ____ bike, and has ____ drink and ____ sandwich before ____ film starts.

7 One evening she was in such ____ hurry to get there that she had ____ accident.

8 She was knocked down by ____ car and had to spend two months in ____ hospital.

9 When I went to visit her, I was shocked to find her swathed in ____ bandages from ____ head to ____ toe.

10 But luckily her injuries looked worse than they really were, and she managed to make ____ very speedy recovery.

The is also used with

a a unique person or object: • *the President* • *the North Pole*
b musical instruments • *He plays the guitar.*
c some adjectives with plural meanings • *the rich*
d nationality adjectives, ships, geographical areas, most mountain ranges, oceans, seas, rivers, deserts, hotels, cinemas, theatres, plural names of countries, island groups, regions
e when talking about a whole species: • *the African elephant*

No article is used when talking about continents, most countries, towns, streets, etc. (except *the High Street*), lakes, and the main buildings of a particular town:
• *Kingston Town Hall*

The is not used with *most* except with the superlative:
• *most people* • *the most incredible sight*

B Correct the sentences if necessary. Tick any which are already correct.

1 Tony had always wanted to explore the foothills of Himalayas.

2 So when he was offered an early retirement package by his firm, he decided to take advantage of the opportunity.

3 First he needed to get really fit, so he spent a month training in Lake District.

4 When he could run up Buttermere Fell without stopping, he considered he was ready.

5 He booked a trip with a well-known trekking company and flew out to the Kathmandu, the capital of Nepal.

6 His group were planning to trek in Annapurna region, but unfortunately Nepalese were beginning to get worried about the amount of damage being done to their ancient mountains by the constant pummelling of climbers' feet.

7 So they temporarily suspended permission for foreigners to climb or use the footpaths in the area.

8 Group leader was very apologetic, but he laid on rafting on River Trisuli and sightseeing in the capital.

9 After a few days, the authorities lifted their ban, and Tony was able to trek through some of world's most beautiful scenery, with breathtaking views of the Mount Everest and Kanchenjunga.

10 At night, group were accommodated in the simple village rooms and ate with Nepalese.

11 Most of group were more experienced trekkers than Tony, and several of them had visited Himalayas before.

12 All in all, Tony reckoned it was most exciting experience he'd ever had, and vowed to return to the Nepal at very first opportunity.

The indefinite article **a/an** cannot be used with uncountable nouns. Most nouns in English are either countable or uncountable, but the following may be used countably or uncountably:
- *cold, country, taste, wine, coffee, tea, cake, cheese, work, hair, life, death*

C Decide whether the nouns in *italics* are being used countably (C) or uncountably (U).

1 I'll have a *coffee* while I sort my papers out.
2 It's a matter of *life* and *death*.
3 They've always dreamed of living in the *country*.
4 Celebrities and critics flooded into the West End to see Harold Pinter's latest *work*.
5 I like a bit of *cheese* after my main course.
6 The reason he's so bogged down at *work* is that he's had a heavy *cold* for the last fortnight.
7 His *death* came as a terrible shock to his colleagues.
8 She's furnished the flat with such *taste*, hasn't she!

Note especially these **uncountable nouns**:
- *furniture, luggage, news, information, progress, knowledge, research, advice*

Many and **(a) few** are used with countables, **much** and **(a) little** with uncountables.

D Match the two halves of the sentences correctly.

1 Scientists have made little
2 It is doubtful whether we have enough
3 I don't suppose there are many
4 I can guarantee he'll give you some
5 The examiner asked both
6 I had to check every
7 I was hoping you could let me have a
8 She's so well-groomed – she never has a
9 He hasn't got much
10 Could you let me know if there's any

A spanner, if I promise to return it tomorrow.
B applicants for that job, are there?
C news about my sister?
D progress in their research into the common cold.
E natural gas for the next fifty years.
F the candidates to sit down.
G excellent advice.
H hair out of place.
I single connection, before I found the fault.
J luggage, has he?

Present tenses

The present simple is used

a to express what happens habitually or regularly:
  • *I go to Italy every summer.*
b to describe facts that are always or usually true:
  • *That road leads to Oxford.*
c to describe natural and scientific laws.
d with verbs that do not normally take the continuous form, such as *dislike, appear, belong, understand.*
  There is a list of these verbs in **Section 1** of the Appendix.
e in the **if** clause of the first conditional.
f with **if** and **when** for parallel facts and conditions:
  • *When you turn the key, the engine starts.*
g for explanations and instructions.
h to describe the sequence of events in a film, play or book.
i for headlines in a newspaper.

(For the future use of the present simple, see **Unit 4**.)

A Match the different uses of the present simple with the categories in the study box above.

1 Local girl wins national contest
2 First you turn the dial, then you press the ignition switch ...
3 The hero meets a girl in a café, falls in love with her and ...
4 We usually take part in the general knowledge quiz on Fridays.
5 It appears that there was some mistake in the information we received.
6 The earth revolves around the sun.
7 Traffic flows much better outside rush hours.
8 If he saves up, he'll soon be able to afford a new computer.
9 The great monastery library now belongs to the state.
10 When you hear the police siren, you slow down and pull in, to allow emergency vehicles to pass.
11 Fisherman finds treasure trove
12 Wood floats on water.
13 Now that he's retired, he watches football every afternoon on satellite TV.
14 I understand that none of the children actually qualified for the award.
15 You separate the eggs, then whip the whites until they're stiff.
16 If you cry wolf too often, people don't pay attention when you really need help.

> **The present continuous** is used
>
> **a** to refer to what is happening now. Key words: **at the moment**, **at present**, **now**, **currently**, **today**, **this week**.
> **b** to describe a repeated action, sometimes with annoyance:
> - *She's always criticising other people!*
> **c** to talk about a temporary habit:
> - *He's smoking a lot these days.*
> **d** to give a running commentary on an event:
> - *Look, the door's opening ...*
>
> (For the future use of the present continuous, see **Unit 4**.)

B Correct the sentences if necessary. Tick any which are already correct.

1 I'm always forgetting to set the alarm.
2 It sounds a marvellous idea.
3 She's studying hard for her exams at the moment.
4 Are you understanding what the lecturer said?
5 I'm thinking that they made a mistake.
6 I'm seeing my friend Jean tonight.
7 The police aren't knowing why he came here.
8 He's constantly leaving his papers all over the place.
9 She jogs around the park three times a week.
10 He commutes to Paris every day this week.

C Decide whether to use the present simple or the present continuous in these sentences.

1 You (look) very worried. What you (think) about?
2 Listen, he (climb) the stairs! What he (do) now? He (ring) the bell!
3 Thank goodness Barbara (take) more exercise these days! She (seem) much fitter, you (not think)?
4 When water (boil), it (give off) steam.
5 Alex never (break) a promise or (let down) a friend.
6 The house (stand) on its own, on a hill that (overlook) the park.
7 I (know) her husband (look for) a new job at the moment, but I (not suppose) he will find one quickly.
8 When you (heat) the pan, the fat (begin) to sizzle.
9 The Foreign Ministers of several EU countries currently (meet) in Luxembourg, where they (attempt) to negotiate a solution.
10 He always (spill) coffee on his shirt! It (make) me furious!
11 At weekends she frequently (drive) up to her mother's in Liverpool, and (spend) an evening with her sister on the way back.
12 I'm a bit worried about Greg. He (work) too hard in his present job. He really (need) a holiday.

The **present perfect** is used to refer to

a actions in a period of time which is not yet finished.
Key words: **already**, **yet**, **so far**, **up to now**, **for** (a period of time), **since** (a fixed point in time), **ever**, **before**.

b actions in the recent past where the time is not known or not important. Key words: **just**, **recently**, **lately**.

c actions in the recent past with an effect on the present.

d habitual actions which started in the past and are still going on.

e states which began in the past and are continuing.

It is also used

f with verbs that do not normally take the continuous form (see above).

It does not make sense to use the **present perfect** with an adverb of finished time, such as **yesterday**, **last week**, **in 1924**.

The **present perfect continuous** is used to stress that

a a present perfect action is continuing.

b the action is very recent.

c the action has a result in the present.

It is not used with clearly defined, completed or quantified activities:

• *I've written ten letters so far this morning.*
Compare: *I've been writing letters all morning.*

D Correct the sentences if necessary. Tick any which are already correct.

1 I am studying English here since August.
2 I've interviewed five applicants and it's still only 11.30!
3 We have met several fascinating people at the conference last week.
4 Once upon a time a beautiful princess has lived in a castle ...
5 Have you ever read any of Hemingway's novels?
6 I've been owning this answerphone for three years.
7 They haven't been selling all the tickets for the Cup Final yet.
8 My friends are married for a long time now.
9 I haven't been feeling at all well lately.
10 A light plane has been crashing in the French Alps.
11 I've already been speaking to the delegates three times.
12 A barrister in a case which is being heard at the High Court in London has accused the authorities of negligence.

E Complete the following sentences with *for* or *since*, and the correct form of the verb in brackets.

1 I (not have) time to do any typing _____ Monday.
2 Nobody (hear) from Amanda _____ she went to the Seychelles.
3 She (wear) the same old clothes _____ a week.
4 He (not ride) a bike _____ 1970.
5 I don't think I (see) you _____ the sales conference.
6 It (not snow) here _____ ages.
7 They (live) in that house _____ it was built.
8 My neighbour (not speak) to me _____ more than two years.
9 I (not buy) a new battery _____ last year.
10 She (wait) for you _____ an hour and a half.

Modal verbs

The verbs **will**, **would**, **shall**, **should**, **can**, **could**, **may**, **might**, **must**, **ought to** and **used to** are called modal verbs, because they convey a particular meaning or mood. Modal verbs have some important grammatical features.

1 Apart from **can** and **could** they do not have past or future forms, or use any auxiliary verb (e.g. **do/did**) either to make a question or a negative:

- *Will she be there?* • *I couldn't help it.*

An exception to this is **used to**, which often takes **did** as an alternative auxiliary:
- *Did you use to be good at maths?* • *Used you to be good at maths?*

2 Modal verbs (except **ought to** and **used to**) take the infinitive without **to**:
- *They can't have arrived yet.*
- *You must have seen her.*
(See **Unit 7** for the different infinitive forms.)

An alternative to **can** is **be able to**, which is used for all tenses:
- *They'll be able to book the tickets soon.*
Could is used as the past simple or conditional of **can**.

An alternative to **must** is **have to**, which is used for all tenses:
- *Surely you didn't have to pay!*
See the study boxes below for differences in meaning of these verbs.

Note the short forms **will not ~ won't**, **shall not ~ shan't**, **cannot ~ can't**.

Dare and **need** can be used either as normal verbs:
- *I didn't dare (to) mention it.*
- *He doesn't need to borrow any money.*
or as modal verbs: • *She daren't tell him the truth.* • *You needn't cry.*

See the study box below for the different uses of **need**.

A Complete the sentences with the correct verb from the box.

will	dare	may	be able	ought	should	used	have

1 How _____ you speak to me like that?

2 He really _____ admit that he is to blame for the whole affair.

3 When she was younger, she never _____ to wear make-up.

4 _____ I use your phone, please?

5 Do you think he'll _____ to come up with the money in time?

6 Steel yourself – it's just possible you might _____ to pay a heavy fine.

7 The authorities _____ to have investigated the incident more thoroughly.

8 There's every likelihood our candidate _____ win the election.

B Correct the sentences if necessary. Tick any which are already correct.

1 Did you must renew your visa last February?
2 Your accountant ought to have give you better advice.
3 The President can't to be re-elected for a fourth term.
4 You could come on the expedition if you wanted to.
5 I might had returned the book. I just can't remember.
6 Will you can help me with my luggage if I tell you exactly when I'm leaving?
7 They didn't could have a picnic because of the inclement weather.
8 The police must have preferred charges against him by now.

Must/mustn't are used

a to express commands or the authority of the speaker:
   • *You must do what I say in future.*

b to express an internal obligation, from the speaker's viewpoint:
   • *I mustn't forget to phone Jake this evening.*

Have got to can be used in all tenses instead of **must** to express external obligation, especially rules or laws made by someone else:
• *We've got to check in at least an hour before take-off.*

The modal form **needn't** is usually used to express the speaker's own opinion or viewpoint: • *You needn't phone me unless there's any problem.*

Don't need to is less personal and is usually used to express lack of external obligation: • *If you're a UK citizen, you don't need to have a work permit.*

Didn't need to do and **didn't have to do** mean that something was not done, because it was not necessary.
Needn't have done means that something was done, although it was not necessary.

C Complete the sentences, using the correct word or phrase from the pair in brackets.

1 You _____ take flowers to your hostess if you don't want to. (mustn't / needn't)
2 She _____ do all the work herself, because nobody will help her. (must / has to)
3 I'm so tired, I really _____ go to bed now.   (must / have to)
4 What a pity you _____ go now! You'll just catch your train if you hurry.   (must / have to)
5 Yesterday all the students _____ read a poem aloud. (must / had to)
6 I was going to book the tickets, but Angus bought them on his way home, so I _____.   (didn't need to / needn't have done)
7 When I turned up at the hospital and saw Natalia surrounded by visitors, I realised I _____ coming.
   (didn't need to bother / needn't have bothered)
8 You _____ smoke in here. It's against the rules. (mustn't / needn't)

Should/shouldn't and ought to/oughtn't to are both used

a   to express the idea of duty or strong advice. **Should** gives the speaker's subjective opinion, whereas **ought to** is a little more forceful, based on objective considerations.

Other uses of **should** are

b   instead of **would** in formal writing:
   • *I should be glad to hear from you as soon as possible.*

c   to convey an assumption:
   • *Jane should have arrived at the office by now.*

d   as a formal or literary alternative to an **if** clause:
   • *Should the star be ill, the concert will be cancelled.*
   to express a remote possibility with an **if** clause:
   • *If they should ever ask about it, tell them the truth.*
   and after **in case**:
   • *We'll hide, in case they should see us.*

e   to make a suggestion or a request for advice:
   • *What should I wear to the wedding?*

f   after **so that**, **in order that**, verbs like **command**, **insist**, **suggest**, and adjectives like **vital**, **essential**, **necessary**, **anxious**, to show that something must be done: • *I'm anxious that he should feel at home.*

D Match the different uses of *should* with the categories in the study box above.

1   Should there be any difficulty, ring me at home.
2   Do you think I should put in an application or not?
3   I took a book with me, in case I should have to wait.
4   The irate customer insisted that the manager should apologise.
5   By this time my brother should be at the station.
6   You really should start planning for your future.
7   If anyone should inquire, kindly take their name and address.
8   It's essential that this should be kept in the strictest confidence.

Could is used to express general ability in the past:
• *I could read when I was three.*

For an achievement on a particular occasion in the past, **was able to/managed to/succeeded in** are used instead:
• *How many letters were you able to write last night?*

Couldn't is used for both general and particular ability.

Used to and **would** are both used to talk about past habits. **Used to** is used for situations and actions, whereas **would** only refers to repeated actions:
• *I used to have a guinea-pig when I was younger.*
• *Lisa would always eat porridge for breakfast.*

E Match the two halves of the sentences correctly.

1 My grandmother would   A better than anyone else.

2 She never used   B very angry every time it curdled.

3 But she could cook   C produce a wonderful meal every time.

4 Somehow she was able to   D select vegetables carefully at the market.

5 We all wondered how   E make was yoghurt.

6 The only thing she couldn't   F to use it up in a cake.

7 She'd get   G to consult any recipes.

8 But she always managed   H she managed it.

F Complete the sentences with *could*, *couldn't*, *was/were able to*, *used to*, or *would*.

1 Unfortunately my cousin _____ see his solicitor that day, as no appointment had been made.

2 When I was a child, I _____ always take the same route to school and back.

3 The boy next door _____ swim when he was five, but he never learnt to sail.

4 In the past people _____ have larger families than they do nowadays.

5 Stephen had to give up half-way round, and _____ finish the marathon.

6 Despite the thunderstorm we _____ climb right to the top of the mountain.

7 I sat on the terrace, drinking coffee. From there I _____ see the vineyards and the olive groves below me.

A **question tag** is composed of an auxiliary verb and a personal pronoun. If there is a modal verb in the main clause, we use this in the question tag:
- *They won't mind, will they?* • *He can swim, can't he?*

Remember that **will you?** is the usual question tag after a command, and **shall we?** after a suggestion with **Let's**.

G Complete the sentences with the correct question tag.

1 We can't see him yet, _____?

2 I ought to pay now, _____?

3 Remember to lock up, _____?

4 You'd rather wait till next week, _____?

5 He must be there, _____?

6 It might rain tonight, _____?

7 They had to do it, _____?

8 Don't tell him about it, _____?

9 Let's have a picnic on the beach, _____?

10 You love him very much, _____?

11 I'd better not say anything, _____?

12 We could stay overnight, _____?

UNIT 4

The future

The **future simple** is used

a in the main clause of a first conditional sentence:
- *If she passes the test, she'll go up to the next class.*
But **will** is not normally used in the *if* clause.

b for predictions after certain verbs like **think**, **expect**, **wonder** and **hope**, and after certain adverbs like **probably** and **perhaps**:
- *I think it'll stay fine for the race.* • *I hope he'll stay in touch.*

c for instant decisions or spontaneous reactions: • *I'll just answer the phone.*

d for offers of help: • *I'll give you a hand, if you like.*

e for promises: • *Believe me, I'll never do it again.*

f for invitations and polite requests: • *Will you come to the theatre with me?*

Except in questions, **will/will not** are usually contracted to **'ll/won't** in spoken English. **Shall** is used mainly in questions with **I/we** to express offers of help, suggestions or requests for advice: • *Shall I give you a lift?* • *Shall we go swimming?*

Avoid using the **future simple** in any situations other than those described above.

A Match the category on the left with the correct sentence on the right.

1	prediction	A	Honestly, I'll work very hard.
2	promise	B	I'm pretty sure he'll win.
3	first conditional	C	Unless it's cheap, I won't buy it.
4	quick reaction	D	Shall we wash up for you?
5	polite request	E	I'll answer the door.
6	offer of help	F	Will you hold the door open, please?

Will is not used after conjunctions of time, such as **after**, **before**, **until**, **when**, **as soon as**. Instead, a present tense is used:
- *I'll ring you as soon as I find out.* • *He'll turn up before we've finished.*

B Put *shall*, *will* or *won't* correctly into the sentences. Tick any phrases or sentences which are already correct.

1 I'm afraid I _____ be able to attend the wedding.

2 He _____ interview you as soon as you _____ arrive.

3 _____ we try the chicken supreme or the steak pie?

4 There _____ be a lot of trouble when the staff _____ find out!

5 By the way, _____ you please take notes?

6 _____ I change your library books for you?

7 Don't worry, you _____ have to stay for the whole session.

8 Make sure you _____ put the rubbish out before you _____ leave.

9 If I _____ see her, I _____ give her your love.

The **present simple** is used to talk about timetables, programmes of events and people's schedules:
- *What time does your train leave?*   • *The President arrives at 9.30.*

The **present continuous** is used to talk about planned future arrangements:
- *Tomorrow I'm flying to Hong Kong.*

A future time-phrase should be used or understood, to prevent confusion with the present uses of this tense.

Going to is used to talk about
a firm intentions: • *I'm going to be an actor when I grow up.*
b predictions based on something in the present: • *Look! He's going to fall!*

The **future continuous** refers to a continuous action which will be happening at a future point in time:
- *I'll be playing football on Saturday afternoon.*

The **future perfect** is used to talk about an action which will have happened by a certain point in the future. **By** is often a key word:
- *He'll have finished his exams by Friday week.*

The **future perfect continuous** is used similarly to the future perfect, but stresses that the action is continuous, or not completed:
- *By the end of May we'll have been living here for three years.*

Remember that many verbs do not have a continuous form; refer to the list in **Section 1** of the Appendix for guidance.

C Correct the sentences if necessary. Tick any which are already correct.

1 What time does your badminton class start?
2 'What will you do tonight?' 'Oh, we will have a barbecue.'
3 By this time next week I'm filling in my tax forms.
4 I promise I'm supporting you whenever you will need me.
5 You won't see him this summer. He'll do his military service then.
6 I'm being an architect when I'm finishing my studies.
7 Don't get up. I'll make the coffee.
8 Do you come to dinner with me tonight?
9 I think he shall probably marry the girl next door.
10 What do you do at 3 o'clock next Sunday afternoon?

D Complete the sentences with the most suitable verb form.

1 If you (not object) we (ask) the committee to approve the proposal.
2 By the time Juan (finish) his maths project next week, he (be) exhausted!
3 What our world (be like) in the year 2050?
4 Anne (not be) happy until she (see) the doctor this afternoon.
5 This time next year I probably (live) on the other side of the world.
6 I (not watch) the horror film that's on tonight. I know it (give) me nightmares.
7 By the end of this week we (raise) over £800 for the children's charity.
8 I swear I (do) my best from now on. Things (be) different, you (see).

Recycling

A Choose the correct word or phrase to complete each sentence. Write the letter in the space.

1 Despite playing under strength, the village team _____ beat their rivals.

a) could   b) were able to   c) couldn't   d) weren't able to

2 She had to do the shopping for her neighbour, _____ she?

a) didn't   b) hadn't   c) does   d) isn't

3 He daren't _____ his boss for a rise just now.

a) asking   b) be asking   c) to ask   d) ask

4 I'll hand over all my files to my assistant before I _____.

a) am leaving   b) leave   c) will leave   d) shall leave

5 By the time Bernard's daughter graduates, _____ retired.

a) he   b) he has   c) he'll being   d) he'll have

6 How long has the property _____ to your family?

a) belonged   b) belonging   c) belongs   d) been belonging

7 Buy me a newspaper on your way back, _____?

a) do you   b) will you   c) have you   d) don't you

8 The noise was so loud that we all _____ wear ear-protectors.

a) must   b) have to   c) should   d) had to

9 This time next year _____ chief translator to the French UN delegation.

a) he is   b) he'll being   c) he'll be   d) he's being

10 It is essential that all top security documents _____ be stamped CONFIDENTIAL.

a) should   b) must   c) will   d) may

11 I suggest Andrea _____ in touch with the organisers.

a) should get   b) to get   c) getting   d) should getting

12 According to _____ surveys, the majority of Britons are in favour of the monarchy.

a) the most   b) most   c) most of   d) the most of

13 The four men who successfully retraced Sir Ernest Shackleton's open-boat voyage across _____ Ocean are resting on South Georgia.

a) Southern   b) a Southern   c) the   d) the Southern

14 You _____ continue. You've made your point clearly enough already.

a) needn't   b) mustn't   c) don't have   d) won't

15 Let's get the house cleared up before he _____.

a) is arriving   b) arrives   c) will arrive   d) arrived

16 In my opinion, the government should _____ action.

a) to take   b) taking   c) take   d) have take

17 Since 1997 my department's work _____ built up considerably.

a) was   b) have   c) is   d) has

18 The bill had already been paid, so I _____ to do it.

a) hadn't   b) didn't need   c) needn't   d) haven't

19 Only _____ research has been carried out in this field.

    a) a little   b) a few   c) few   d) not much

20 It's 4 p.m. Marc _____ have arrived in Istanbul by now.

    a) would   b) can   c) should   d) ought

21 If Molly _____ to her guns, she'll probably get what she wants.

    a) will stick   b) would stick   c) stuck   d) sticks

22 By December Tim _____ enough to buy a mountain bike.

    a) saves   b) will have saved   c) has saved   d) will be saving

23 _____ anyone object, the plan will be reconsidered.

    a) If   b) Do   c) Should   d) Might

B Think of **one** word only which can be used appropriately in all three sentences in each group.

1 Having had a _____ of cruising last winter, he's been thoroughly bitten by the bug.

You know, this chicken has hardly any _____ at all!

She always dresses with such _____, doesn't she?

2 The club's best player seemed to have lost his _____, and was beaten by a junior.

I'm fine now, thanks – it was just a rather annoying _____ of flu.

Do keep in _____ once you get to Australia, won't you?

3 I _____ say that mobile phones will be superseded in due course.

Kim didn't _____ to move from her seat while the invigilator was watching her.

How _____ you threaten me like that!

4 The books dropped to the floor with a surprisingly _____ thud.

If you're found guilty, you'll have to pay a _____ fine.

Hazel had to drive through _____ rain on her way home.

5 The missing _____ of clothing was later discovered in the lost property cupboard.

I first read about McNulty's new film in a magazine _____.

The _____ is one of the parts of speech that cause most difficulty to students.

6 Jane has just _____ twenty, although you'd never think it to look at her.

As the evening wore on, the conversation _____ to football.

The milk in the pantry _____ rancid in the unaccustomed heat.

7 The opposition party _____ the government for an answer to their questions.

With great daring I _____ the button, and the machine started clicking and whirring.

Henry had to have his suit _____ at the hotel before attending the meeting.

8 You'll be able to _____ the audience's attention if your speech is lively enough.

I realise you're in agony, but just _____ on till the doctor gets here.

How many files is that drawer really supposed to _____?

C Complete the passage by putting **one** word in each space. The main focus of this task is on grammar rather than vocabulary.

Chile 1) _____ over a hundred potentially active volcanoes. Several teams of international geology experts have 2) _____ collaborating with Chilean colleagues on two of 3) _____ most interesting, known 4) _____ Lascar and Sollipulli. A recent study of Lascar has shown that glaciation seems 5) _____ have had 6) _____ important influence on its eruptions. When the ice retreated at the end of 7) _____ Ice Age 20,000 to 15,000 years ago, Lascar suffered 8) _____ most violent eruption. Scientists hope that further study of this volcano 9) _____ produce valuable data leading to some definite conclusions.

A British team 10) _____ led the investigations into the Sollipulli volcano, where 11) _____ glacier fills the main depression. At 12) _____ moment the ice cap 13) _____ melting at a rate of about 5 cm a day. This 14) _____ indicate a high risk factor for the surrounding countryside, as the ice cover normally plays a useful role 15) _____ preventing the violent release of volcanic gases 16) _____ cause explosive eruptions. 17) _____ the ice cap continues retreating, the volcano is very likely to erupt. This is a serious threat to the rich agricultural lands and tourist areas which 18) _____ Sollipulli.

Work is 19) _____ on both volcanoes, as, fortunately, the teams 20) _____ received a guarantee of international funding for further study for the next two years.

D In **most** lines of this text there is **one** unnecessary word. It is either grammatically wrong or does not make sense in the text. Write the unnecessary words next to the numbers on the right. Tick any lines that are correct.

Women can see their doctor on average five times a year	1 _____
in the UK compared with a men, who visit their doctor	2 _____
about three times. Two out of three women do leave	3 _____
from their GP's surgery clutching a prescription. Yet women	4 _____
have been taking tablets without knowing what effect they	5 _____
may to have on their bodies, because of a scientific	6 _____
anomaly – the most drugs are tested on men. In addition,	7 _____
there are being well-known examples of the way drugs and	8 _____
other substances should work differently in women. The	9 _____
different balance of fat and muscle in men's and women's	10 _____
bodies affects the speed with which alcohol is are absorbed	11 _____
and broken down, for example. It is predicted that natural	12 _____
remedies will be continue to gain in popularity as women,	13 _____
in particular, are become more aware of the possible side-	14 _____
effects of the powerful drugs currently being prescribed.	15 _____

Past tenses

The past simple is used

a for completed past actions at a known time. The time can be stated or understood:
   • *He bought his car last month.*   • *She worked there as a teacher.*

b with **when**, enquiring about past time: • *When did you last see her?*

c for habitual past actions and states: • *She always wanted to be loved.*

d for a definite period of past time: • *They spent five years in York.*

The past continuous is used for

a continuous past actions sometimes interrupted by the past simple:
   • *He was just getting into bed when the phone rang.*
   or setting the scene for a story:
   • *The sun was shining and the birds were singing as he walked down the lane.*

b simultaneous past actions: • *She was ironing while he was bathing the baby.*

c repeated past actions: • *I was always trying to save my pocket money.*

d past intentions, often not carried out:
   • *She was planning to ring her friend, but she forgot.*

The past perfect is used for

a a past action that happened before a past simple action:
   • *She had worked in Bonn before she moved to Stuttgart.*

b an action that happened before a stated time:
   • *He had completed the work by tea-time.*

But if two past actions are close in time or closely connected, we often avoid the use of the past perfect:
• *When he reached the airport, he checked in immediately.*

The past perfect continuous is used to stress that a past perfect action was continuous or repeated. Remember that many verbs do not have a continuous form; refer to the list in **Section 1** of the Appendix for guidance.

A Complete the sentences with the correct past tense of the verb in brackets.

1 Helena (receive) hospital treatment for a year before the doctors finally (tell) her their diagnosis.
2 The party chairman only (make) a statement after there (be) a lot of speculation in the press.
3 Julia (try) several computer dating agencies by the time she (meet) and (fall in love) with George.
4 Sharon eventually (find) the job she (want) last year, although she (graduate) the year before.
5 The official I (ask) to speak to (not be) there. Apparently he (go) abroad on business.

6 When the doctor (arrive) at the scene of the accident, he (realise) the victim still (breathe).

7 The workmen (spend) all morning digging the trench, and by lunchtime they (finish) it.

8 When the ship (hit) the reef, most of the crew (play) cards, and the passengers (have) dinner.

9 It (rain) and (begin) to get very cold as I (set out) on my long walk home.

10 When she (be) a child, she always (want) to do the most dangerous things.

11 I suddenly (recognise) the town square. I (be) there ten years before.

12 When my friend (open) the door, I (feel) like hitting him. I (ring) his doorbell for at least twenty minutes!

13 When Oscar (go back) into the room, his colleagues still (quarrel) about the coffee.

14 I (not answer) the phone immediately, because I (try) to finish some work.

15 When you (get) your first job?

16 Between 1989 and 2000 they (work) in three different countries, and (move) house five times.

B Correct the sentences if necessary. Tick any which are already correct.

1 My aunt worked in London before she had moved to Norwich.

2 The lawyer had a nervous breakdown because he had been working for years without a break.

3 We were packing the cases while the removal men were loading the furniture into the van.

4 The judge had brought the trial to an end yesterday.

5 The writer spent most of his childhood in abject poverty.

6 Pierre was owning a sailing boat for several years.

7 The company thought of giving their assistant manager the sack, but he resigned.

8 He was delighted with his purchase. He had been saving up to buy the motorbike for months.

9 The Norwegians planted their flag at the summit just before the British team were arriving.

10 A police car was almost knocking me over as I had crossed the road.

11 When did you leave school and go to college?

12 'Who are they?' 'Oh, a group of students who had arrived in Oxford a week ago.'

13 The First World War ended in 1918.

14 Until he explained a second time, I didn't understand what he meant.

15 The mountain was seeming very high as the weary group started to plod uphill.

C Read the two texts on the Princes in the Tower, a mystery which remains unsolved after over five hundred years. Answer questions 1–4 with a word or short phrase. You do not need to use complete sentences. Then write a summary according to the instructions in question 5, based on evidence from both texts.

Who killed the Princes in the Tower – the 12-year-old Edward V and his younger brother? The year is 1483, the place is the grim and forbidding Tower of London, and the victims are the two young sons of the late Edward IV. Suspect number one has always been their uncle Richard, Duke of Gloucester, the so-called villain of the piece. The boys stood between him and the throne, and, as one of their closest relatives, he was ideally placed to arrange their murder. He had both the motive and the opportunity. But did he do it? Evidence against him is merely circumstantial.

What we do know is that sometime during 1483 the two royal princes disappeared while in the care of their uncle, and that he immediately assumed the throne, becoming Richard III. No bodies, no trail of blood, not a shred of proof. But if not Richard, then who? There *was* someone else who wanted the crown, someone who wanted it so much that he was prepared to raise an army and fight Richard for it. When he became king two years later, he even married the boys' sister Elizabeth and had their cousin executed, in order to protect himself from claimants to the throne. His name was Henry Tudor.

1 Which phrases in the first paragraph imply that the writer does not agree with the general assumption of Richard's guilt?

2 In your own words, give two reasons for suspecting Henry Tudor of the murders.

At the Battle of Bosworth in 1485, Henry Tudor defeated and killed the reigning English monarch, Richard III, and was subsequently crowned Henry VII. For thirty years there had been intermittent conflict between two great families, the houses of York and Lancaster. The Wars of the Roses, as they were known, were thus brought to an end when Henry, as leader of the Lancastrians, conquered Richard and his Yorkist supporters. Henry was eager, not only to impose his authority, but also to keep the peace, and with that in mind he united the two warring houses by marrying Elizabeth of York. In order to flatter him, Tudor chroniclers were at pains to disparage his predecessor, and Richard has therefore gone down in history as a malicious, vengeful usurper, who murdered his innocent nephews. It is true that Richard never denied the contemporary rumours of his guilt, and may well have committed this heinous crime. Nevertheless, it seems likely that if *he* had defeated *Henry* at Bosworth, Yorkist historians would have painted a very different picture of events.

3 Explain briefly in your own words how the Wars of the Roses came to an end.

4 According to the text, why did Henry marry Elizabeth of York?

5 In a paragraph of 50–70 words, summarise the reasons why Richard III is generally thought to have killed the Princes in the Tower.

Gerund and infinitive

The gerund (the **-ing** form used as a noun) is used

a as the subject of a sentence: • *Swimming is Dorothy's favourite sport.*

b after certain verbs, including most verbs of liking and disliking. See **Section 3** of the Appendix.

c after all prepositions, including adjective-plus-preposition phrases, and verb patterns ending in a preposition:
  • *I'm tired of not having a garden.*
  • *He drove off without looking in his rear mirror.*
  Remember that **to** has two uses. It can either be used with the infinitive:
  • *They want to pay the bill.*
  or it can be a preposition, in which case it is followed by the gerund:
  • *I'm looking forward to seeing them.* • *You'll soon get used to not drinking coffee.*
  Object to, **be/get used to**, **look forward to**, **in addition to** are all followed by a noun or gerund.

d after phrasal verbs: • *He went on peeling the potatoes.*

e after common expressions such as: **It's (not) worth, waste/spend time, burst out.**

In formal English, possessives (**my**, **her**, **their**, etc.) are used with the gerund:
• *I hope you don't mind my asking.*
but in informal English the pronouns **me, her, them** etc. are more common:
• *I hope you don't mind me asking.*

The passive gerund can be used:
• *I remember being teased by my classmates at boarding school.*

A Correct the sentences if necessary. Tick any which are already correct.

1 To take regular exercise is becoming quite a trend these days.

2 I don't mind to be interviewed in the street by market researchers.

3 Excuse my interrupting, but I can give you the directions you want.

4 Since he's been in Ireland, he's got used to driving on the left.

5 The company achieved its productivity target by offering incentives to the work-force.

6 You can go to sightsee in London from the top of a double-decker bus.

7 In addition to lose all my money, I realised my credit card had been stolen.

8 I can't stand him coughing and sneezing all over us. He should stay at home if he's got a cold.

9 It's no use to tell me all your problems. You'll have to see the student counsellor.

10 She burst out crying as soon as she saw our shocked faces.

11 Most cats enjoy be stroked.

12 I'm afraid I just can't face to go into the witness box and tell all those people what happened.

The **infinitive** has several forms.

to do: • *They hope to visit you.*
to be doing (for a continuous action):
• *It's nice to be leading such an exciting life.*
to have done (for a completed or past action):
• *We were sorry to have missed you.*
to have been doing (to stress the frequency or length of the action):
• *He appears to have been making phone calls from the office every day.*

For passive infinitives see **Unit 9**.

The infinitive is used with **to** after certain verbs, including **ought**, **have**, **used**, and **be able**. See **Section 4** of the Appendix.
Notice the position of **not** before **to**:
• *Try not to worry.*   • *He's determined not to give in.*

The infinitive is used without **to** after most modal verbs, **would rather**, **had better**, **let**, ***make**, ***see**, ***hear**, ***feel**, **watch**, **notice**, ***help** (informally).
*If these verbs are used in the passive, the infinitive with **to** is used. Compare:
• *I saw her take the money.*
• *The champion was seen to shake hands with his opponent.*

Notice the very common **It is + adjective + to + infinitive**:
• *It is difficult to understand what you mean.*   • *It was nice to see you.*

Also notice the construction **object + to + infinitive** after certain verbs:
• *I want you to enjoy yourselves.*   • *She begged him not to go.*

The idea of purpose is usually expressed by **to + infinitive, in order to + infinitive** or **so as to + infinitive**:
• *He tiptoed upstairs so as not to wake the children.*

Notice: • *I have work to do.*   • *Nobody is to blame.*   • *The house is to let.*

B Correct the sentences if necessary. Tick any which are already correct.

1 They didn't ask that I leave early.
2 The army made him to complete his training course.
3 I hope to drop in on you next time I'm in the area.
4 Try to don't keep interrupting the speaker this time.
5 It's easier to learn a language in the country where it's spoken.
6 The doctor seems to have left a prescription here for you.
7 I was delighted to receive your most appreciative letter the other day.
8 In my view parents should not let their children to watch too much television.
9 He enrolled at a language school in Pisa for learn basic Italian.
10 It seems strange to be standing here, looking out at Sydney Harbour.
11 She didn't want that you go to all this trouble for her.
12 No wonder he was sacked! He seems to have been fiddling the accounts for years.

The following verbs can be used with either **the gerund or the infinitive**, depending on the meaning required:

a remember, forget, stop, go on, regret
b interested in, interested to
c try
d need
e used, be/get used to
f like, enjoy, love, hate, prefer
g allow, advise, forbid, permit
h mean.

The differences in meaning are explained in **Section 5** of the Appendix, but try to work them out for yourself before doing the next exercise.

C Complete the sentences with the gerund or the infinitive of the verbs in brackets.

1 Humility means (be) able to admit you're sometimes wrong.
2 You will not be permitted (enter) the building without the Chief Fire Officer's permission.
3 I'd be interested (know) if the chair in astrophysics is still vacant.
4 I'll never forget (see) the factory chimney collapse in a cloud of smoke and rubble.
5 Bankers advised the owners of the ailing theme park (reduce) entry charges in a bid to attract more visitors.
6 All the report's recommendations need (review) in the light of the committee's statements to the press.
7 The politician was accused of trying (stir up) trouble in his constituency as a ploy to divert attention from his own affairs.
8 I don't think my uncle will ever get used to (be) at home all day instead of (go) out to work.

D Match the first half of each sentence with the correct ending.

1 He objected
2 We'd rather not
3 She's looking forward
4 I insist on
5 Kindly allow me
6 I think you need
7 Everyone should be able
8 You'd better
9 I'm afraid it means
10 I always enjoy
11 He was made
12 She always used
13 His father wants him

A to write a polite letter.
B write a polite letter.
C to writing a polite letter.
D writing a polite letter.

Conditionals, wishes and regrets

> The main linking words for conditional clauses are **if** and **unless**, but **even if,
> as/so long as, supposing, whether ... or, however** (+ adjective/determiner),
> **whoever, wherever, whenever,** etc., **providing/provided (that),
> no matter who/how/when** etc. can also be used:
>
> - *If they're short of money, they don't eat out.* (**zero conditional**)
> - *You'll have a tussle with the management if you go ahead with that plan.*
>   (**first conditional**, possible future action)
>   Note that *if you should go ahead...* or *should you go ahead...* are more formal.
>
> - *If they had a bigger garden, they could grow their own vegetables.*
>   (**second conditional**, hypothetical but possible)
> Similarly:
> - *If you were to join the committee, we'd be very pleased.*
>   Note that *Were you to join...* is more formal.
> - *If you hadn't been late, you would have understood the lecture.*
>   (**third conditional**, referring to a past situation)
>
> There are also **mixed conditionals**:
> - *If you hadn't been late, you'd know what we're talking about now.*
>
> and a more formal version of the **third conditional**:
> - *Had you arrived on time, you would have understood the lecture.*

A Complete the sentences with the correct tense of the verbs in brackets.

1 If you (make) a run for it, you'll catch the train.
2 If Laura (not eat) so much, she wouldn't have put on weight.
3 If they (have) their car serviced regularly, it never lets them down.
4 The earthquake would have caused less damage if the houses (be) of stronger construction.
5 If there (be) a good breeze on Sunday, we'll go hang-gliding.
6 You can get there more quickly if you (take) the short cut across the playing field.
7 If you (leave) the milk out of the fridge in this weather, it'll go off.
8 Would you contribute to the fund if I (ask) you?
9 If I (drop) Eve's vase, she'd have been furious.
10 If you (be) really my friend, you'd lend me the money.
11 Had the councillors been re-elected, your proposal (be) accepted.
12 Productivity will improve if manufacturing procedures (be) streamlined.
13 (Be) you to take out the relevant insurance policy, you would be completely covered.
14 No matter what (happen), I'll always stand by him!
15 Supposing the computer (break down), what would you do?
16 You can invite whoever you (like) to the barbecue.

B Complete the second sentence so that it means the same as the first one, using the word given. You must use between **three** and **eight** words, including the word given. (Contractions count as two words.)

1 Should you persist in your defiance of instructions, disciplinary action will be taken.

go

If you _____ disciplinary action.

2 If you changed your mind, you'd be welcome to join our staff.

change

Were you _____ delighted to have you on the staff.

3 If I find that what you've told me is true, I'll resign my post.

out

Should your information _____ in my resignation.

4 If he fails the final examination, he won't be able to graduate.

be

Unless he _____ unable to graduate.

5 Sally's dog wasn't muzzled, and so it bit the postman.

have

If Sally's dog _____ the postman.

6 Because the evidence was withheld, the prisoner was found guilty.

presented

Had the evidence _____ acquitted.

I wish/If only + past simple are used to express a wish or regret about a current situation, by imagining its opposite:

- *I wish (that) Mark knew about it.* • *If only Mark knew about it!*
  (Sadly, Mark doesn't know about it.)

Notice also:
- *I would rather Mark knew about it.* (a preference rather than a wish)
- *It's time (that) Mark knew about it.* (In my opinion he should.)

I wish/If only + would are used for a future wish – something we would like to happen:
- *If only Mark would come back!* (I'm afraid he won't.)
- *I wish you'd stop doing that.* (You're annoying me.)

I wish/If only + past perfect are used for a past wish or regret:
- *I wish someone had told Mark about it.*

Note that we use **could** instead of **would** with **wish** when the subject pronouns are the same:
- *I wish I could see him.* (NOT *I wish I would see him.)

Were is often used instead of **was** after **wish** and **If only**:
- *I wish Luke were here.*

As if/as though are often used in similar hypothetical situations:
- *Don't treat me as if I were a child.*
- *He spoke as though he had been insulted.*

C Match the correct wish or regret on the left with the situation on the right.

1 If only he would tell her!
2 I wish he had stayed.
3 If only we knew what to do!
4 I wish he had told her.
5 I wish we'd known what to do.
6 It's time he stopped smoking.
7 I'd rather he stayed.
8 If only he'd stopped smoking!

A It's a pity he didn't tell her.
B We have no idea what to do.
C We didn't know what to do.
D I'd like him to tell her.
E It's a pity he didn't stay.
F I'd like him to stay, if possible.
G I think he should stop smoking.
H He should have stopped smoking.

D Complete the sentences, using the correct tense of the verb in brackets.

1 No matter how many people (come) tonight, we'll have a great time!
2 He looked at me as if I (just land) from the moon.
3 Supposing she (not agree), what would you do next?
4 However late you (be), there'll be a warm welcome for you.
5 Wherever they (end up), I'm sure they'll be happy.
6 It seemed as though nobody (spot) the obvious flaw in the plan.
7 We'll go along with the deal, provided we (receive) our fair share of the profits.
8 I wish the firm (not go) bankrupt, but the shares would still have been worthless.
9 Supposing the police (not come), what would you have done?
10 I'd be on your side even if you (not be) my friend.
11 He stared at me. It was as if he (not hear) a word I'd said.
12 However difficult you (find) the test, just try to complete it.

E Make a new sentence for each situation, starting with *I wish*.

1 What a pity he's so boring!
2 It was a mistake of mine, accepting that job.
3 How unfortunate that they all heard about it!
4 It'd be useful to have shares in the company, but I haven't any.
5 I'd like him to contribute his opinions more tactfully.
6 I should have gone to the conference.
7 I simply can't remember Myra's address.
8 Is it ever going to stop snowing?

UNIT 9

Passives

Passives are used whenever an action is more important than the agent – for example, in reporting the news or scientific experiments:
- *A woman has been arrested for the abduction of baby Emily Smith.*

The object of the active verb becomes the subject of the passive sentence, and the verb **be** is used in the correct tense with the past participle of the relevant verb. **By** + the **agent** is used only if it contributes important information:
- *Coastal buildings have been damaged by gales.*

Intransitive verbs, e.g. **arrive**, cannot become passive, because they have no object. Certain other verbs, e.g. **let**, **fit**, **lack**, **resemble**, **suit**, cannot normally become passive.

After modal verbs, **passive infinitives** are used (see **Unit 7**):
- *He ought to be arrested.*   • *You might have been killed.*

Passive -ing forms are possible:
- *She likes being driven to work.*   • *Having been fed, the dog went to sleep.*

A Complete the passage with the correct passive form of the verbs in brackets.

An ingenious device like a bed of nails, which 1) _____ (originally use) by the great Carthaginian general Hannibal to restrain his elephants, is currently 2) _____ (put) to a similar use in parts of Britain. It 3) _____ (know) as the Stinger, and recently it 4) _____ (successfully deploy) in Greater Manchester and the Midlands. When a joyrider in a stolen vehicle 5) _____ (involve) in a police chase, the Stinger can 6) _____ (lay out) on the road in front of the speeding driver, bringing the car to an abrupt halt. Last week a car chase in Bolton, which had lasted 90 minutes, 7) _____ (end) in 30 seconds, when the fugitive's tyres 8) _____ (puncture) by the Stinger. It 9) _____ (hope) that this device will save police time and enable more joyriders to 10) _____ (catch), as well as reducing the length of dangerous high-speed chases.

B Follow the same instructions as for Exercise A.

A recent front-page story in the British press revealed a truly sensational musical discovery – six Haydn piano sonatas 1) _____ (find) in Germany. Apparently the long-lost sonatas 2) _____ (discover) by a German music teacher in the home of an elderly lady. Strangely enough, the manuscripts, which 3) _____ (pronounce) genuine by several eminent musicologists, 4) _____ (not make) available in their original form, so no scientific tests could 5) _____ (carry out) in order to verify their authenticity. The musical world 6) _____ (throw) into a state of great excitement by this news. Preparations 7) _____ (make) for a

prestigious recording of the sonatas, and an authoritative article
8) _____ (publish) in the BBC's *Music Magazine*. Since then,
however, a note of doubt has crept in, and experts now say that unless
the originals 9) _____ (hand over) very soon, the manuscripts must
10) _____ (regard) as a forgery, albeit a very clever one.

Many verbs, like **give**, **award**, **lend**, can have two objects. When putting
these verbs into the passive, it is more usual to make the 'person object', rather
than the 'thing object', the subject of the passive verb:
• *I was given back my change.* (NOT *My change was given back to me*).

C Improve the sentences if necessary by putting the 'person object' first. Tick any which are already correct.

1 I was promised a review of my case in due course.
2 The news was told to the whole community.
3 The volunteers are being lent suits of protective clothing.
4 She will be sent a free gift with her mail order catalogue.
5 A lucky mascot has been given to me, to use in my exams.
6 A postgraduate diploma will be awarded to her as soon as she has completed her practical assignments.
7 A chance to participate in the Olympic Games is being refused him, on the grounds of his unreliability.
8 However, he has been offered a place in the national team for the forthcoming international matches.
9 You will be shown your living quarters for the duration of your stay in the camp.
10 A bribe seems to have been offered to the officials in charge of the institution at the time.

Passive constructions are often used with verbs like **say**, **believe**, and **know**.

It + passive + that-clause:
• *It is said that three people died in the accident.*
• *It was once believed that the earth was completely flat.*

Subject + passive + to + infinitive:
• *Three people are said to have died in the accident.*
• *The earth was once believed to be completely flat.*

Sometimes there are two passive constructions in the same sentence:
• *It is known that York was invaded by the Vikings.*
• *York is known to have been invaded by the Vikings.*

Other verbs which are used in this way include: **consider**, **think**, **understand**,
report, **allege**, **expect**, **fear**, **claim** and **deny**. The verb **be rumoured** only
exists in the passive form.

See **Unit 7** for a list of infinitive forms.

D Complete the second sentence so that it means the same as the first one, using the word given. You must use between **three** and **eight** words, including the word given. (Contractions count as two words.)

1 It is expected that tax increases will be announced in tomorrow's budget statement.

to

Tax increases _____ in tomorrow's budget statement.

2 We understand that inner-city crime rates are going up in most areas.

be

Inner-city crime rates _____ in most areas.

3 They say the rock star's wife has had at least two facelifts.

have

The rock star's wife _____ at least two facelifts.

4 We fear that nine crew members were lost overboard in the storm.

are

Nine crew members _____ overboard in the storm.

5 It was considered that Ralph's speech was one of the best.

to

Ralph's speech _____ one of the best.

6 We can't deny making certain mistakes in the early stages.

that

It _____ made in the early stages.

7 Police reported that a man had been helping them with their inquiries.

was

A man _____ police with their inquiries.

8 The accused was alleged to have committed fraud.

had

It _____ committed fraud.

If **phrasal verbs or verbs with prepositions** become part of a passive sentence, they must not lose their particle:

• *The child was extremely well looked after.*

E Complete the sentences if necessary, by choosing the correct particle from the box. Tick any which are already correct.

up	down
in	away
out	off

1 What a mess! Sam's toys haven't been put.

2 He wasn't here last night. His bed hasn't been slept.

3 The situation is serious, but it'll have to be faced, I'm afraid.

4 This is the third time our meeting's been put.

5 All cigarettes must be extinguished before you enter the building.

6 The girls were brought on a farm near the Welsh border.

7 Cheques should be made to Wellingtons plc.

8 I must warn you that if you have anything to say, it'll be taken and may be used in evidence against you.

Recycling

A Choose the correct word or phrase to complete each sentence. Write the letter in the space.

1 We regret _____ you that you have exceeded your overdraft facility.

   a) to inform   b) informing   c) to tell to   d) telling

2 Why don't you try _____ the key anti-clockwise?

   a) to turn   b) on turning   c) turning   d) turn

3 The company's apology _____ regarded as an exercise in damage limitation.

   a) were   b) was   c) would   d) had

4 We don't allow _____ in the classrooms.

   a) that people smoke   b) smoke   c) people to smoke
   d) to smoking

5 The accused denied _____ in the vicinity of the murder scene.

   a) to have ever been   b) have ever been   c) having been ever
   d) ever having been

6 Why don't you do what you're told, instead of _____ such a song and dance about it?

   a) to make   b) making   c) made   d) make

7 The children _____ to stay up late.

   a) don't allow   b) aren't let   c) aren't allowed   d) would rather

8 I rashly posted the parcel without _____ it.

   a) weighing   b) weigh   c) weighed   d) to weigh

9 I suppose you just went to the disco _____ improve your conversational skills!

   a) so as   b) for   c) in order to   d) too

10 He wasn't responsible. He wasn't _____.

   a) blame   b) to blame   c) blaming   d) for blame

11 What a dangerous thing to do! You _____ have been killed!

   a) may   b) can   c) must   d) might

12 For the rest of his life he lived in fear of _____ tracked down.

   a) having   b) be   c) being   d) been

13 All that rubbish will have to be _____ at once.

   a) get rid of   b) got rid of   c) got rid   d) getting rid of

14 You'll get a free month's subscription, _____ you renew your membership by the end of January.

   a) unless   b) however   c) were   d) provided

15 By the time I applied, all the holiday vouchers _____ used up.

   a) had been   b) have been   c) was   d) are

16 I felt as if I _____ a confidence.

   a) have betrayed   b) would betray   c) had betrayed
   d) am betraying

17 I wish I _____ more about the logistics of the expedition.

    a) would know   b) knew   c) know   d) can know

18 _____ bread is regarded by some as a therapeutic activity.

    a) To make   b) Made   c) Making   d) Having made

19 It's time she _____ promotion, in my view.

    a) get   b) got   c) will get   d) have got

20 The candidate _____ to have withdrawn her application.

    a) claimed   b) said   c) denied   d) reported

21 There's nothing I like more than _____ for a brisk walk along the seashore.

    a) go   b) out   c) walking   d) going

22 How can you waste all that money on _____?

    a) gamble   b) to gamble   c) gambling   d) the gamble

B Think of **one** word only which can be used appropriately in all three sentences in each group.

1 Oh, do let me! I'd really much _____ do your work than my own.

You know, I can't face reading much more of this article – it's _____ dull.

Some people feel that the prisoner is _____ to be praised than condemned.

2 Can you please _____ that the children are in bed by seven.

I was very sorry I wasn't able to _____ Luke off at the airport.

The solution was obvious to me, but Jade just couldn't _____ it.

3 So long as you bring a group with you, you're allowed a _____ ticket.

When there's a _____ cubicle, I'll pop in and change, and then see you in the pool.

For a man with a large overdraft, he's surprisingly _____ with his money.

4 You'd better take a vote if you can't _____ a consensus.

The effects of environmental pollution will _____ right across the planet.

We've been trying to _____ Graham all day, but he's not answering his phone.

5 The Stinger device may help the police to _____ more joyriders.

If your body's resistance is low, you're more likely to _____ a cold.

Sorry, I didn't quite _____ what you said just then.

6 The manuscripts of the piano sonatas are not available in their original _____ .

A fine is a _____ of punishment for a minor offence.

Now Heather's moved to the local state school, she's in the same _____ as her cousin.

7 The theft of their savings _____ the Dodgson family into a panic.

At the second fence the horse reared up and _____ its rider.

Rushing to the controls, Will _____ a switch, and the engine juddered to a halt.

C Complete the passage by putting **one** word in each space.

A central feature of 1) _____ 12th and 13th centuries in Europe was the concern of the great aristocratic families to ensure that their landed estates 2) _____ handed down intact to future generations. In 3) _____ to prevent their inheritance from 4) _____ divided, it 5) _____ traditional to insist that their younger sons 6) _____ remain unmarried. It was usual for the eldest son 7) _____ have his bride chosen for him, probably from another related noble family, and if the wife 8) _____ not 9) _____ in producing the male heir needed to carry on the line, she 10) _____ be discarded, and another bride would be chosen. 11) _____ potentially anarchic situation subsequently arose, 12) _____ loveless marriages on 13) _____ side, and rebellious bachelor knights on the other. 14) _____ social problem was brilliantly 15) _____ by the invention of courtly love, in which an unmarried knight 16) _____ swear eternal love, respect and obedience to a married lady. The energies of younger sons 17) _____ thus cleverly channelled into adventurous exploits and chivalrous deeds, all 18) _____ the sake of their noble lady. 19) _____ in all, courtly love went a long way 20) _____ palliating the internal contradictions of mediaeval aristocratic society.

D In **most** lines of this text there is **one** unnecessary word. It is either grammatically wrong or does not make sense in the text. Write the unnecessary words next to the numbers on the right. Tick any lines that are correct.

Sergeant Bob Mann was one among the survivors of an ill-fated army	1 _____
expedition to the wilds of Borneo. He has still a fascinating tale to tell of	2 _____
alternative medical treatment in a remote jungle village. Despite of his	3 _____
precautions, he seriously injured his right hand while cutting a path through	4 _____
the jungle, and the wound became so badly infected that he was feared the	5 _____
onset of the gangrene. Several days later, when he and his companions	6 _____
reached to a hamlet, he was treated by a local witch doctor, who plunged	7 _____
his hand into a jar of snake flesh and herbs. 'It was very amazing,' said	8 _____
Sergeant Mann. 'My own wound looked completely clean when I took	9 _____
my hand out. The people in here know so much about natural remedies.	10 _____
Without them, I might have had to have my hand quite amputated.'	11 _____
Bob Mann's hand has recently been operated on in a Hong Kong	12 _____
hospital, where the authorities have confirmed that the wound is being	13 _____
recovering well, and that the witch doctor's treatment was so beneficial.	14 _____
But snake flesh, venom and saliva are traditionally considered to have	15 _____
healing properties for all kinds of wounds and infections.	16 _____

Reported speech

When direct speech is changed into **reported speech**, with a reporting verb in the past, the verb tense, the pronouns and the time-phrase may all have to be changed to indicate the time shift to the past:

- *'We'll be getting married this year,' he said.* (direct speech)
  He says (that) they'll be getting married this year.
  (reported speech with a present reporting verb)
  He said (that) they would be getting married that year.
  (reported speech with a past reporting verb)

It is usually better style to use more precise **reporting verbs** than **say** or **tell** when turning (usually informal) direct statements into (usually more formal) reported ones. Examples are: **advise**, **apologise**, **congratulate**, **promise**, **remind**.

See **Section 6** of the Appendix for a complete list of these verbs and their different grammatical patterns.

A Match the direct speech on the left with the most appropriate reporting verb on the right.

B Now put the direct statements in Exercise A into reported speech, using the verbs you have chosen, and starting each sentence with *She*.

1 'I've had better marks than anyone else all term!'
2 'You did it! I saw you! You stole my watch!'
3 'If you don't give me your money, I'll hit you!'
4 'I'm very sorry I didn't get round to writing earlier.'
5 'Why don't we all go for a drive in the country?'
6 'I must, I simply must see the manager at once!'
7 'Please, please, don't tell anyone you've seen me!'
8 'That's right. Your flight's taking off at midnight.'
9 'Don't forget to bring the binoculars, will you?'
10 'I imagine Mexico City has about 20 million inhabitants by now, but I could be wrong.'

A threaten
B accuse
C suggest
D boast
E insist
F estimate
G beg
H apologise
I confirm
J remind

C Follow the instructions for Exercise A.

D Now follow the instructions for Exercise B, starting each sentence with *He*.

1 'It's five o'clock already, you know.'
2 'Yes, that's fine. I'll be able to help.'
3 'Don't worry, there'll be no difficulty, believe me.'
4 'How kind of you to bring me the flowers!'
5 'If I were you, I'd keep it under my hat.'
6 '.... and another thing, there'll be a 2% surcharge.'
7 'I didn't do it! I didn't rob the old lady!'
8 'No, I'm afraid I'm not prepared to make a speech.'
9 'Be careful when you cross the road, won't you?'
10 'Well done! You've passed the test first time!'
11 'I'm sure it was Charlotte who let us down.'
12 'Yes, it was my fault. I caused the accident.'

A assure
B blame
C deny
D warn
E admit
F refuse
G congratulate
H add
I point out
J advise
K thank
L agree

The modals **should**, **would**, **could**, **ought** and **might** do not change tense in reported speech, and neither do the **second** and **third conditionals**. With a reported second or third conditional, **that** is needed, and a comma is necessary to separate the two clauses if the **if** clause comes first:

• *He pointed out that if she had bought him a ticket, he could have seen the play too.*

E Turn the sentences into reported speech.

1 'If I had known, I'd have come earlier,' she said.

2 He said, 'Unless John tells the truth, somebody'll get hurt.'

3 'I really think you should join the tennis club this summer,' she said.

4 'If you practised more, you might be able to make a career out of music,' her teacher said.

5 'I wouldn't have had the accident if the brakes had been repaired properly,' he said.

6 'He'll be sent to prison if he commits a further offence,' said the magistrate.

7 'You can stay here as long as you like,' he said.

8 'I wish Bob would buy himself a new suit,' said Maggie.

Notice how **reported questions** are formed from the two types of direct question in English.

a questions starting with a question-word:
• *'When will you next be in Paris?'*
  He asked when she would next be in Paris. (NOT ... *when would she next be in Paris*)
• *'When does your plane take off?'*
  She asked when his plane took off.
Notice that no *do/did* auxiliaries are needed in reported speech, and that the word order is the same as in a statement.

b questions starting with a verb:
• *'Can you come tomorrow?'*
  She asked if/whether I could go the next day/the day after/the following day.
If/whether connect the reporting verb and this type of question.
If has no connection here with conditional **if**. **Whether** must be used before an infinitive: • *He was not sure whether to believe them.*
• *I didn't know whether to laugh or cry.*

F Correct the reported questions if necessary. Tick any which are already correct.

1 I asked how far was it to the station.

2 They wondered how many people lived in Tokyo.

3 She asked me unless I could do the shopping for her.

4 Her father asked her was what she had told him true.

5 The committee enquired whether she might accept the job.

6 The traffic warden asked why had I parked there.

7 I asked the old man what was his recipe for long life.

8 We wondered how did our neighbours manage to keep their garden so neat.

9 The officials asked him what did he want.

10 I only wanted to know where he had been for so long.

Reported requests or commands usually involve the use of the **infinitive** with **to:**
- *'Take that away!'*   *He told me to take it away.*
- *'Please don't talk.'*   *She asked us not to talk.*

Use **ask** for a polite request, **beg** for an earnest request, **instruct** or **tell** for a command, and **order** for an authoritative command:
- *She ordered the children to sit down and be quiet.*

G Match the direct request or imperative on the left with its reported version on the right.

1 'Kindly stand back, would you!'

2 'Please don't cry!'

3 'Leave the room now!'

4 'Would you mind opening the door?'

5 'Stand back!'

6 'You mustn't cry!'

7 'Would you leave the room, please?'

8 'Open the door!'

A She asked us to stand back.

B She ordered us to stand back.

C He begged me not to cry.

D He told me not to cry.

E He told me to leave the room immediately.

F He asked me to leave the room.

G She ordered me to open the door.

H She asked me to open the door.

H Complete the second sentence so that it means the same as the first one, using the word given. You must use between **three** and **eight** words, including the word given. (Contractions count as two words.)

1 'You've passed the exam? Oh, well done!' my aunt said to me.

on

My aunt _____ the exam.

2 'I'm sorry I forgot to set the security alarm,' said the receptionist.

for

The receptionist _____ set the security alarm.

3 'Why don't you postpone your trip till the autumn, Jim?' suggested Sarah.

off

Sarah suggested _____ till the autumn.

4 'Don't forget to enclose a cheque, will you?' the clerk said to me.

in

The clerk reminded _____ the envelope.

5 'It's a good idea to rehearse your speech in front of a mirror,' George told me.

run

George advised _____ in front of a mirror.

Linking words and discourse markers

The main linking words expressing **concession and contrast** are **despite, in spite of, however, although, even though, much as, as/though** (after adjectives), **but, yet, all the same, even so, nevertheless**.

Despite and **in spite of** can only be followed by a noun or gerund:
- *In spite of having a fax machine, he couldn't send the documents.*
The alternative construction is **in spite of/despite the fact that**:
- *She married him, in spite of the fact that he treated her badly.*
All the other conjunctions and connectors are followed by a verb clause.

Note how **as** and **though** are used after adjectives:
- *Intelligent though she is, I don't think she'll win the competition.*
- *Brave as he was, the soldier dreaded the onset of battle.*

Although, even though and **much as** can come at the beginning of the sentence or introduce the second or additional clause:
- *Much as I enjoy his company, I don't want him here the whole time.*

But and **yet** normally introduce the second or additional clause:
- *She's charming, yet there's something a little odd about her.*

All the same, even so, nevertheless and **however** all need a comma or commas to separate them from the rest of the sentence:
- *He decided to go, all the same.*   • *All the same, he decided to go.*

However is a more formal alternative to **but**. It is rarely used in spoken English:
- *Klaus was a loyal friend. However, she found him irritating at times.*

A Correct the sentences if necessary. Tick any which are already correct.

1 In spite of he revised hard for his exams, he didn't pass.
2 Much as I approve of her enthusiasm, I'm worried she'll overdo her weight training.
3 He doesn't all the same know what he's talking about.
4 She would love the opportunity, although it seems unlikely at the moment.
5 There are no grants available. Nevertheless, you may be awarded a scholarship.
6 My first reaction was one of distaste, yet there was an element of humour in the situation.
7 Despite his extended illness, he managed to complete his doctoral dissertation.
8 Quiet this spot seems now though, you ought to see it when the tourists are here in August!
9 'Try a bit harder!' 'However I don't want to!'
10 I can't accept, but it's very kind of you to offer, all the same.

11 Even though your lack of agreement, you must admit it's a strong case.

12 Even so his creditors are baying for satisfaction, he has just bought a BMW!

The main linking words expressing **cause** are **as**, **since**, **because**, **participles** (see **Unit 18**) and **adjectives** like *aware*, *distraught*, *horrified* which express feelings that would cause certain behaviour:

- *As I hadn't had time for lunch, I bought a sandwich.*
- *Realising that no one would help him, he abandoned the idea.*
- *Suddenly aware of the pain, she keeled over on the ground.*
- *Distraught that Susan had rejected him, Toby rushed wildly out of the room.*

Notice that **as**, **since**, and **because** are followed by a verb clause, **participles** by a verb clause with **that**, and **adjectives** either by a preposition + noun or by a verb clause with **that**.

For is a more formal alternative to **but**. It is not normally used in spoken English, and cannot be used to begin a sentence.

On account of, **due to**, **owing to** and **because of** are followed by a noun or gerund:

- *Stevenson moved to the South Seas because of the climate.*

B Use these words to complete the sentences. Do not use any word more than once.

| disgusted | because | for | horrified | deprived | told |
| surprised | embarrassed | sad | alone | due | aware |

1 Gillian blushed, _____ that she might have embarrassed him.

2 _____ of sweets in his childhood, Antonio had fortunately never acquired a sweet tooth.

3 _____ again in her tiny room, Lucy couldn't help crying a little.

4 _____ it could publish any late news in its evening edition, the local paper had an advantage over its competitors.

5 _____ at the thought of missing the party, Sandra tried to cheer herself up by watching a video.

6 The toddler was crying bitterly, _____ he'd lost his mother.

7 _____ to hear the unexpected news, Peggy phoned her mother and told her immediately.

8 _____ to wait until he was needed, the boy sat down and watched the rest of his team play.

9 _____ at the catastrophe, the onlookers panicked and fled.

10 _____ to serious problems with the track, trains to Manchester Victoria will not be running until further notice.

11 _____ by the attention they were receiving, the boys tried to creep out of the room.

12 _____ by the mess, the residents set to work to clear it up before it became a health hazard.

The main linking words expressing **result** are **therefore**, **consequently**, **as a result**, **(and) so**, **so that**, **so ... that**, **such ... that**, **enough**, and **too ... (for someone) to** + infinitive. **As a result of** comes before a noun or gerund.

Such can be used with a noun, or an adjective + noun:
* *It was such a nice day/such nice weather that we went out.*
* *It was such a surprise for Percy!*

So ... that is used with an adjective or adverb, and also with **much**, **little**, **many**, **few** + noun:
* *He talks so fast that you can't understand him.*
* *We had so little time that we didn't manage to see everyone.*

Enough comes before a noun but after an adjective or adverb:
* *There wasn't enough time to see him.*   • *He isn't old enough to join the navy.*

C Rewrite the sentences, using *too* or *enough*.

1 The matter is so important that you should deal with it yourself.
2 She didn't study much, so she didn't pass the end-of-term test.
3 The door was so narrow that we couldn't squeeze through.
4 She had so little energy that she couldn't keep going all day.
5 The leisure centre is so inaccessible that hardly any tourists find it.

D Rewrite the sentences using *so* or *such ... that*.

1 They had very little money, and couldn't afford to run a car.
2 There was a lot of food. We could have fed ten hungry men with it!
3 You're a really experienced worker, so you should know what to do.
4 He hasn't had much acting experience, so we can't give him the part.
5 I draw very badly, so I can't do a very good sketch map.

In case is used to explain precautions or things done in advance. It is followed by a present or past tense, or (less often) by **should** (see **Unit 3**):
* *I'll take an umbrella in case it rains.*
* *I took an umbrella in case it rained/should rain.*

DO NOT use **will** or **would** after **in case**.

E Complete the sentences with the correct tense of the verb in brackets.

1 I went on a first aid course, in case I ever (need) to know about it.
2 Take your money with you in case you (see) any good souvenirs to buy.
3 I always pack my shorts in case the weather (be) fine.
4 I've been looking for her everywhere, in case she (get lost).
5 I think I'll lock my briefcase in the boot in case someone (spot) it and (try) to break into the car.
6 He was planning to work out every day, in case he (be select) for the match.
7 I'm looking for other jobs, in case I (not get) this one.

Discourse markers are words or phrases which play an important part in the structure of a spoken or written text by signposting the logical progression of ideas. They may do this by:

a referring the listener or reader back to previous events or statements:
  - *following the incident, in such circumstances, at that time, hitherto, be that as it may, accordingly, in those days*

b introducing new topics:
  - *With regard to finance, Financially speaking, In terms of finance, As for finance, in financial terms, As far as finance is concerned, Regarding finance*

c clarifying the chronology of events or ideas:
  - *The first point is, In the first place, Firstly, A further point is, Moreover, Similarly, One final thought is, Last but not least, In conclusion, To sum up*

d making specific references to people, facts or events:
  - *the aforementioned, the following terms, the former, the latter, the undersigned, respectively, the facts are as follows, the above address*

e indicating the speaker's or writer's views:
  - *as I see it, in my view, frankly, I suppose*

F Complete this letter with the most appropriate discourse markers from the study box. Then answer the questions, using the clues provided by the discourse markers.

Dear Sir,

We, 1) _____ , are writing to you to complain about the proposed closure of the Midwest Bank in the village of Little Stopping. The facts 2) _____ . Since both Gourlays and Boyds closed their branches in the nearby villages of Hopwell and Stopton 3) _____ , local people have been left with no option but to travel the eleven miles to Merryford or the twenty miles to Worchester. 4) _____ , although nearer and therefore more accessible by public transport, only offers banking facilities three days a week. 5) _____ , while providing a good choice of banks, is regarded by most people as too far away to be of much use.

6) _____ of public relations, the 7) _____ closure of your branch in Little Stopping would be a disaster, in blatant disregard of the wishes of many of your 8) _____ loyal customers.

We urge you to reconsider your decision. Kindly send any comments you have on this issue to us at 9) _____ .

Yours faithfully,

Joan Morris   Jamie Rogers   Edward Patching   Liz Fowler

10 How many times is the closure of the Midwest Bank mentioned?

11 Which bank had a branch in Hopwell?

12 Which town only offers banking facilities three days a week?

13 What are the two main points made in the letter?

14 In your opinion, which discourse markers from the text should only be used in a very formal style, as in this letter?

Relative clauses

Relative pronouns connect a relative clause to a main clause. They are **who, whom, which, that, whose, where, why, when** and **what**.

Who/whom refer to people. **Which/that** refer to animals or things, although people who love animals often use **who** when speaking of them. **Whom** is very unusual, especially in informal English, and is generally omitted or replaced with **who**:
• *We'll take Timmy to the specialist (who) we've heard so much about.*

Whose is possessive, for people or things:
• *She works for a company whose chief executive has been arrested for fraud.*

Where is used after nouns referring to place, **when** after nouns referring to time, and **why** after the word **reason**. **Where/when** can often replace **in/on/at which**:
• *I think that's the church where/in which my grandparents were married.*
• *It was a day when everything seemed to go wrong.*
• *Is there any reason why he can't come?*

What means 'the thing that':
• *I'll explain what he said.*
• *What I like for breakfast is hot buttered toast.*
• *She'll give you just what you want.*

A Correct the sentences if necessary. Tick any which are already correct.

1 There's the woman who she sold me the oranges.
2 This is my brother, who's wife's French.
3 Did you ever meet the model who's married Jeff's cousin?
4 I don't like people which talk too loudly.
5 That's the car whose brakes are being repaired.
6 I know a little taverna at where you can get a wonderful meal.
7 Do you understand what he said?
8 I suppose that's the house where we'll have to stay in.
9 Could we arrange a time when we'll both be free?
10 I'm afraid I haven't sent exactly what he asked for.
11 That I can't stand is queuing in the rain.
12 Have you any idea to whom I'll be speaking to?
13 Is that the school which you studied?
14 Deirdre will show the new students which to do.
15 You'd better tell me the reason for he didn't turn up.
16 That's the old chap whom you met at the bus stop last week, isn't it?
17 That was the day when I mislaid my passport.
18 What he told you is hopelessly inaccurate.

Defining relative clauses give us the necessary information to know which person or thing is referred to:
- *I did the work (that/which) he asked me to do.*

In this type of clause there is no comma. **That** or **which** can be used, or the pronoun can be omitted if it is the object.

Which and **that** are often interchangeable. In defining clauses, however, **that** is commonly used instead of **which** after **superlatives**, **every(thing)**, **all**, **only**, **some(thing)**, **any(thing)**, **no(thing)**, **none**, **little**, **few** and **much**:
- *It was the strangest case that had ever come to Dr Martin's notice. No disorder that he had read about had such bizarre symptoms.*

Which is used

a to refer to a whole previous sentence, and needs a comma before it:
  - *Nicholas never offers to pay, which always annoys me.* (NOT *what always annoys me*)
b with a preposition/particle:
  - *This is the room in which Wagner died.* (formal).
  - *This is the room (which) Wagner died in.* (informal)
c in **non-defining clauses**, which give information that is not really necessary:
  - *I did the work, which was well paid.*
  A comma is used to separate the relative clause from the main clause. **That** cannot be used to introduce this type of clause.

B Explain the difference in meaning between each pair of sentences.

1 a) She decided to take the first train that stopped in Strasbourg.
  b) She decided to take the first train, which stopped in Strasbourg.
2 a) The people, who hadn't seen the weather forecast, were caught unawares by the hurricane.
  b) The people who hadn't seen the weather forecast were caught unawares by the hurricane.
3 a) We couldn't eat the food, which was bad.
  b) We couldn't eat the food that was bad.
4 a) I was hoping to visit my cousin, who lives in New Zealand.
  b) I was hoping to visit my cousin who lives in New Zealand.
5 a) They picked all the fruit that had ripened.
  b) They picked all the fruit, which had ripened.

If **who**, **which** or **that** is the **object** of the relative clause, not the subject, the pronoun can be, and often is, omitted:
- *I received the order you despatched last week.* (which/that = object)
- *I've received the goods, which are in my office now.* (which = subject)

Notice that we do not use a possessive adjective in the following type of sentence:
- *It's the bike Dad gave me.* (NOT *It's my bike Dad gave me.*)

C Combine the sentences to make one new sentence, including a defining relative clause. Make any necessary changes, and omit the relative pronoun if possible.

1 The bus goes up Edward Avenue. It doesn't stop at the railway station.
2 The debate went on all night. The backbenchers had demanded it.
3 The escaped convicts stashed away the gold bars. They had stolen the gold in an earlier bank raid.
4 It was her dream cottage! She had always wanted one like that.
5 They booked into the hotel. They had stayed there on their honeymoon.
6 The bodyguards were flanking the King. They had revolvers concealed inside their jackets.
7 It wasn't their dog. No, I was taking care of their cat.
8 The tree had died. They cut it down.
9 That's the cruise. I've always wanted to go on that one.
10 I think it was the manager. I was speaking to him.

D Correct or improve the sentences if necessary. Tick any which are already correct.

1 It's the tallest building which I've ever seen.
2 Everything she had told us turned out to be true.
3 He was arrested for speeding, which unfortunately was reported in the local newspaper.
4 There is very little that escapes the senior partner's eagle eye.
5 He'll be playing with the same racquet, with which he always plays.
6 Next Tuesday I'll have to visit the dentist again which I detest.

In non-defining clauses, determiners like **some**, **all**, **neither**, **none**, **(a) few**, **(a) little**, **both**, **most**, **much** and **several**, superlatives and expressions of quantity can be used with **of whom** (for people) and **of which** (for things):
• *They'll introduce you to a lot of people, most of whom you'll forget immediately.*
• *I was offered lamb or chicken, neither of which I like.*

E Combine the sentences to make one new sentence, including a relative clause.

1 She had invited a hundred guests. I didn't know any of them.
2 Growling in the corner were two big dogs. They both looked extremely dangerous.
3 The manager called in my new colleagues. I had met one or two of them already.
4 There were several large holes in the road. Three of them had to be repaired urgently.
5 There were some vegetables left over. I was able to use a few of them in some soup for supper.
6 The talk was attended by over two hundred delegates. Most of them took notes.
7 The researchers reported back on the questionnaires. The most interesting ones showed a marked change in leisure habits among older people.
8 He comes from a large family. All of them now live in Australia.

UNIT 14

Adverbs

Adverbs can modify verbs, adjectives, other adverbs, prepositions and whole clauses or sentences:
• *He kicked the ball well past the goalie. Unfortunately, that never happened again.*
Adverbs of **frequency**, **time**, **manner** and **place** are the most common.

Most adverbs are formed by adding **-ly** to an adjective or **-ally** after **-ic**:
• *slow~slowly* • *spasmodic~spasmodically*
If the adjective ends in **-le**, the **-e** is replaced with **-y**: • *reliable~reliably*
If the adjective already ends in **-ll**, only add **-y**: • *full~fully*

Most adjectives ending in **-y** change like this: • *angry~angrily, happy~happily*
Some adjectives ending in **-ly**, e.g. *likely, lovely, lonely, ugly, deadly*, are usually used as adverbs like this: • *friendly~in a friendly way*
Others ending in **-ly**, e.g. *early, daily, weekly, monthly*, can be used as adjectives or adverbs with no change.

Some adverbs have the same form as adjectives. For example:
• *hard, fast, far, near, early, late, direct, straight*
Notice also: • *good~well*

A Write the correct form of the adverb for these adjectives.

1 graceful	6 hard	11 inevitable
2 good	7 heavy	12 fast
3 important	8 cruel	13 noisy
4 full	9 timid	14 jolly
5 straight	10 illegal	15 increasing

Avoid putting an adverb between the verb and its object:
• *I like riding very much/I very much like riding.* (NOT *I like very much riding.*)

Time adverbs normally go right at the beginning or end of the clause:
• *Tomorrow I'm going there/I'm going there tomorrow.*

Frequency adverbs, e.g. **always**, **never**, **sometimes**, usually go between the subject and verb: • *I always drink coffee.*
or between two parts of the verb: • *She's never been late.*

Many **adverbs of manner** can be used in different positions in a clause, although the end position is most typical:
• *He tore the letter up slowly.* • *She quickly left the room.*
Front position gives the adverb more emphasis: • *Suddenly the door flew open.*

Long adverbs and **adverbial phrases** usually go at the end of the clause:
• *She read it aloud monotonously.* • *He crossed the road without looking.*

B Correct the sentences if necessary. Tick any which are already correct.

1 Tomorrow is the boss having a day off.

2 She likes very much watching videos at home.

3 She turned to him with a contemptuous smile.

4 I went to the principal's office immediately.

5 They yesterday mowed their lawn.

6 I've always enjoyed reading, travelling and playing music very much.

7 He slammed suddenly the book down on the table.

8 Alma stamped out angrily of the office.

9 I always make sure I do every day my homework.

10 We go frequently for a picnic in the forest.

11 Always the foreman gives the workmen a ticking off.

12 The nurse suddenly rushed out of the operating theatre.

Some common adverbial phrases are **with hindsight/in retrospect**, **in the wake of**, **by no means**, **by ...%**, **in monthly instalments**, **without more/ further ado**, **with reference to**, **at the expense of**.

C Complete the sentences with the phrases from the study box above.

1 _____, he realised he should not have resigned.

2 The army was sent to the province, _____ popular unrest there.

3 The news sent the stock market plummeting _____.

4 They are paying for their new car _____.

5 _____, he put on his coat and left the room.

6 He was an extremely prolific writer, but his huge output was achieved _____ his health.

7 _____ your letter of 15th February, please note that I shall be consulting my legal advisors forthwith.

8 No, I'm afraid he's _____ the sort of friend I would have chosen for you.

D Choose the correct word or phrase from the pair in brackets to complete each sentence.

1 I simply can't remember what happens _____ of the book. (in the end/at the end)

2 We waited and waited, and _____ our turn came. (eventually/at the end)

3 There's a marvellous shot _____ of the film, with the heroine running along a deserted sandy beach. (in the beginning/at the beginning)

4 I'm sorry I won't be able to help you with the decorating. I'm _____ very busy myself. (presently/actually)

5 They climbed steeply for a hour and a half, and _____ they reached the summit. (at last/lastly)

6 He had to jump-start the car, but he _____ got it going. (in the end/finally)

There are many **confusing pairs** like **dead/deadly**, which do not follow normal adjective/adverb rules.
Deadly is an adjective, meaning *lethal*, while **dead** can be used as an adjective meaning *not alive*, or as an adverb meaning *completely*:
• *You're dead right.* (informal)

E Choose the correct word from the pair in brackets to complete each sentence. Refer to Section 7 of the Appendix for a brief definition of the words if necessary.

1 The vicar lives _____ to the church.   (close/closely)

2 Take it _____! I didn't mean to be rude!   (easy/easily)

3 Make sure the onions are _____ chopped.   (fine/finely)

4 He's a _____ good golfer, so I think he'll beat you. (pretty/prettily)

5 They'll be moving to Leeds _____.   (short/shortly)

6 Hold _____! Here comes a speed hump!   (tight/tightly)

7 I can ——- recommend that restaurant.   (high/highly)

8 The villagers campaigned _____ for the bypass to be re-routed. (hard/hardly)

9 It's _____ known that he's the best in his field.   (wide/widely)

10 Be there at nine o'clock _____, or you'll miss all the bargains. (sharp/sharply)

11 You can get in _____ with this voucher.   (free/freely)

12 I feel very hard done by. He just isn't playing _____. (fair/fairly)

13 I couldn't believe it when they turned me down _____! (flat/flatly)

14 They drove _____ from Milan to Paris without stopping. (direct/directly)

15 They turned up very _____ for the celebrations.   (late/lately)

16 They _____ refused to consider my proposition.   (flat/flatly)

17 Don't make a noise. The baby's _____ asleep.   (sound/soundly)

18 He cut her _____ with a wave of the hand.   (short/shortly)

19 I _____ forgot my passport. I only remembered it at the last minute.   (near/nearly)

20 She hit the target _____ in the centre.   (right/rightly)

See **Unit 16** for the use of **negative adverbs** at the beginning of a sentence.

Recycling

A Choose the correct word or phrase to complete each sentence. Write the letter in the space.

1 They'll explain _____ you need to know to complete your report.

 a) what   b) that   c) which   d) how

2 The TV company _____ contract is up for renewal is losing money.

 a) which   b) whose   c) the   d) who's

3 In _____, it was obviously the wrong thing to do.

 a) hindsight   b) the wake   c) retrospect   d) the whole

4 I'll have to do overtime tonight, _____ is very tiresome.

 a) which   b) what   c) that   d) so

5 There were _____ few tickets sold that the concert was cancelled.

 a) a   b) very   c) so   d) such

6 The piano was _____ heavy for us to carry from the removal van.

 a) far   b) much   c) so   d) too

7 I'm afraid that's the best _____ can do for you.

 a) which   b) I   c) that   d) what

8 He _____ that he had three Rolls-Royces at home.

 a) threatened   b) reminded   c) boasted   d) informed

9 You've got to be _____ certain before you decide.

 a) deadly   b) deathly   c) dead   d) dearly

10 She burst into tears when he spoke to her _____.

 a) sharp   b) sharpish   c) sharper   d) sharply

11 Her cousin is _____ related to the Hapsburg family.

 a) nearly   b) close   c) closely   d) near

12 We accused him _____ a blatant lie.

 a) to telling   b) to tell   c) in telling   d) of telling

13 You _____ assumed that we'd be starting at 8.00.

 a) right   b) rightly   c) fairly   d) fair

14 The witness _____ ever having seen the prisoner.

 a) denied   b) admitted   c) insisted   d) objected

15 Police are reported _____ found illegal drugs in a secret hiding place in the star's home.

 a) they have   b) having   c) to have   d) have had

16 No, he _____ ever jogs round the park these days.

 a) doesn't   b) occasionally   c) hardly   d) almost

17 It's by _____ means the best book I've ever read.

 a) no   b) all   c) far   d) some

18 She waited for twenty minutes and _____ arrived at the head of the queue.

 a) lastly   b) finally   c) at the end   d) eventual

B Read this jumbled memo from an employer to members of staff, and put the sentences in the correct order, using the discourse markers to help you.

To: All staff

From: Chief Executive

Date: 22.08.01

Re: Break-in incident

a Be that as it may, the police have always advised against this type of direct action, if intruders are spotted on the premises. Therefore the company would like all staff to maintain a low profile if such a situation recurs.

b Last but not least, please remember that the company is ultimately responsible for the safety of its employees while on the premises, and it is our policy to encourage you to safeguard yourselves from harm at all times.

c Following the recent incident during the lunch break, when an attempt was made by opportunistic thieves to steal computers from the main office, I want to remind staff of company policy on intruders.

d Accordingly, do NOT follow Don's and Neil's example. Instead, restrict yourself to challenging a possible intruder verbally. On no account should you resort to physical restraint or violence.

e Firstly, however, I must thank two members of staff, Don and Neil, for their bravery and presence of mind. As no doubt you all know by now, they confronted and succeeded in capturing the intruders.

C Complete the second sentence so that it means the same as the first one, using the word given. You must use between **three** and **eight** words, including the word given. (Contractions count as two words.)

1 At the moment people think the accident is Nick's fault.

   blamed

   Nick is currently _____ the accident.

2 'I didn't harm anybody!' cried the accused.

   to

   The accused denied _____ anybody.

3 Even though the invaders were short of ammunition, they won the battle.

   a

   Despite _____ by the invaders.

4 Your scheme is brilliant, but it won't succeed.

   doomed

   Brilliant though _____ failure.

5 Although it's fun being with her, I think she talks too much.

   company

   Much as I _____ too talkative.

6 There is a rumour that the principal is planning to retire early.

   rumoured

   The principal _____ early retirement.

7 There was no further delay in awarding the prizes.

   more

   The prizes _____ ado.

8 I was in the middle of my speech when Pippa interrupted me.

   cut

   Pippa _____ through my speech.

D Complete the passage by putting **one** word in each space. The main focus of this task is on grammar rather than vocabulary.

A substance produced 1) _____ disease-transmitting insects 2) _____ provide the key to fighting these same diseases. Mosquitoes and blackflies transmit malaria and river blindness respectively, both of 3) _____ cause a large number of deaths every year. However, scientists 4) _____ now discovered, in some of these insects, a substance called a peptide 5) _____ kills the viruses and parasites 6) _____ carry. 7) _____ introduced techniques have allowed researchers 8) _____ study these minute insects in 9) _____ to find out more about the peptides.

Professor John Wells said yesterday that if his team 10) _____ identify the genes responsible for 11) _____ the peptides, they 12) _____ introduce into the world genetically altered mosquitoes 13) _____ were incapable of 14) _____ the disease. In the 15) _____ of these exciting developments, it 16) _____ hoped that science 17) _____ be able to eradicate some major tropical diseases sooner rather than later.

E Choose from the list A-J the best phrase to fill each gap. Use each correct phrase only once. There are more answers than you need.

THE JARGON JUNGLE

According to a recent survey, one in five office workers in Britain no longer understands 1) _____ . At meetings many people are left floundering, confused by management jargon and specialised 'babble' – the kind of language 2) _____ these days. Secretarial recruitment firm Office Angels administered the survey to over 1000 office staff and found 3) _____ derived from corporate gurus, American slang and the internet. Some employees complained that the phrases were irritating and distracting at meetings, while others dismissed speakers 4) _____ as pretentious and untrustworthy. Provided that puzzled listeners can find the courage to seek clarification, they may discover what the speaker really means. But most do not ask, 5) _____ .

A spokesperson for Office Angels said the survey showed 6) _____ in the workplace. She added that jargon can either help to bring individuals and teams together, as companies and sectors develop their own phraseology, 7) _____ to exclude and confuse people, as well as masking inexperience and lack of expertise.

A for fear of revealing their ignorance
B that 65% had to cope with jargon
C which is often heard at work
D that corporate buzz words were rife
E which speaker really means it

F who used them frequently
G to pretend they are in control
H what his or her colleagues are talking about
I who liven up meetings
J or it can be used

UNIT 16

Verb inversion

In formal English the subject and verb are occasionally inverted, to give emphasis or literary or dramatic effect. This should be avoided in spoken or informal English.

Inversion may take place in

a adverb clauses beginning with **Scarcely/Hardly... when/before, No sooner... than**:
  • *Hardly had he raised the alarm(,) when the fire engine arrived.*
  • *No sooner had she told him her address than she regretted it.*

b negative adverb clauses beginning with **Under no circumstances, On no account, In vain, At no time, In no way, Never/Not for one moment, Seldom, Rarely, Never**:
  • *In vain did they try to persuade him.*

c conditional clauses in which **if** is replaced by **had, had... but, had... only, should**:
  • *Should the rope break, the dinghy will float away.*
  • *Had Colin but informed the police, he would be safe now.*

d clauses with **so + adjective** (or **little, few, much, many**) or **such + noun**:
  • *So little did he know about her(,) that he was not even sure of her name.*
  • *Such was my annoyance(,) that I tore up the letter.*

A Rewrite the sentences, putting the words in italics at the beginning, and making any other necessary changes.

1 They had *seldom* participated in such a fascinating ceremony.

2 I pleaded with him *in vain*. He was adamant.

3 Miss Weaver will not be offered the job *under* any *circumstances*.

4 If the film *should* be a box-office success, there may be a sequel.

5 He was *so surprised* to be addressed by the Queen that he didn't answer at once.

6 If only they *had* confirmed by phone, the airline could have warned them.

7 He had *hardly* entered the house when the police arrested him.

8 I *never* for one moment thought the consequences would be so far-reaching.

9 She has *rarely* travelled more than fifty miles from her village.

10 You must *on no account* lift heavy weights like that again.

11 I had *scarcely* put down the phone when it rang again.

12 The defendant did not express his misgivings *in* any *way*.

13 The task was *so* difficult that expert assistance was required.

14 If they *had* accepted our offer, we would have moved house by now.

B Match the two halves of the sentences correctly.

1 No sooner had Karen parked her car

2 Such was her fury that

3 Scarcely had the plane landed

4 Should you need any help,

5 Nowhere else in the world

A I'll be available all afternoon.

B when it was surrounded by photographers.

C than a lorry crashed into it.

D can you find palaces as fine as these.

E she threw the book across the room.

Inversion also takes place

a after **only** and **as**:
  - *Only yesterday did I hear the news.*
  - *They live in Hollywood, as do most of the other stars.*
  Also note the use of **Not only... but also**:
  - *Not only did we get wet, but we also lost our passports.*

b in clauses with ***here** and ***there**, and other adverbial expressions of place. Note that **do/did** are not used: • *Here are the answers.*
  - *Up jumped the cat.* • *In the corner sat a large pig.*
  Note also that continuous tenses are rare:
  - *There goes the bus!* NOT ***There is going the bus!**
  In this case inversion does not take place if the subject is a pronoun:
  - *Here you are!* • *Down it jumped.* • *Round the corner she ran.*

  *Inversion after these words is normal, not just a formal use.

c in short answers with **neither**, **nor** and **so**, formally and informally:
  - *Neither do I.* • *Nor is he.* • *So are you.*

C Correct the sentences if necessary, beginning with the same word. Tick any which are already correct.

1 Over fell I, and broke my leg.
2 'I'd rather have a walk in the morning.' 'So I would.'
3 Not only she twisted her ankle, but she also dropped her purse.
4 Down in the valley lay a fertile-looking vineyard.
5 Only recently did scientists discover a cure for certain types of leukaemia.
6 Charlotte Brontë died of tuberculosis, as did all her sisters.
7 Up the stairs did the plump old housekeeper puff.
8 Look, there go the children on their way to school.
9 Right through the underwater tunnel swam she.
10 Only if you pay cash will you get the car.
11 Into the valley of death rode the six hundred.
12 There is the famous statue of Admiral Lord Nelson standing.
13 Only last week found I the information I'd been looking for.
14 Here the police come! Someone must have called them.

D Complete the second sentence so that it means the same as the first one, using the word given. You must use between **three** and **eight** words, including the word given. Be careful, because inversion may not be required in every sentence.

1 It isn't worth considering his suggestion for a moment.
   giving
   Not for one moment _____ consideration.

2 He was so disgusted at the way she behaved that he refused to speak to her.
   her
   Such _____ he refused to speak to her.

3 Adele tries hard, but she doesn't get anywhere.
   hard
   However _____ nowhere.

4 The volunteers' efforts to avert the catastrophe were unsuccessful.
   attempt
   In vain _____ avert the catastrophe.

5 I was never shown how to operate the machine.
   ever
   At no time _____ the machine work.

6 The firm had never celebrated anything so lavishly before.
   such
   Never _____ laid on by the firm.

7 It wasn't until last week that the minister admitted he was wrong.
   error
   Only last week _____ of judgement.

8 Tick the box if you wish to take advantage of the offer.
   accept
   Should _____ tick in the box.

9 We may have to reject applications in a few cases.
   be
   In a few cases, applications _____ down.

10 Invitations were sent out as soon as the date was chosen.
   been
   Hardly _____ invitations were sent out.

11 In order to stay open, the charity shop needs at least four helpers.
   enable
   No fewer _____ the charity shop to stay open.

12 If his father hadn't advised him against it, he might have become a record producer.
   for
   Had it not _____ a record producer now.

13 The employees insisted on being given a full bonus.
   satisfy
   Nothing but _____ the employees.

14 This computer data is strictly confidential.
   revealed
   Under no circumstances _____ to anyone.

Comparison and similarity

As is used in three main ways to express **similarity**.

a as a preposition, when it describes a function:
- *He was disguised as a security guard.*
- *I used the encyclopedia as a doorstop.*

b as a conjunction with a verb clause or prepositional phrase:
- *He stayed at the Raffles Hotel, as he had done the previous time.*
- *In Greece, as in Spain, people are hospitable to strangers.*

c in expressions such as **as you know**, **as you like**, **as you suggested**.
(See **Unit 16** for inversion after **as** in formal English.)

Like is a preposition, followed by a noun or pronoun, used for **similarity or comparison**:
- *I'm a teacher, like my father.*   • *Like her friends, she loves rock concerts.*

Like can be used as an alternative to **such as**, when offering an example:
- *The great French Impressionists, such as/like Monet, ...*

Note that **like** is sometimes used instead of **as** with a verb clause:
- *They ignored the ban on smoking, like they did last time.*
However, this is not generally considered correct.

A Complete the sentences, by inserting *as* or *like*.

1 You don't look anything _____ your mother.

2 _____ we expected, the singer didn't arrive on time.

3 _____ your teacher, I advise you to read more in order to widen your vocabulary.

4 He dug a snow hole and waited for help, _____ he had been instructed to do.

5 Her father was a great sportsman, just _____ her grandfather.

6 Her father was a great sportsman, just _____ her grandfather used to be.

7 We don't need the box, but we can use it _____ firewood.

8 She went to the party dressed up _____ Cleopatra.

9 Several state museums, _____ in other countries, are imposing admission charges.

10 _____ you say, we shouldn't argue about it.

11 She worked _____ a bilingual secretary for two years.

12 The local council, _____ others in the area, is taking a strong line on parking offences.

13 _____ his colleagues, Yves has a postgraduate qualification.

14 The twentieth century produced a number of female political leaders, _____ Indira Gandhi and Margaret Thatcher.

15 _____ you, Colette experienced considerable difficulty in adapting to an alien environment.

As...as is used with adjectives or adverbs. As much/many...as is used with nouns or verbs:

- *The road's as straight as a ruler.*
- *Exercise as much as you can.*
- *Take as many oranges as you want.*

Negative comparisons are made with **not as/so + adjective/adverb + as**:
- *The proposal isn't as attractive as it seemed at first.*

Twice, **three times**, **half** etc. can precede comparisons, and they can be modified with **(not) nearly**, **just**, **nothing like**, **almost**, **every bit**, **exactly**:
- *He's twice as old as you are.*   • *It wasn't half so difficult as I thought.*
- *My cake's every bit as nice as yours.*

B Correct the sentences if necessary. Tick any which are already correct.

1 She's nothing like so good at tennis like her friend.
2 Mine cost three times as much as yours.
3 Have as many potatoes that you like.
4 His hand is so steady as a rock.
5 The cottage isn't as well-built as we thought.
6 She works just as hard as you do.
7 Eat as much as you can, now you're feeling better.
8 Last night's current affairs programme was almost as interesting as last week's.
9 The dictionary wasn't nearly as helpful than I had hoped.
10 Their population is twice as large as ours.
11 Laurie drank half as much beer like Hugo.
12 Their offer is every bit as acceptable than yours.

The same...as is used before a noun, pronoun, verb clause or prepositional phrase:
- *Her name's the same as her cousin's.*

The same...that can also be used before a verb clause, and **that** may be omitted if it is the object:
- *He's living in the same house (that) he used to live in.*
- *It's the same dog that's been hanging around all week.*

C Correct the sentences if necessary. Tick any which are already correct.

1 That's same formula you told me last week.
2 They're the same people we went to the theatre with.
3 I borrowed the same book as I'd taken out the week before.
4 That's same man that we saw in the bank robbery!
5 The medicine will have the same effect as last time.
6 The rules are same same in my country.
7 The traffic's probably the same on the bypass as in the town centre.
8 Did you pay the same than I did?

The **comparative** of most two-syllable adjectives is formed by adding **-er**. With adjectives ending in **-y**, the **-y** is replaced with **-ier**. With most other adjectives, **more/less** are used:
- *a smaller dog*   • *a prettier flower*   • *a less interesting book*

Than is always used in a comparison: • *Yours is better than mine.*

Comparatives can be modified with **a bit, a little, even, much, a lot, far, a great deal**:
- *Today's puzzles are far more difficult to do than yesterday's. They're a great deal more complicated.*

Double comparatives convey the idea of change:
- *She's getting thinner and thinner.*
- *He's becoming more and more cantankerous.*

When two changes happen together, we sometimes use **The..., the...**:
- *The older you get, the more you learn.*

The superlative of most short adjectives and adverbs is formed with **the + -est**. Longer words take **the most/least**. Note these irregular superlatives:
- *best*   • *worst*   • *furthest/farthest*

Superlatives can be modified with **by far** for emphasis:
- *She's by far the most talented musician in the group.*

D Correct the sentences if necessary. Tick any which are already correct.

1 More you work, more money you earn.
2 The more it is difficult, more harder he tries.
3 He's been working longer that you.
4 This meat's tougher as yesterday's.
5 I found myself becoming more and more terrified.
6 You're the more infuriating person I've ever met.
7 He's a great deal the best boxer in the world.
8 The patient looked worse a week ago than yesterday.
9 My cousin is very taller than me.
10 We all live a long way away, but Jim lives the furthest.
11 I think the driver is a bit the tireder than me.
12 At the moment he's less neurotic than I've ever seen him.
13 The more, the merry.
14 Our plans are getting more and more out of hand.
15 It was the dreariest hotel I'd never had the misfortune to stay in.
16 That one's the slowliest train.
17 The view from the penthouse suite is by far the best.
18 Your work's more impressive then anyone else's.
19 The greater your input, the more satisfaction you get out of a project.
20 I suppose you've chosen the least unpleasant option.

Participles

Present participles (e.g. *going, breaking, starting*), and **past participles** (e.g. *gone, broken, started*) are used with auxiliary verbs to form continuous, perfect and passive forms, or as adjectives:

- *He's just dashing after her.*   • *It'll be done as soon as possible.*
- *It's an exhausting job.*   • *She's got a broken arm.*

Note the difference between **adjectives ending in -ing** and **-ed**. The present participle (e.g. *exciting, interesting, boring*) describes the person or thing that is initiating the action. The past participle (e.g. *excited, interested, bored*) describes someone's reactions to something:

- *I thought the race was very exciting.*   • *We weren't very interested in the film.*

Participles can be used to give a **reason** for doing something, or to show a **time connection** between clauses/phrases:

- *Realising she was wrong, she apologised.*   • *Having paid the bill, he left the hotel.*

The subject of the participle clause should be the same as in the main clause, but note the following exceptions to this rule: **generally/broadly speaking, taking everything into consideration/account, supposing, providing, considering, judging by/from**:

- *Generally speaking, these plants grow better in chalky soil.*
- *Providing no one objects, I'll reschedule the meeting.*

A Complete the sentences by filling the gaps with a suitable participle.

1 _____ delivered the message, the boy went home.

2 We were awfully _____ by the company's decision, which seemed quite wrong to us.

3 He was thrilled by the film and thought it very _____.

4 The burglar must have got in through the _____ window.

5 _____ you had no money, what would you do?

6 _____ rather exhausted, she decided to give the meeting a miss.

7 The departmental head spoke to his assistant, _____ why he was being so uncooperative.

8 _____ packed our cases, we took a taxi to the airport.

9 _____ everything into consideration, I think you're right.

10 How can we motivate the children? They always look so _____ when we talk to them.

11 Claudia entered the room, _____ a tray of soft drinks.

12 _____ unable to concentrate, I fell asleep.

13 _____ unexpectedly into the room, she took the intruder by surprise.

14 _____ by his appearance, Timothy doesn't spend much on his clothes.

15 He was sitting in his usual corner, _____ miserable and _____ his pipe.

Present participles can be used after certain verbs and their objects, e.g. **see**, **hear**, **feel**, **smell**, **notice**, **watch**:
• *I heard a warbler singing in the woods.*
• *Did you notice the man sitting in the corner?*
This suggests that we heard/noticed an action which continued, whereas if an **infinitive without to** is used instead, it suggests that we heard/noticed the whole of the action, including its completion. Compare:
• *I saw her plant the tree.* (I saw her finish the planting.) with
• *I saw her planting the tree.* (I saw her in the middle of planting.)

B Decide whether to use a present participle or an infinitive (without *to*) in these sentences.

1 We watched her (close) the door. (The door is shut now.)
2 I saw him (repair) the fence. (I didn't see him finish it.)
3 Can you smell the chicken (cook)? (It isn't ready to eat yet.)
4 She heard a door (bang). (just once)
5 I didn't notice them (stand) there. (I didn't see them leave.)
6 I felt anger (well) up inside me. (a brief feeling of anger which soon passed)
7 He saw a man (throw) something that glinted in the sun. (It was a quick action that is now over.)
8 He watched the customs official (open) his case and (take) out his clothes garment by garment.

After, on, until, as, once, when, while, whenever, before and since can all be followed by participle clauses:
• *Once correctly installed, the system will give years of trouble-free use.*
• *On being accused, the young man immediately confessed.*
• *After buying the flowers, he took them to the hospital.*
• *Whenever sunbathing, make sure you use a sunscreen.*

Remember that the subject of the main clause should also be the subject of the participle clause, apart from certain exceptions (see study box on **page 60**).
So the following sentence is wrong:
Once correctly installed, you will have no trouble with the system.

C Complete the sentences with one of these words: *as, since, when, after, once, on.* Use each word only once.

1 _____ taken out of the oven, the cake should be left to cool on a wire rack.
2 She's been bedridden _____ undergoing her last operation.
3 _____ making the arrangements for the wedding, don't forget to order the flowers.
4 _____ having concluded the interviews, they spent some time discussing the respective merits of the candidates.
5 _____ being welcomed to the town, Lady Higginbottom gave an eloquent speech in reply.
6 He struck me _____ being rather eccentric.

Some **past participles used as adjectives** change their meaning according to their position.

Concerned after a noun means *relevant* or *affected*, but before a noun it means *worried*:
- *The grant will be given to the family concerned.*
- *Concerned parents have expressed their anxiety.*

Adopted after a noun means *chosen*, but before a noun it usually refers to a child who officially becomes part of someone else's family:
- *There was uproar over the policies adopted.*
- *The adopted child will never discover the identity of his parents.*

Involved after a noun means *relevant* or *affected*, but before a noun it means *complicated*:
- *I'll have a word with the people involved.*
- *He gave us a long and involved explanation.*

D Correct the sentences if necessary. Tick any which are already correct.

1 When booking a room for myself and my wife the other day, the receptionist was rather rude to me.

2 Looking at my diary, there were several double-booked appointments.

3 Remember to use unleaded petrol whenever filling the tank.

4 I hope you've mentioned this to the concerned people in the matter.

5 Not having written about the required topic, the teacher gave my presentation a low mark.

6 It was an extremely involved story. I couldn't make head or tail of it.

7 While working in California, my house was damaged by an earthquake.

8 Being such a sunny day, I got up early and went for a swim.

9 Judging from his expression, you're about to be disciplined!

10 Do you know anyone having been to the Canary Islands?

11 The employees involved will have their pay docked.

12 The club approved of the solution adopted by the sub-committee.

13 Whenever leaving the premises, please ensure that the security system is switched on.

14 Once ensconced in his comfortable armchair, the television didn't bother him at all.

Adjectives

> **Adjectives** are used to modify nouns or as complements to verbs like **be** and **seem**:
> • *a romantic novel*   • *Martin seems happy, and Tracy is cheerful.*
>
> Notice these similar adjectives: **asleep/sleeping, afloat/floating, afraid/frightened, ajar/open, awake/waking, ablaze/blazing, alone/lone, alight/burning, alive/live**. The first one of each pair cannot be used before a noun, and is normally used with the verb **be**:
> • *He is awake.*   • *The ship was afloat.*   • *The house was ablaze.*

A Complete each sentence with the correct adjective from the pair in brackets.

1 All the guests are fast _____. (asleep/sleeping)

2 Her mother hated living all _____. (alone/lone)

3 The firemen had to carry the _____ children to safety. (afraid/frightened)

4 The salvage teams watched the_____ wreck from the shore. (ablaze/blazing)

5 They can't get to sleep. They're wide _____. (awake/waking)

6 I think I can smell a(n) _____ cigarette in the room. (alight/burning)

7 It's a (n) _____ concert, coming to you via satellite from Rome. (alive/live)

8 Flies buzzed in through the _____ door. (ajar/open)

9 As soon as we're _____, we'll set sail for France. (afloat/floating)

> With certain verbs, like **be**, **seem**, **sound**, ***look**, ***appear**, ***taste**, ***feel** and ***smell**, adjectives, not adverbs, are used:
> • *This dish tastes delicious.*   • *The house looks dirty.*
>
> *****These verbs can be used with an adverb when they refer to an action rather than a state:
> • *She tasted the dessert appreciatively.*   • *He looked seriously at me.*
>
> Certain other verbs, e.g. **sit**, **lie**, **stand**, **fall**, **become**, **go**, **get** and **turn**, can also be followed by adjectives, when the adjective describes the subject:
> • *I went red with embarrassment.*   • *She fell ill and died.*
> • *The mountain stood powerful and threatening ahead of me.*

B Correct the sentences if necessary. Tick any which are already correct.

1 She turned palely with fear.

2 I felt the bird's wing gently.

3 The boy stood motionless in the corner.

4 This trick seems easy to do, but it isn't.

5 I'm feeling more enthusiastic now you've explained it all to me.

6 He became angrily when he saw what had happened.

7 This pasta tastes garlicky.

8 Don't look at me so resentfully. It wasn't my fault.

9 Your friend Carrie sounds charming.

10 The patient was lying unconsciously on the bed.

Adjectives can be used in certain expressions with **the**, when we are generalising, to indicate a whole group of people: • *the rich, the poor, the old, the disabled, the dead, the unemployed, the blind, the deaf*
Some adjectives of nationality can also be used like this, including all nationality adjectives ending in **-sh** or **-ch**: • *the British, the Spanish, the French*

Plural nouns with numbers become singular when they are used as adjectives: • *a ten-mile walk, a three-hour journey*

C Correct the sentences if necessary. Tick any which are already correct.

1 The new toilets in town are for the disabled people.

2 It will probably be a two-hours lecture.

3 Dominic works at a special school for blind.

4 The eleven-year-old girl won first prize.

5 In many societies it is true that the rich get richer, and the poor get poorer.

6 French negotiated with Spanish over the return of the wanted fugitives.

The order of adjectives is important where there is more than one adjective in front of a noun. The following order should generally be observed:
opinion, size, age, shape, colour, origin/nationality, material/purpose, NOUN.

However, some adjectives and nouns are used so often together that the above rule does not apply:
• *We drank some delicious Spanish white wine.*   NOT **white Spanish wine*

D Unscramble the following sentences.

1 saw a I silk sweet green little scarf

2 was huge castle a there mediaeval stone hill the on

3 beautiful ship at quay moored white a sailing was the

4 battered is table leather a there old suitcase the on

5 live ancient cottage the sea by they fisherman's in an

6 was her striped bag shopping carrying she canvas a heavy arm full vegetables of on

7 introduced a handsome executive she to young was remarkably

8 wearing smart business a a jazzy suit grey waistcoat he was with

9 cakes butter the Danish unsalted makes with she only best

10 an oriental extremely carpet exotic he bought just has

E Match the adjectives, connected with people's emotions or character, with their approximate opposites.

1	unperturbed	A	sensitive
2	lazy	B	cheerful
3	gloomy	C	forgiving
4	strict	D	garrulous
5	thick-skinned	E	slapdash
6	reserved	F	sceptical
7	defensive	G	integrated
8	gullible	H	apprehensive
9	indecisive	I	unreliable
10	methodical	J	easy-going
11	alienated	K	aggressive
12	sincere	L	purposeful
13	carefree	M	devious
14	vindictive	N	anxious
15	dependable	O	energetic

F Complete the sentences with the correct adjective from the box. Use each word only once.

> sworn   dire   gruelling   blatant   mere   burgeoning
> insatiable   first-hand   innovative   primary   abortive
> contemporary   fierce   lucrative   heinous

1 He committed the offence in _____ disregard of the rules.
2 The children have a(n) _____ appetite for sweets.
3 The company made a(n) _____ effort to improve productivity, but finally had to call in the receivers.
4 Her father's always been a(n) _____ critic of modern art.
5 You can't expect him to know any better – he's a(n) _____ child.
6 Overwork and a(n) _____ reading tour of the USA contributed largely to Charles Dickens' death.
7 Howard Barker is hailed by some as one of our most _____ playwrights.
8 Police consider the murder one of the most _____ crimes in recent years.
9 The island was quite content with its _____ prosperity.
10 From the moment the boys saw each other, they were _____ enemies.
11 The company is in _____ need of financial assistance.
12 You need to find a(n) _____ market for your products.
13 It is hard for _____ authors to achieve the status of earlier writers who have become household names.
14 Unemployment is the _____ focus of concern in many people's minds.
15 Josephine's actually worked in the diplomatic service, so she has _____ experience.

Recycling

A Choose the correct word or phrase to complete each sentence. Write the letter in the space.

1 He'll believe anything. He's so _____.
   a) garrulous   b) gullible   c) credible   d) believable

2 At _____ time did I ever promise you a pay rise.
   a) any   b) no   c) all   d) some

3 He's got plenty of _____ experience as he's worked in that field already.
   a) second-hand   b) first-hand   c) primary   d) tertiary

4 The feuding families have been _____ enemies for years.
   a) sworn   b) promised   c) cursed   d) blood

5 Not only was there no tea, _____ there was no food either.
   a) and   b) nor   c) but   d) so

6 The girl felt _____ with hunger.
   a) faintly   b) fainting   c) fainted   d) faint

7 Here is an example of an ancient _____ Chinese vase.
   a) beautiful   b) tiny   c) patterned   d) exotic

8 People in this village have got an _____ appetite for news.
   a) inexorable   b) inevitable   c) insatiable   d) inedible

9 Hardly had he sat down _____ he was sent for again.
   a) when   b) than   c) after   d) that

10 Even the other convicts considered it a _____ crime.
   a) guilty   b) hard-bitten   c) heinous   d) hell-bent

11 Nothing was arranged – it was all very _____.
   a) take away   b) worn out   c) slapdash   d) slap up

12 She gave me the same advice _____ you did.
   a) like   b) than   c) as   d) who

13 _____ you are, the more you laugh.
   a) The happier   b) More happy   c) The happy   d) Happier

14 She's _____ about her nursing exams, but I'm sure she'll do well.
   a) alienated   b) keen   c) stressed   d) apprehensive

15 All the way along the winding street _____.
   a) he came   b) came he   c) did he come   d) comes he

16 Don't worry about making a noise. The children are wide _____.
   a) waking   b) awake   c) woken   d) awoke

17 She's always been one of your _____ critics.
   a) fiercest   b) most violent   c) wildest   d) hardest

18 _____ has such a stunning achievement been recorded.
   a) Always   b) Seldom   c) Today   d) Recently

19 When _____ money into the slot, be sure to use undamaged coins.
   a) on inserting   b) having inserted   c) to insert   d) inserting

20 The mother sat by her _____ child's bedside all night.
   a) asleep   b) sleep   c) sleeping   d) overslept

B Choose from the list A-K the best phrase to fill each gap. Use each correct phrase only once. There are more answers than you need.

GETTING TO SLEEP

If you suffer from insomnia, there are several natural remedies 1) _____ the next day. Start with essential oils, 2) _____ or by diffusion in the lungs when you inhale them. A combination of lavender and geranium oil is highly recommended 3) _____ after travelling.

If you have an aversion to aromatherapy, why not try listening to soothing sounds? The right kind of sound can help you drop off 4) _____ to a sleep-ready state. Playing relaxing music or sounds from the natural world can facilitate the transition 5) _____ to sleep mode.

Another solution is to sleep with a hop pillow under your head. The hop plant, 6) _____ for its use in beer, provides the stuffing for an aromatic pillow, 7) _____ for centuries.

Perhaps the most popular sleep therapy at the moment is the use of flower essences. It was native Australians 8) _____ the different healing properties of certain flowers, and nowadays many people combat sleeplessness by using blends of flower essences.

A by slowing down your bodily processes
B which makes you fall asleep
C which won't leave you feeling terrible
D by raising your heart rate
E although better known
F who originally discovered
G whose calming qualities have been known
H from alert, wakeful state
I which has incredible holistic value
J for help with getting to sleep
K which work either via skin absorption

C Complete the passage by putting **one** word in each space. (Do not use contractions – they count as two words.)

Education was not formally integrated into the European Union policy portfolio 1) _____ the 1993 Maastricht Treaty, although the first Community legislation with an impact on the education sector was adopted as long ago as the 1960s. These early 2) _____ dealt with mutual recognition of qualifications. Achieving recognition by one member state of a qualification obtained in 3) _____ was an important pre-condition for implementing the free movement of workers.

Citizens of EU countries 4) _____ are students now enjoy the same rights of access to higher education in all member states 5) _____ they do in their home country, 6) _____ that they have the relevant qualifications for entry. Growing numbers of student exchange activities 7) _____ been developed, of 8) _____ the oldest and most famous is the 1987 Erasmus programme. 9) _____ recognising course credits, Erasmus allows university students to study for one year in a different member state. A separate programme, Leonardo, gives young school leavers, students and graduates the 10) _____ to receive vocational training.

Few EU initiatives enjoy 11) _____ wholehearted and widespread political support as these higher education programmes. The key issue for future initiatives is to build on this success 12) _____ being over-ambitious. Unfortunately, these programmes are becoming 13) _____ expensive, and this is now the primary 14) _____ of concern.

D Read the following message left by a parent. Use the information in the message to complete the letter to an employment agency which follows. Use either **one or two** words for each gap. The words you will need do not occur in the message.

Diane

The employment agency rang. Good news and bad news! The bad news is that the Paris job is only paying £20,000. The good news is that the agency's got details of a job in Frankfurt instead. You'll probably want to drop the Paris one and get them to pass your c.v. on to the German firm. Can you let them know? Better ask them what they know about the Frankfurt job. And you could mention that you'll be away on Thursday and Friday of next week, in case they want to fix a time to see you. Make sure you tell them what a good job they're doing for you!

Mum

Dear Mr Sampson,

Thank you for getting 1) _____ again recently. I understand that the 2) _____ for the Paris job has turned out to be quite a bit 3) _____ I was expecting, so I would like you to 4) _____ my application for that one. Please do 5) _____ my c.v. to the German company, however, and send me 6) _____ you have on that 7) _____. If they wish to arrange 8) _____, I shall be 9) _____ any day next week 10) _____ Thursday and Friday.

I really am 11) _____ for all your help, and can assure you I 12) _____ your efforts on my 13) _____.

Yours sincerely,

Diane Woolley

Prepositions

> **Prepositions** are words or groups of words, normally used before a noun or pronoun to express a relationship between one person/event etc. and another:
> * *She walked into the operating theatre.*   * *He seemed strangely out of breath.*
>
> Prepositions may relate to space, time, cause, origin, purpose, source, agent, instrument, possession, topic or abstract ideas:
> * *They arrived at midnight.*   * *He's done it for his own reasons.*
> * *The shirt is made of cotton.*   * *We live in hope.*
>
> Refer to **Section 8** of the Appendix for a list of expressions with **above**, **over**, **beneath**, **below**, **under**, **at**, **by**, **between**, **among**, **in**, **on**, **out of**.

A Use an expression with *above, over, under, below* or *beneath* to complete each sentence.

1 He's too young to be allowed in this bar. He's _____.

2 Nobody would ever suspect her. She's _____.

3 There'll be no trouble about repairing the television if it goes wrong. It's _____.

4 Don't let those children get too wild! Keep them _____.

5 He's taller than most people. He's of _____.

6 The main thing is, don't hurt him. _____, keep him safe.

7 That's rather unfair. You're hitting _____.

8 I'm afraid I can't work for anyone else. You see, I'm _____ to my present employers for two years.

9 He whispered the answer. 'Yes,' he said, _____.

10 Someone who robs an old lady of all her savings is _____, and deserves to be punished.

11 Use one of the _____ prepositions to complete these sentences.

12 It's very frosty this morning. The temperature must have dropped _____.

13 Shall we discuss the problem after lunch, _____?

14 He's a freelance film director, and travels all _____ making his films.

15 The village is well _____, and at risk of being flooded if the sea wall is breached by a particularly high tide.

16 Doctors think heart attacks are sometimes brought on by being _____ at home or at work.

17 You'll have to tell me the truth. Stop trying to pull the wool _____!

18 If you don't bargain with the market traders, you'll be paying _____ for their goods.

B Match each expression with *at* on the left with its approximate paraphrase.

1	at a loss	A	unoccupied, with no purpose
2	at short notice	B	going very fast
3	at any rate	C	deep down inside (a person)
4	at present	D	no matter what it takes
5	at a loose end	E	without much advance warning
6	at once	F	fighting another country
7	at heart	G	immediately
8	at hand	H	unsure what to do
9	at first sight	I	taking the most hopeful view
10	at times	J	near, ready, available
11	at war	K	sailing, on a ship
12	at all costs	L	in danger
13	at sea	M	the first time (I) saw (her)
14	at best	N	anyway
15	at risk	O	occasionally
16	at high speed	P	now

C Complete the sentences with the correct preposition, choosing from *between*, *among*, *out of* and *over*.

1 Bob's been _____ work for six months now.

2 _____ you and me, Smith hasn't got much of a future in the firm.

3 That book's too high up on the shelf. It's just _____ my reach.

4 She's _____ jobs at the moment, so she's struggling to make ends meet.

5 Unfortunately the catering committee can never agree _____ themselves.

6 I went on waving until the car was _____ sight.

7 We'll discuss the affair _____ a cup of tea.

8 It's no good trying that snack machine – it's _____ order.

9 The boys were hiding _____ the bushes in the garden.

10 There's a footpath _____ the canal and the main road.

11 No, I certainly won't give permission. It's _____ the question!

12 I can only admire his conscientiousness. It's _____ and above the call of duty.

13 I'm afraid those sandals are _____ stock at the moment, madam.

14 General Gibson settled in quite happily _____ the Polynesian natives.

15 I'm hoping to be reimbursed for my travelling expenses, otherwise I'll be rather _____ pocket.

16 The lift wasn't working, so she was _____ breath by the time she reached the top floor.

17 A prize was awarded to Fawzia, _____ others.

18 Children, put your coats on if you want to play _____ doors.

19 The photo's _____ focus, unfortunately, but you can still make out the figure in the doorway.

20 This information is rather _____ date, so we can't use it in our new brochure.

D Complete each sentence with the correct preposition from the pair in brackets.

1 _____ second thoughts, I'll have the lentil soup after all. (In/On)

2 Giles was mortified to discover that he had sent Cordelia a photograph of his ex-girlfriend _____ mistake. (by/at)

3 The results will be published _____ due course. (in/on)

4 'Could I possibly use your phone?' 'Oh, _____ all means.' (by/in)

5 The intrepid women explored the remotest part of the sierra _____ horseback. (by/on)

6 _____ all likelihood, we will never know the real reason. (In/On)

7 Kindly sign the contracts in triplicate and send back to head office _____ return. (by/on)

8 Nobody helped him. He managed it all _____ his own. (by/on)

9 The company is keeping its head above water this year, but it will have to become more efficient _____ the long run. (in/on)

10 The proposal looks good _____ paper, but there may be snags in its practical application. (in/on)

11 The victims of the industrial accident should, _____ rights, be compensated by the factory owners. (at/by)

E Complete the passage by putting a suitable preposition in each space.

1) _____ the whole, Flora was content with her life. 2) _____ day she was a librarian in a large city library, but 3) _____ her spare time she lived in a world of dreams. Her secret, all-devouring passion was reading – novels 4) _____ particular – and she had read almost all the classics that the library had 5) _____ stock. She read voraciously, 6) _____ her lunch hour, her tea break, and the long evenings 7) _____ home. She would even read 8) _____ her way home, walking slowly 9) _____ her book open.

The small flat where she lived 10) _____ herself was piled high 11) _____ books. She knew her favourites 12) _____ heart, empathising with the characters and thinking 13) _____ them as real people. 14) _____ short, she had found that books fulfilled her emotional needs better than people did, and 15) _____ any case, she had now completely forgotten how to relate to people other than characters in novels.

Difficult verbs

Make usually conveys the idea of creating or producing something new:
• *make a speech, a fuss, a noise, the beds, a (new) thing, (someone) ill/well/better, a mistake, a change*

Do is used with work, obligations or general activities:
• *do homework, housework, military service, your duty, a favour, (someone) good, with/without*

A Complete the sentences with the correct form of *make* or *do*.

1 If you agreed, you'd be _____ me a great favour.

2 It's no good playing with Victoria. She _____ such a fuss if she doesn't win.

3 The visiting foreign dignitaries were invited to _____ speeches at the ceremonial opening of parliament.

4 What on earth have you _____ with the paper I was reading just now?

5 If you _____ any noise, they'll hear us and call the police.

6 A complete rest would _____ you an awful lot of good.

7 Well, there just isn't any coffee. You'll have to _____ without.

8 The housekeeper always _____ the beds straight after breakfast.

9 He's having a new suit _____, as he can't find one in his size.

10 What do you feel like _____ this weekend? Walking? Eating out? Going for a swim?

11 Now that he's over eighteen, he'll have to _____ his military service.

12 Doctor, is this treatment really going to _____ me better?

13 Try to avoid _____ so many mistakes in the final version.

14 I didn't manage to _____ my homework, as I was at a rehearsal last night.

15 I expect the new manager will be _____ a few changes in some departments.

16 He always _____ the hoovering, but not without a bit of grumbling!

17 John, have you got a moment? I could _____ with some help.

18 I don't see what the problem is, Jess. You're _____ a mountain out of a molehill.

19 Shall I _____ a beef casserole for dinner?

20 I'm afraid I can't make it to the meeting tonight. I've got too much to _____.

Say is used for direct or reported speech, with no personal direct object:
• *He just stood there and said nothing.*

Tell is followed by a direct object:
• *tell the truth, a lie, fortunes, a story, someone something*

Speak is often used for a single utterance or for knowledge of languages:
• *Can you speak French?*
Note: • *He stopped speaking to me after our argument.*

Talk is less formal, more conversational than **speak**, and refers to a longer activity:
• *The trouble with Marian is she talks too much.*
• *Can the baby talk yet?*
Note: • *talk something over, talk about* (discuss)

B Complete the sentences with *say, tell, speak* or *talk*, in the correct form.

1 She was _____ to go home.
2 They _____ quietly to each other for a long time.
3 'Come in,' he _____.
4 The postman didn't _____ me he had delivered a parcel.
5 How many languages do you _____?
6 _____ me! I must know! What did he _____ to you?
7 Don't believe him. He always _____ lies.
8 Now, stop _____, everybody, and listen to me.
9 You must be silent while the judge is _____.
10 There is nothing more to be _____ on the subject.
11 You can always _____ the supervisor if you don't feel well.
12 I've just got one thing to _____, so listen carefully.
13 They will have to be _____ to pull their socks up.
14 Everything will be all right if you _____ the truth.
15 I was so surprised I couldn't _____ a word.
16 Every time he tries to _____, he stutters.

Arise/arose/arisen means to occur (of a problem, difficulty or need) or to stand up (formal or poetic):
• *Should any problems arise, let me know.*

Rise/rose/risen means to move upwards or stand up, and cannot take a direct object:
• *He rose to his feet.*

Raise/raised/raised means to move something upwards, or cause something to grow or appear, and takes a direct object:
• *He raised his eyes from his work.*
Note: • *raise a smile/laugh, an army, a family, a protest, doubts, fears, suspicions*

C Correct the sentences if necessary. Tick any that are already correct.

1 I watched the sun, a great red ball, raise slowly over the horizon.

2 Please raise your hand if you need the invigilator's help.

3 Wait until the dough has rose before kneading it again.

4 The actress rose from her sofa and swept out of the room.

5 The comedian just about managed to raise a laugh from his listeners.

6 Arise, Sir Galahad! Henceforth, you will serve your queen as her knight.

7 As the curtain was slowly raised, there were gasps of admiration from the audience.

8 If any more difficulties should rise, just let me know.

9 Taxes will probably raise next year.

10 Inflation is rising steeply in some countries, and more gradually in others.

Lie/lay/lain means to be flat or horizontal: • *She's lying on the beach.*

Lie/lied/lied means not to tell the truth: • *He's lying, I tell you!*

Lay/laid/laid means to put something down: • *Lay the book on the table.*
• *The hen's laying an egg.*
Note: • *lay the table, lay the blame on someone or something, lay bare (reveal), lay hold of someone/something*

D Complete the sentences with the correct form of *lie* or *lay*.

1 Yesterday the mayor _____ the foundation stone of the new leisure centre.

2 How long do you think those fossils have _____ there?

3 All the blame was _____ on the hospital management.

4 Would you mind _____ the table for supper, please?

5 How long have you been _____ to your friends? Why don't you tell the truth for a change?

6 I'm afraid Mrs Worth won't be coming tonight. She's _____ down at the moment, with a migraine.

7 In some cases, both birds take their turn at sitting on the eggs that the hen bird has _____.

8 Despite the sweltering heat outside, Sharon _____ down on her bed and tried to sleep.

9 The international mediators are hoping that both sides will _____ down their weapons and sit down at the negotiating table.

10 'Don't speak!' he said, _____ a finger on his lips.

11 You may not like the photo, but remember, the camera never _____.

12 We're having the new carpet _____ tomorrow.

13 Take your time. The ultimate decision _____ with you.

14 The city of Paris _____ on the River Seine.

Transformation

> **Transformation** exercises require you to rewrite sentences using a key word and keeping approximately the same meaning. There are two areas to focus on:
>
> **a grammatical**
> You need to be familiar with all the main structures, such as passives, conditionals, wishes, regrets, reported speech, inversion of the verb, gerund and infinitive. (See relevant units for practice of these points.)
>
> **b lexical**
> You need to have a good knowledge of advanced vocabulary, including idioms and phrasal verbs.
>
> Transformation items may be grammatical, lexical or 'lexico-grammatical' (a combination of both). See **Units 8**, **9**, **11**, **15**, **16** and **25** for CPE-format transformation exercises.

A Match the phrase or clause on the left with its approximate paraphrase on the right.

1	get a word in edgeways	A be extremely busy
2	bark up the wrong tree	B find a solution to
3	be made redundant	C bears no resemblance to
4	give their verdict	D make them angry
5	have their hands full	E manage to interrupt
6	resolve the problem of	F evade the issue
7	incur their wrath	G take the full force of
8	there's no similarity between	H say what they have decided
9	bear the brunt of	I be mistaken
10	beg the question	J lose your job

B For each sentence, write a new sentence which is as similar as possible in meaning. Use the word given, but do not alter it in any way.

1 The prisoner answered the question honestly.
   honest
2 It is said that he was born in Segovia.
   reputed
3 We had nearly finished when Isabel arrived.
   about
4 They've been behaving very strangely recently.
   recent
5 His medical treatment appears to have had a serious effect on his mental state.
   affected

6 The star was surrounded by screaming fans as soon as he arrived at the stage door.

arrival

7 The staff have always esteemed the headmaster very highly.

esteem

8 The electrician advised me to have the wiring checked.

advice

9 The guided tour takes place every hour.

intervals

10 She herself admits to being rather selfish.

admission

C Follow the instructions for Exercise A.

1 except for
2 I infer from what you say
3 there's no difference of opinion between them
4 instead of
5 voice their disapproval of
6 it's none of my business
7 take everything into account
8 be no match for an opponent
9 have misgivings about
10 brace themselves for

A as an alternative to
B it doesn't concern me
C consider all the facts
D say they are against
E have no chance of winning
F apart from
G prepare themselves for
H be worried or doubtful about
I they agree
J I understand from what you imply

D Follow the instructions for Exercise B.

1 She is certainly not a good cook.

means

2 I had no idea it was a breach of protocol.

unaware

3 The store should definitely give you your money back.

refund

4 The tourists were most impressed with the castle.

impact

5 Building societies will have to guard against their rivals.

laurels

6 They're faced with the choice of two alternatives.

horns

7 Taxpayers had to pay the cost of the privatisation plan.

foot

8 I did all I could to expedite the matter.

utmost

9 Juliet simply couldn't wait for his return.

long

10 By the time we all sat down to dinner, the Morrises still hadn't arrived.

sign

11 I think you've misunderstood the situation.

stick

12 The firm didn't go bankrupt, because they took Gerry's advice.

thanks

13 You'd feel much healthier if you had a relaxing break.

do

14 When the assembly line was introduced, five hundred workers were dismissed.

advent

15 His colleagues were shocked to hear of Ahmed's illness.

came

16 Alan complains all the time.

nothing

17 She'll probably win first prize.

stands

18 The policeman pointed out the speed limit sign to us.

drew

E Fill in the boxes to complete the missing words.

1 You can only get this product here. It's _____ to this store.

E ☐☐☐☐☐☐☐

2 She became a _____ name, after hosting her own TV chat show.

H ☐☐☐☐☐☐☐

3 What the crowd _____ in numbers, it made up for in enthusiasm.

L ☐☐☐☐☐

4 I really didn't know what to do. I was in a _____.

Q ☐☐☐☐☐☐

5 It's stalemate. Both sides refuse to negotiate. How can we break the _____?

D ☐☐☐☐☐☐

6 I hate throwing food away. It goes against the _____ to waste anything.

G ☐☐☐

7 There's no need to _____ tears over his problems. He can cope.

S ☐☐☐

8 No review can do _____ to Steven Spielberg's amazing new film.

J ☐☐☐☐☐

9 Be more _____ with electricity. Switch the lights off when you go out.

E ☐☐☐☐☐☐☐☐☐

10 Reggie has a _____ to get irritable when he's tired. He's often cross with the children then.

T ☐☐☐☐☐☐☐

Dependent Prepositions

Many **adjectives and nouns** are followed by a particular preposition:
- *They have every confidence in his judgement.*
- *Margarine is a substitute for butter.*

See **Section 9** of the Appendix for a list of common adjectives and nouns with their **dependent prepositions**.

Note that if adjectives or nouns have similar or opposite meanings, they often take the same preposition:
- *be ready/prepared for school*
- *be married/engaged/ related to someone*
- *be furious/angry/irritated with someone*
- *be frightened/scared/terrified of snakes*
- *be happy/sad about something*

A Complete the sentences with the correct prepositions.

1 I understand you will be eligible _____ promotion soon.

2 We regret the delay _____ despatching your order.

3 She was very conscious _____ her lack of experience on her first day at work.

4 He's come up with a new solution _____ the problem.

5 At least here you'll be safe _____ unwarranted intrusion.

6 There's no doubt _____ his feelings for you.

7 She's always been lacking _____ tact.

8 I would like to take this opportunity _____ thanking my hosts.

9 I have complete confidence _____ his ability to handle the situation.

10 Be very patient _____ Ryan. He's suffered a lot, you know.

11 It's a strange smell, isn't it? It's peculiar _____ this type of plant.

12 How very typical _____ her! Nothing is ever her fault!

13 Is there any chance _____ our meeting in the near future?

14 Despite her age, she takes pleasure _____ pitting her wits against all comers.

15 The island is rich _____ minerals and other natural resources.

16 It's obvious he's incapable _____ holding down a job.

17 I really don't see any point _____ continuing this conversation any longer.

18 Without the certificate, you won't be sufficiently qualified _____ the job.

19 There's no question _____ your leaving us so soon.

20 Would you kindly inform me who is responsible _____ the travel arrangements?

21 We had great difficulty _____ hearing the station announcements.

22 She's convinced _____ the justice of her case.

23 I must point out that I'm not in the habit _____ walking around in my pyjamas.

24 He's always been rather envious _____ his older brother.

25 He takes pride _____ showing off his prize cucumbers.

Many **verbs** are followed by a particular preposition:
• *I've been puzzling over the problem for hours.*
See **Section 10** of the Appendix for a list of common verbs with their **dependent prepositions**.

Remember that verbs of similar or opposite meanings often take the same preposition: • *apply/send/ask for information*
• *care/worry about someone* • *agree/disagree with someone*

B Complete each space in the conversation between two business colleagues with the missing verb or preposition.

'Come in, Harold!'

'I must 1) _____ for arriving so late. The traffic, you know.'

'Oh, don't 2) _____ about that. The meeting's been put off anyway. Come in and help yourself 3) _____ coffee. Let me be the first to congratulate you 4) _____ your promotion.'

'Oh thanks, Paul. Yes, I'm delighted. But it hasn't been announced officially yet. Could you possibly 5) _____ it to yourself for a bit?'

'Well, of course, Harold. When do you think you'll be taking up the new post, then?'

'I'm not sure. It all 6) _____ on the contract, which I haven't seen yet. They're sending it to me this week. I was determined to 7) _____ on a pretty big salary increase, I can tell you.'

'Quite right too. It's a lot more responsibility.'

'Yes, and my outgoings are considerable these days. I still have to provide 8) _____ Julie and the kids, of course, even though we split up over two years ago. What about you, Paul? Any jobs *you've* 9) _____ for lately?'

'Not a thing. You're the only one here who's moving on. But don't worry, we won't 10) _____ it against you!'

'Good. Of course there's no need 11) _____ us to lose touch. I value your judgement, you know.'

'Well, thanks, Harold. I'm always happy to advise a friend.'

'I've been thinking, Paul. I may have difficulty 12) _____ adjusting to living in Munich – I must confess 13) _____ a slight feeling of apprehension.'

'Oh, I have every confidence 14) _____ you, Harold. You'll be a huge success 15) _____ our German colleagues, just wait and see!'

C Match the two halves of the sentences correctly.

1 You should insure property

2 The local restaurants are well supplied

3 The coach was blamed

4 The charity is devoted

5 The accused pleaded guilty

6 Jonathan struggled

7 After the row, Jane was seething

8 The sales assistant is attending

9 The intruder was mistaken

10 She's always fishing

A to a customer at the moment.

B with the youth who had attacked him.

C with resentment.

D for compliments.

E for a doctor.

F to the charge of arson.

G against fire and theft.

H with organically grown vegetables.

I to raising money for the disabled.

J for his team's poor performance.

D Complete the passage with the correct verb, noun or preposition.

Scientists are still curious 1) _____ the effects of the oceanographic phenomenon called El Niño, which occurs in the south-west Pacific Ocean. There is no 2) _____, however, about the reason 3) _____ its occurrence. Every few years, a rise 4) _____ surface temperatures due to a temporary decrease in trade winds makes sea levels rise, and waves head north-east up the coast of South America. El Niño is noted 5) _____ its effect on local climates, but recent research has shown that it is also 6) _____ for wider atmospheric changes, resulting, for example, 7) _____ temporary drought in the Sahel or failure of the maize harvest in Zimbabwe.

Now scientists involved 8) _____ oceanographic research are 9) _____ on a new theory, that El Niño can produce changes 10) _____ ocean patterns that may last for decades. Computers at the Naval Research Laboratory in Mississippi, fed 11) _____ the latest satellite information on sea temperatures and wave heights, show that the giant waves that roll across the Pacific may be the result 12) _____ a previous El Niño, which will continue to affect the circulation of the North Pacific for years to come.

The 1982 El Niño, the strongest of the 20th century, is 13) _____ of causing the flooding of the Mississippi basin in 1993, with the loss of life and serious 14) _____ to crops and property that resulted.

Recycling

A Choose the correct word or phrase to complete each sentence. Write the letter in the space.

1 Your car's very _____. It hardly seems to use any petrol at all.

   a) economical   b) economic   c) ecumenical   d) ecological

2 I'm in a terrible _____. I just don't know what to do.

   a) problem   b) quandary   c) loss   d) trouble

3 _____ to the bank manager's loan, Gerald's struggling company managed to stay solvent.

   a) With thanks   b) Thank you   c) Thanks   d) Gratefully

4 We have every confidence _____ his powers of diplomacy and organisation.

   a) on   b) in   c) with   d) by

5 Is there any chance _____ the machinery repaired?

   a) to have   b) of having   c) for having   d) of being

6 By appearing on the soap powder commercials, she became a _____ name.

   a) housewife   b) housekeeper   c) house   d) household

7 Now that John has decided he doesn't want to stand, we'll have to find a substitute _____ the post.

   a) to   b) as   c) for   d) in

8 It's hard to do _____ to such a masterpiece.

   a) judgement   b) justice   c) fair play   d) fairness

9 It's crucial that he _____ attend the ceremony.

   a) should   b) must   c) will   d) ought

10 At the moment the ruling party is on the _____ of a dilemma.

   a) hooves   b) points   c) feet   d) horns

11 How you invest your money is none of my _____.

   a) affair   b) business   c) matter   d) care

12 I'm afraid you've got the wrong end of the _____.

   a) loaf   b) pot   c) leg   d) stick

13 I'm _____ a complete loss to understand why you reacted so violently.

   a) at   b) in   c) on   d) by

14 _____ you cut down your carbohydrate intake, you'd have lost weight by now.

   a) Did   b) Were   c) If   d) Had

15 If the level of VAT is _____ this year, small businesses will be affected.

   a) raised   b) risen   c) arisen   d) raising

16 Don't _____ anything to him if you can help it.

   a) speak   b) say   c) talk   d) tell

17 I couldn't hear what he said, because he was muttering _____ his breath.

a) out of   b) under   c) in   d) on

18 I object _____ to do all the work myself.

a) to being asked   b) to asking   c) being asked   d) on being asked

19 The stones have _____ buried in the sand for a thousand years.

a) lied   b) lying   c) laid   d) lain

20 I want _____ clear up the mess you've made!

a) that you   b) you to   c) you do   d) you should

21 We shall review the salary arrangements _____ due course.

a) in   b) on   c) by   d with

22 The magistrate _____ his disapproval of the young man's behaviour.

a) said   b) told   c) voiced   d) spoke

23 Nobody would question the PM's integrity. He is above _____.

a) contempt   b) suspicion   c) average   d) all

24 I'll _____ you just one more story before you go to sleep.

a) tell   b) speak   c) say   d) talk

25 If only I _____ lost my temper in the meeting!

a) wouldn't have   b) wouldn't   c) hadn't   d) didn't

B Complete the second sentence so that it means the same as the first one, using the word given. You must use between **three** and **eight** words, including the word given. (Contractions count as two words.)

1 The villagers, though few in number, were incredibly friendly.

lacked

What the villagers _____ in friendliness.

2 My business partner and I are in complete agreement.

difference

There is _____ my business partner and me.

3 In the end they left me to settle up with the restaurant.

foot

In the end I _____ the restaurant bill.

4 He himself admits to having wasted a lot of money.

admission

By his _____ wasted a lot of money.

5 Getting upset over Michael's departure is pointless.

tears

There's no _____ over Michael's departure.

6 The effects of the gale were felt mainly along the south coast.

brunt

The south coast _____ the gale.

7 All she does is sit in the office drinking coffee.

but

She does _____ drinking coffee.

C Complete the passage by putting **one** word in each space. (Do not use contractions – they count as two words.)

The Great Pyramid of Giza is probably the most famous 1) _____ the seven wonders of the ancient world. It 2) _____ built by King Khufu (known as Cheops to 3) _____ Greeks) around 2450 BC, and its neighbour, 4) _____ is a little smaller, was constructed later 5) _____ his son Khefren. By the time of the beautiful Queen Cleopatra, they 6) _____ already stood against the desert skyline through the reigns of more 7) _____ a hundred kings or pharaohs. 8) _____ centuries archaeologists have puzzled 9) _____ the reasons for their construction. Now a new solution 10) _____ the mystery 11) _____ been proposed, according to 12) _____ the Great Pyramid was intended 13) _____ a focus for 14) _____ pharaoh's complicated funeral ceremony. Astronomers think 15) _____ narrow passages 16) _____ from the royal burial chambers 17) _____ aligned with certain stars in the 26,000-year cycle of the constellations, 18) _____ that the dead king's soul could 19) _____ launched to the stars. The latest discovery is a hitherto unopened door in the depths of the Pyramid. Who can imagine what 20) _____ behind it?

D In **most** lines of this text there is a spelling or punctuation mistake. Write the correct spelling or punctuation next to the numbers on the right. Tick any lines that are correct.

A japanese monk has just become a Buddhist   1 _____

'saint', by completing a grueling course of 1,000   2 _____

marathons he is only the eleventh person in a   3 _____

hundred years to complete this ancient ritual. As   4 _____

a comitted disciple of Tendai Buddhism, the   5 _____

35-year-old has sort enlightenment through   6 _____

physical endurance and a level of stamina that   7 _____

we might find hard to acheive. Not all Tendai   8 _____

monks, who attempt the marathon ordeal survive,   9 _____

and this monk, who's name is Gyosho Uehara, is   10 _____

still very weak as a result of his experience, which   11 _____

has badly effected his ankles and knees. Now   12 _____

they're are seven marathon monks, instead of six,   13 _____

residant on Mount Hiei, which is a centre of Buddhist   14 _____

retreat an ascetic monasticism not far from the large   15 _____

and bustling city of Kyoto.   16 _____

Phrasal verbs with *down*

blow	break	bring	calm	chop	close	come	crack
cut	fall	flag	get	go	hand	jot	let	lie	mark
narrow	note	pelt	play	pour	pull	put	run	sit
slam	slow	squat	tear	tie	tone	track	tumble
turn	wind

Down often has the meaning of a downward movement, or a decrease, or of stopping an activity.

A Rewrite the sentences, using a phrasal verb with **down**, to produce the opposite meaning of the words in italics. Choose from the verbs in the box above.

1 We all *stood up* when the managing director walked in.
2 The building society has *set up* a branch in Warmsley.
3 Inflation has been *rising* steadily since January.
4 When Caroline heard the terrible news, she *remained calm*.
5 Rain was *gently falling*.
6 The teacher *quietly put the book* on the table.
7 The company will probably want to *publicise* the results.
8 The old lady was adamant that her cat should be *kept alive*.
9 After three days of continuous bombardment, the White Tower *remained standing*.
10 Having Bruce to stay has really *cheered me up*.
11 He *got very excited* after his meeting with the trade union officials.
12 The secretary *carefully put the notice up on* the board.

B Use verbs from the box above to complete the sentences.

1 You'll have to ☐☐☐☐ down when you come to the crossroads.
2 The town council decided to ☐☐☐☐ down the building, as it was unsafe.
3 The small boy ☐☐☐☐☐☐ down on the ground and examined the insect.
4 The force of the gale ☐☐☐☐ down hundreds of trees.
5 I know you're angry, but you should ☐☐☐☐ down the language you're using. It's too aggressive.
6 From the time of his arrival in prison, Jones was ☐☐☐☐☐ down as a troublemaker.
7 It's a difficult choice, but at least we've ☐☐☐☐☐☐☐ it down to five out of the hundred applicants.
8 The escaped convict was finally ☐☐☐☐☐☐ down to a hiding place in the Far East.

9 The aim of the popular uprising was to ☐☐☐☐☐ down the government.

10 As fewer orders came in, the firm began to ☐☐☐☐ down its sales force.

11 If there is any more subsidence, that cottage will ☐☐☐☐☐☐ down into the sea.

12 The reporter ☐☐☐☐☐ down the details of the court case for inclusion in his article.

C Complete each sentence with a phrase from box A followed by a phrase from box B. Do not use any phrase more than once.

A	B
flagged down	they offered me.
I turned down the job	on fraud everywhere.
I felt badly let down	at the moment.
wind down	a taxi.
and jotted down	chopping down the tree.
rather tied down	the professor's points.
running down	properly.
have been handed down	his wife's achievements.
will prevent them from	by him.
cracking down	through the centuries.

1 Family traditions _____

2 Jeremy is forever _____

3 The man in a business suit _____

4 With two small children, she's _____

5 The preservation order _____

6 I listened to the lecture _____

7 The authorities are _____

8 After the interview _____

9 When Steve wouldn't help, _____

10 The holiday gave us a chance to _____

Phrasal verbs with *after*, *back* and *about*

after
go   look   take

back
bring   call   cut   fall   get   give   go   hold   keep   pay
put   ring   set   take   talk   turn

about
bring   go   put   set

Back often has the meaning of returning something (to someone) or of remembering the past.

A Match each phrasal verb with the correct definition. (There may be other possible definitions.)

1 bring about	A	pursue
2 ring back	B	return something to its correct place
3 take after	C	take care of
4 answer back	D	cause
5 go about	E	be like an older relative
6 turn back	F	delay or hinder the progress of something
7 cut back	G	not tell the whole truth
8 put (it) about	H	reduce
9 put back	I	reply rudely or defiantly to someone in authority
10 set back	J	return someone's phone call
11 go after	K	retreat
12 look after	L	recover something that had been taken away
13 fall back	M	approach or tackle (a problem)
14 keep (something) back	N	make someone return the way they have come
15 get back	O	spread (a rumour)

B Complete each sentence with the correct form of a phrasal verb from the box above.

1 The gangsters lay in wait for their victim, and _____ him with their fists.

2 The salesman has left us a brochure to look at. He said he'd _____ soon, to see if we want to place an order.

3 I can lend you some money for a sandwich. You can always _____ me _____ tomorrow.

4 Legends about the Green Man _____ right _____ to the Middle Ages.

5 Especially when you're tired and under stress, it's important to _____ yourself and your health.

6 Alex _____ mending the clock, but he soon had to admit defeat.

7 We were halfway across the bay when two of the boys felt seasick, so we thought we'd better _____ and put them ashore.

8 Everyone _____ their daily tasks as if nothing had happened.

9 I was just leaving the office when the receptionist _____ me _____. She'd forgotten to give me a message.

10 Police had difficulty in _____ the demonstrators, who were threatening to break through the security cordon.

11 You've been to Austria recently, haven't you? When did you _____?

12 If we don't get any applications for the job, we'll just have to _____ on part-time staff as a temporary measure.

C Complete each sentence with a phrase from box A followed by a phrase from box B. Do not use any phrase more than once.

A
held back
bring back
ring you back
set my roses back
bring about
go about
went after
take back

B
memories of a person or place.
raising the money?
his anger.
a change in the law.
the pickpocket.
what you said about him.
when I get home.
by several weeks.

1 We are campaigning to _____

2 You'll have to _____

3 A passer-by _____

4 I'll _____

5 How are you going to _____

6 A severe frost could _____

7 Sometimes a certain smell can _____

8 For the children's sake he _____

Phrasal verbs with *off*

be	break	call	clear	come	cordon	cut	doze	drop	fight
get	give	go	keep	laugh	lay	let	live	pay	pick	pull	put
ring	rip	round	scare	scrape	see	send	set	shake	shave
show	switch	take	tell	throw	turn	wear	work	write

Off often has the meaning of a movement away, or of separating people or things.

A Decide whether the definitions are true (T) or false (F). Give the correct definition(s) if necessary.

1	pick off	collect a person from a place
2	live off	survive
3	round off	complete, give the finishing touch to
4	be off	separate someone from another person
5	scare off	frighten someone away
6	switch off	stop concentrating
7	show off	make someone feel embarrassed by behaving badly
8	set off	cause to explode
9	see off	be present at someone's departure
10	rip off	steal from or cheat someone

B Complete each sentence with the correct form of a verb from the box above.

1 When Roger saw the restaurant kitchen, it completely _____ him off eating there.

2 If milk smells bad, you can be certain it has _____ off.

3 He always leaves his room in a mess. I'm forever _____ him off about it.

4 The mixture in the saucepan was beginning to _____ off a very unpleasant odour.

5 The police had to _____ off the embassy to protect staff from the demonstrators.

6 Detectives cannot interview the victim until the operation is over and the effects of the anaesthetic have _____ off.

7 Maria's car was so badly damaged that her insurance company _____ it off.

8 Just fill in the application form, and _____ it off.

9 I've been trying to _____ off this cold for the last week.

10 Surely you don't mean that! _____ off it!

11 I must _____ off soon. I've got to collect Louise from school.

12 With a bit more planning, his idea might have worked, but I'm afraid it didn't really _____ off.

C Add **it** where necessary to the following sentences, and say what **it** means or might mean.

1 The party's been cancelled. She called off last week.

2 I have great confidence in the PM. I'm sure he'll pull off.

3 I went for a long walk to work off the effects of the huge meal.

4 You don't need the light on in here. Turn off, please.

5 Eva suddenly rang off in the middle of our conversation.

6 I'll drop off at your house on my way to work tomorrow.

7 How on earth are you ever going to scrape all off?

8 His father dozed off while watching the news.

9 I knew they disapproved of me, but I just laughed off.

10 I suppose Noel will shave off one day!

11 Jane decided the moment had come to break off.

12 Don't you know this is private property? Clear off, will you!

D Complete each sentence with a phrase from box A followed by a phrase from box B. Do not use any phrase more than once.

A	B
will be laying off	without a penny.
put off	in two hours' time.
set off	all too quickly.
will pay off	as he is hoping.
let off	by what people say.
wore off	before first light.
kept off	500 workers until after the summer.
will be taking off	very lightly in the accident.
got off	fireworks in their garden.
cut her off	during the cricket match.

1 The plane _____

2 Fortunately Zoë _____

3 The factory _____

4 I don't think his gamble _____

5 Her family _____

6 The boys _____

7 The rain _____

8 James refuses to be _____

9 The effects of our holiday _____

10 We'll have to _____

Phrasal verbs with *through*, *for* and *by*

> **through**
> break   check   fall   get   go   look   pull   put   run   see
> sleep   think
>
> **for**
> account   apply   ask   call   care   fall   fish   go   look
> make   mistake   pay   send   stand
>
> **by**
> get   go   put   stand   tick
>
> **Through** often has the meaning of doing something completely or thoroughly.

A Match each phrasal verb with the correct definition. (There may be other possible definitions.)

1	mistake for	A	not wake up during an emergency, alarm etc.
2	stand for	B	arrange for someone to come
3	check through	C	provide the necessary money for
4	see through	D	be connected (on the phone)
5	get by	E	go in the direction of
6	apply for	F	look through to see if everything is correct
7	make for	G	not be deceived by, see the truth behind
8	sleep through	H	pass (of time)
9	go for	I	confuse with
10	get through	J	have just enough (usually money) to manage
11	call for	K	ask for (a job)
12	send for	L	attack
13	think through	M	collect someone (from their home, office etc.)
14	pay for	N	consider all the aspects
15	tick by	O	represent

B Complete the crossword with verbs from the box above, using the clues provided.

Across:

1 I hope I'll be able to stay on in the job long enough to _____ the project through.

4 You shouldn't _____ compliments like that! (4, 3)

7 Although he's in a critical state after the accident, the doctors think he'll _____ through.

8 Could you just _____ through these accounts and see if they're correct?

10 A good friend will always stand _____ you.

11 It's hard to _____ for the old lady's disappearance.

12 Do you think Ellen and Roy will be able to _____ by on one salary?

13 When he moves to Edinburgh, he'll have to _____ for a flat.

Down:

2 If you need anything, just _____ me for it.

3 I was enjoying myself so much that I hardly noticed the time _____ by.

4 Her plan cannot possibly succeed. I'm sure it'll _____ . (4, 7)

5 She's so beautiful, he'll _____ for her as soon as he sees her.

6 Can we _____ through the instructions again, please?

7 Luckily, I had some money _____ by for a rainy day.

9 When her mother died, Agatha had to _____ for her invalid sister single-handedly.

10 Journalists are hoping to _____ through the secrecy surrounding the royal family's decision.

Recycling

A Choose the correct word or phrase to complete each sentence. Write the letter in the space.

1 The road was closed, so we had to _____ and find an alternative route.

  a) put down b) turn back c) go about d) go off

2 They _____ for Paris at midnight.

  a) set off b) made for c) went off d) got down

3 I knew your family would stand _____ you.

  a) for b) off c) by d) about

4 How could you have _____ him for your brother?

  a) confused b) considered c) thought d) mistaken

5 It is vital that we _____ a change in people's attitudes.

  a) bring down b) bring back c) bring about d) look after

6 Giuseppe's secretary _____ a call to the office in Milan.

  a) put through b) applied for c) put by d) set about

7 We'll have to _____ down the options before coming to a decision.

  a) slow b) narrow c) bring d) wind

8 Rosa certainly _____ her mother in her devil-may-care approach to life.

  a) looks after b) calms down c) cares for d) takes after

9 Ingrid broke _____ in tears when we told her about the accident.

  a) off b) through c) down d) for

10 I'm so tired I think I'll probably _____ off in the cinema.

  a) doze b) sleep c) turn d) fall

11 If a bus doesn't come, you can always flag _____ a taxi.

  a) after b) for c) down d) off

12 Look, I _____ it all back. I should never have spoken like that.

  a) take b) put c) call d) give

13 I think a couple of coffees will _____ off the meal nicely.

  a) go b) send c) round d) wear

14 The official _____ quickly through my file, and then handed it back to me.

  a) saw b) looked c) got d) turned

15 If you're interested in *Mastermind,* you can send _____ free tickets and be part of the studio audience next time they record it.

  a) off b) by c) about d) for

16 You shouldn't have sent Sebastian that Valentine's card. I think you've scared him _____!

  a) back b) down c) off d) through

17 The rain was simply _____ down on the deserted street.

  a) pelting b) spraying c) showering d) dripping

18 She talks so fast, it's difficult getting a word in _____!

  a) sideways b) halfway c) edgeways d) any way

B Read the text and underline the **ten** phrasal verbs. Give a definition for each one, according to its meaning in the text.

When Laura was a university student, she found it very difficult to get by on her grant, so she decided to look for a part-time job. When she spotted an advertisement in the local paper for snack bar staff, she sat down to apply for the job. She wasn't sure how best to go about presenting herself on paper, so she just jotted down the details of her qualifications and experience, and sent the application off immediately.

The owner of the snack bar, a Mr Edwards, rang a couple of days later to ask her to come for an interview the following Saturday. When she arrived at Tasty Bites, she was very nervous because she felt sure he could see through her claims to have worked as a waitress before, and would turn her down as a matter of course. But finally the interview was over, and when he shook hands with her and said 'See you next week, then!', she realised she had pulled it off.

C Match the first half of each sentence with the correct ending.

1 How do you account for
2 I'm not sure you've
3 If your car's out of action,
4 Surely he didn't sleep through
5 She's putting it about
6 I can't stand the way
7 Have they cordoned off

A thought this through sufficiently.
B he's always showing off.
C that his wife has left him.
D all that noise!
E the discrepancies in your reports?
F the scene of the crime?
G I'll call for you tonight.

D Complete the passage by putting **one** word in each space. (Do not use contractions – they count as two words.)

THE CUCKOO ROLLER OF MADAGASCAR

This bird is about the same size 1) _____ the European roller, and has many features in common 2) _____ its near relatives.
3) _____ the European family, however, the cuckoo roller can reverse its outer toes, 4) _____ it to perch 5) _____ gripping a branch with two toes forward and two back. Its eating habits are also quite different.
6) _____ nearly all other rollers take food on the wing or pluck reptiles or large insects from the ground, the cuckoo roller stays high up in the forest canopy, 7) _____ on caterpillars, stick insects and, 8) _____ important of all, chameleons.

Subtly blending its colours to the forest backcloth, and 9) _____ leaving the safety of the branches except to cross from one tree to 10) _____, the chameleon is an elusive prey. 11) _____ on open ground, 12) _____ myriad dangers it normally avoids, the chameleon's slow, swaying walk 13) _____ it difficult to see against the leaves. 14) _____ good is its camouflage that the cuckoo roller has to 15) _____ up with long periods of watching and waiting, 16) _____ a tell-tale movement betrays its victim's presence. At 17) _____, experts assume this is 18) _____ happens, because 19) _____ the fact that this bird is widespread throughout Madagascar, 20) _____ observer has yet seen it in the process of catching its prey.

Phrasal verbs with *up*

blow	bottle	break	bring	build	call	catch	cheer
clear	crop	cut	draw	dress	eat	end	fill	fix
flare	get	give	go	grow	hang	hurry	hold	keep
liven	look	make	own	pick	pull	put	seal	settle
shoot	show	shut	speak	split	stay	stir	sum	take
tie	turn						

Up often has the meaning of an upward movement, or of approaching, completing or increasing.

A Match each phrasal verb with the correct definition. (There may be other possible definitions.)

1	stir up	A	confess, admit
2	sum up	B	come to a stop (of a vehicle)
3	own up	C	summon for military service, conscript
4	draw up	D	put on smart clothes
5	hang up	E	try to cause (trouble)
6	call up	F	raise your voice
7	liven up	G	not go to bed early
8	dress up	H	summarise
9	settle up	I	make more lively
10	speak up	J	suddenly become angry
11	stay up	K	pay all that is owed
12	flare up	L	finish a phone call

B Rewrite the sentences, using a phrasal verb with **up**, to produce the opposite meaning of the words in italics. Choose from the verbs in the box above.

1 His visit certainly *depressed me*.
2 Have you *let the dog loose?*
3 The child *left her food untouched*.
4 Jeremy tends to *express his emotions openly*.
5 When did Ramon and Anna *start their relationship?*
6 He was determined to *continue* smoking.
7 My uncle usually *goes to bed* at 9 o'clock.
8 The officer *emptied* his wine glass.
9 The lawyer *opened* the envelope with a flourish.
10 As soon as controls were lifted, prices *came down*.
11 Ted *stopped* playing tennis when he was sixty.
12 I'll *drop you off* at seven o'clock.

C Use verbs from the box on page 94 to complete the sentences.

1 She quickly ☐☐☐☐☐☐ up the basics of the language.

2 You'll have to ☐☐☐☐☐ up your strength by eating properly.

3 Be quiet! Just ☐☐☐☐ up!

4 How long can you ☐☐☐☐ up this pretence?

5 I'll ☐☐☐ you up with a room. Leave it to me.

6 The carpet was ☐☐☐ up into three smaller pieces.

7 An accident ☐☐☐☐ up the flow of traffic in the town centre.

8 Guy Fawkes and his fellow-conspirators did not succeed in ☐☐☐☐☐☐☐ up the Houses of Parliament.

9 The Brontë sisters all ☐☐☐☐ up in Yorkshire.

10 First Sam worked in Canada, then Florida, but he finally ☐☐☐☐☐ up in France.

11 Come on! ☐☐☐☐☐ up, or we'll be late!

12 I waited for ages, but my cousin never ☐☐☐☐☐☐ up.

D Complete each sentence with a phrase from box A followed by a phrase from box B. Do not use any phrase more than once.

A	B
clear up	last month.
put you up	if you need to stay overnight.
made up,	if you ask me.
crop up	his room before doing his homework.
pulled up	on her farm in Cornwall.
look Lorenzo up	in front of the hotel.
brought him up	if we pass through Rome.
shot up	at the meeting.

1 We should _____

_____

2 The taxi _____

_____

3 The boy was told to _____

_____

4 Tom's grandmother _____

_____

5 Prices simply _____

_____

6 I didn't expect that topic to _____

_____

7 I can easily _____

_____

8 The story was obviously _____

_____

Phrasal verbs with *out*

branch	break	carry	check	come	cross	cry	drop
eat	find	get	give	hand	keep	lay	leave	let
lock	look	make	measure	pass	pick	point	pull
put	rub	rule	set	share	slip	sort	stick	storm
take	think	throw	try	turn	wash	wear	work

A Decide whether the definitions are true (T) or false (F). Give the correct definition(s) if necessary.

1 slip out — leave quietly and unobtrusively
2 wear out — disappear
3 carry out — perform (an operation, an experiment or a duty)
4 cross out — delete
5 sort out — distribute
6 break out — make an escape
7 leave out — omit
8 storm out — leave angrily
9 work out — calculate
10 make out — manage to see
11 rule out — erase
12 find out — study
13 set out — begin (a journey)
14 keep out — prevent from entering
15 pick out — pluck or scratch
16 branch out — split

B Complete each sentence with the correct form of a verb from the box above.

1 I really don't feel like cooking. Couldn't we _____ out?
2 We're _____ my mother out for the day on Sunday.
3 Jason never completed his university course. He _____ out halfway through.
4 In the end it _____ out that the police had suspected Ferguson all along.
5 Her clothes were all neatly _____ out on the bed, ready for packing.
6 I happened to _____ myself out of the house last week.
7 We'll have to _____ out to him that he simply can't throw his weight around like that.
8 Liz has always been squeamish about the sight of blood. Last week she actually _____ out when she cut her finger.
9 The driver picked up speed and _____ out into the main stream of traffic.

10 Volunteers are going to _____ out soup and bread to the homeless.

11 He hasn't been _____ out yet, has he? Surely he hasn't served his sentence yet?

12 It's no good covering up for him. The truth will have to _____ out in the end.

13 It's rude to _____ your tongue out at people, Marian.

14 You're not going to _____ those bottles out, are you? We could take them to the bottle bank.

C Add **it** where necessary to the following sentences, and say what **it** means or might mean.

1 I want to try out before agreeing to buy.
2 There'll be enough for all of us. I'll measure out.
3 I think the diary's stuck behind the radiator. Can you get out?
4 The girl cried out in pain as the doctor dressed her wound.
5 Do you think this ink stain will wash out?
6 Look, you've spelt my name wrong! Rub out!
7 Are you sure you've really thought out?
8 If there's a lot of work to do, we can share out.
9 I wonder if Jamal has got it right. Could you check out?
10 You want the file on the Kingman family? I'll look out for you when I have time.

D Complete each sentence with the correct verb from the pair in brackets.

1 I'm afraid the authorities have already _____ out the bypass option. (ruled/rubbed)
2 As glass, paper and plastic are all disposed of separately now, we have to _____ out our rubbish before it's collected. (share/sort)
3 I'm not sure Jenny's coming with us. She said she might have to _____ out at the last minute. (get/drop)
4 If I were you, I'd _____ out the recipe before the dinner party. (measure/try)
5 The cleaners _____ out all the lights, then set the burglar alarm and left the building. (put/took)
6 The ex-President's memoirs, currently being serialised in a leading newspaper, are _____ out next week. (coming/getting)
7 The bank clerk called the police when he saw what looked like a gun _____ out of the man's jacket pocket. (pulling/sticking)
8 Civil Service mandarins have designed a complicated and lengthy interview procedure, whose purpose is to _____ out candidates of the highest calibre. (work/pick)
9 To implement the Common Agricultural Policy, farming subsidies have been _____ out on a massive scale by the EU. (handed/laid)
10 When his car hire business showed signs of imminent collapse, Jason decided to _____ out into another, potentially more lucrative, field – the property market. (slip/branch)

UNIT 33

Phrasal verbs with *over*, *apart* and *with*

over
blow   boil   bowl   check   cloud   get   go   hand   look   pull
run   stop   take   think   turn

apart
come   take   tell

with
confuse   deal   do   fight   go   identify   part   reason   side   toy

A Match each phrasal verb with the correct definition. (There may be other possible definitions.)

1 get over   A see the difference between
2 deal with   B match
3 take apart   C consider
4 check over   D recover from
5 reason with   E make sure something is in good condition
6 hand over   F transfer, surrender
7 tell apart   G support someone holding a particular view
8 stop over   H handle, do
9 go with   I move to one side when driving
10 side with   J cease (of a storm)
11 think over   K break a journey (especially for a night)
12 confuse with   L try to persuade
13 blow over   M dismantle
14 pull over   N mistake for

B Complete each sentence with the correct form of a phrasal verb from the box above.

1 Sadly, the old lady will have to _____ her beloved budgie when she moves into the old people's home. They don't allow pets there.

2 I opened the back of the watch to put a new battery in, and the whole thing suddenly _____ in my hands! I hope I can get it repaired.

3 Could you please _____ those instructions again? Kate wasn't listening the first time.

4 There was a terrible smell in the kitchen. The soup had _____ and put the gas out.

5 You simply can't _____ the twins _____ if they're wearing identical outfits.

6 No wonder Ryan often comes home from school with a black eye. He's always _____ the other boys!

7 I always get Madeleine to _____ my reports before I hand them in to the boss. He's a stickler for spelling and punctuation, and she's got a good eye for that sort of thing.

8 The company's personnel department need good management systems to _____ their workload effectively.

C Complete each sentence with a phrase from box A followed by a phrase from box B. Do not use any phrase more than once.

A	B
got over	later on today.
will cloud over	the feminist cause.
toy with	the small private company.
has always identified with	her tragic loss.
could do with	by the success of the plan.
was quite bowled over	the fourth time I tried it.
finally turned over	some financial assistance.
took over	the food on her plate.

1 The engine _____
2 The state airline _____
3 My sister _____
4 Everyone _____
5 I expect it _____
6 The newly-weds _____
7 Sally could only _____
8 It was a long time before she _____

D Complete the text with phrasal verbs from the box on page 98, in the correct form.

It all started when the milk 1) _____ over, on the little stove in the workshop. Tony was supposed to be keeping an eye on it. Bill didn't even notice. He never made the coffee – he was always much too busy 2) _____ apart the old radios that came to be repaired. However, it was the last straw for Roger.

'Can't I trust you to do anything right?' he shouted.

Tony turned, surprised. He tried to 3) _____ with his brother. 'Well, Rog, you're the one who wants hot milk in your coffee.'

Bill looked up and 4) _____ with Tony. 'Tony's right. Why don't *you* keep an eye on it in future?' he said gruffly.

Roger looked at his brothers in despair. There had to be a better way of 5) _____ with the constant friction between them, but he hadn't found it yet. 'Sorry, Tony, I'm a bit irritable at the moment, I know. I could 6) _____ with a holiday, that's what it is,' he said.

'So could I,' said Tony, turning back to his work and 7) _____ idly with his pen. 'So could we all,' said Bill grumpily.

There was silence in the workshop again. The row had 8) _____ over for the time being.

Phrasal verbs with *on*

add	bring	call	carry	catch	count	get	go	hang
have	hold	keep	let	live	look	move	pass	pick	put
ramble	send	soldier	switch	take	touch	try	turn	

On often has the meaning of attaching or continuing.

A Match each phrasal verb with the correct definition. (There may be other possible definitions.)

1	look on	A	ask someone for help
2	get on	B	continue
3	take on	C	continue bravely despite difficulties
4	count on	D	employ
5	bring on	E	become popular
6	let on	F	be a spectator
7	soldier on	G	induce or cause
8	call on	H	rely on, have confidence in
9	catch on	I	make progress
10	keep on	J	reveal information

B Rewrite the sentences, using a phrasal verb with **on**, to produce the opposite meaning of the words in italics. Choose from the verbs in the box above.

1 Toby *took off* his three-piece suit.
2 You'll have to *let go* when I tell you to!
3 The little girl *stopped* talking when the teacher came in.
4 Remember to *switch off* the electricity at the mains.
5 He *spoke briefly and to the point* about the arrangements.
6 Are you going to *keep to yourself* what happened?
7 The tax was *deducted* before the bill was paid.
8 Are you *being serious with me*?

C Use verbs from the box above to complete the sentences.

1 The fashion editor wondered if the trend would ☐☐☐☐☐ on.
2 Would you like to ☐☐☐ that suit on, sir?
3 Tonight, ladies and gentlemen, I'd just like to ☐☐☐☐☐ briefly on one or two topics of general interest.
4 The old man only has his state pension to ☐☐☐☐ on.
5 If I'm in trouble, I can always ☐☐☐☐☐ on Rosemary to help me.
6 ☐☐☐☐ on a minute! Wait for me.
7 My grandmother is ☐☐☐☐☐☐ on a bit now. She's over eighty.

8 They [ ][ ][ ][ ] on to the next item on the agenda without answering his question.

9 If the boss asks you, don't [ ][ ][ ] on that I've told you. Keep it to yourself.

10 A chain letter is a letter which is [ ][ ][ ][ ][ ] on from one person to another, until someone breaks the chain.

11 Perhaps we should [ ][ ][ ][ ] on Gabriela when we pass through London.

12 It'll be a muddy walk, so we'd better [ ][ ][ ] our boots on.

D Complete each sentence with a phrase from box A followed by a phrase from box B. Do not use any phrase more than once.

A	B
was brought on	his unsuspecting assistant.
is being sent on	by overwork.
is getting on well	somewhere in the street.
have carried on	without a pay rise.
soldier on	in her new job.
was picked on	until we find someone suitable.
turned on	to the new address.
take on	to clean the whiteboard.
keep on advertising	too much extra work.
going on	their business for 100 years now.

1 For no apparent reason, the professor _____

_____

2 The workers decided to _____

_____

3 Philippa _____

_____

4 The new boy _____

_____

5 Car manufacturers _____

_____

6 Dave's nervous breakdown _____

_____

7 Her mail _____

_____

8 Be careful not to _____

_____

9 We'll have to _____

_____

10 There was a loud party _____

_____

Recycling

1 Don't _____! I haven't finished explaining yet!

    a) hang up   b) hold on   c) hang on   d) call up

2 The motorist must have run _____ the fox without noticing.

    a) out   b) on   c) over   d) up

3 It _____ out that the mayor had bribed several councillors to vote for him.

    a) resulted   b) pointed   c) broke   d) turned

4 I expect the new trend will soon _____ here.

    a) catch up   b) catch on   c) take up   d) identify with

5 It's difficult to tell identical twins _____.

    a) on   b) out   c) apart   d) over

6 Paloma will have to _____ her antiques, because she needs the money.

    a) part with   b) take out   c) move on   d) clear up

7 I'll use my credit card to _____ up before we check out.

    a) take   b) sum   c) bottle   d) settle

8 Scientists _____ a carefully controlled experiment on the mystery virus.

    a) carried over   b) measured out   c) carried out   d) put up

9 As darkness fell, there was nothing for it but to _____ for the nearest village.

    a) call   b) go   c) make   d) stand

10 There is no time to do anything but _____ briefly on the most important points.

    a) touch   b) run   c) go   d) pick

11 Owning an animal can really tie you _____.

    a) out   b) down   c) back   d) off

12 The terrorist headquarters was blown _____ in the army attack.

    a) down   b) up   c) out   d) over

13 Don't worry if you make a mistake. Just _____ it out.

    a) rule   b) slip   c) leave   d) cross

14 It's no good trying to _____ with Eddie. You'll never change his mind.

    a) deal   b) discuss   c) reason   d) side

15 Thank goodness you'll be there. I'm _____ on your support.

    a) holding   b) calling   c) hanging   d) counting

16 The lecture hall gradually emptied as Professor Jackson _____ on.

    a) kept   b) passed   c) rambled   d) touched

B Read the text and underline the **eleven** phrasal verbs. Give a definition for each one, according to its meaning in the text.

For her first evening's work at Tasty Bites, Laura dressed up in a black skirt and white blouse, as she had been told to look smart. However, when she turned up, she found out that the proprietor had been less than honest with her about the job. Not only did she have to serve the customers, but she also had to work in the kitchen. When she pointed this out to Mr Edwards, he was not at all apologetic. Still, she decided to go on working at the snack bar for the time being. After all, she was getting on well in the job. 'And I can really do with the money!' she told herself.

Three months later, she saw an advertisement in the paper for a Saturday sales assistant at a department store. She thought it over carefully, and decided to apply for it. 'But I won't let on to Mr Edwards until I'm sure I've got the new job!' she thought. The prospect of doing something different cheered her up considerably.

C Complete each sentence with a phrase from box A followed by a phrase from box B. Do not use any phrase more than once.

A	B
picked out	to the disco.
set out,	of the station.
took her out	the best display.
keep foxes out	I bought another one just like it.
make out	from under his school cap.
ruled out	of the chicken shed.
laid out	there was a clap of thunder.
pulled slowly out	the banquet in the palace.
wore out,	the possibility of a cure.
stuck out	Marcella's handwriting.

1 We haven't entirely _____

2 The competition judges _____

3 The little boy's ears _____

4 Tracy's boyfriend _____

5 The steam train _____

6 The royal servants _____

7 The farmer found it hard to _____

8 I can't quite _____

9 When my favourite sweater _____

10 Just as we _____

Phrasal verbs with *away, across* and *around*

away
back   blaze   break   call   clear   die   fade   gamble   give
get   go   pass   pull   put   scare   send   stow   take   throw

across
come   get

around
crowd   fool   get   hang   look   shop

Away often has the meaning of movement away from the speaker.

A Decide whether the definitions are true (T) or false (F). Give the correct definition(s) if necessary.

1	put away	return something to its correct place
2	give away	lend or borrow something
3	call away	summon someone (often on business)
4	back away	go backwards in fear or dislike
5	go away	continue
6	get across	convey (a message)
7	get around	be (socially) active
8	shop around	consider a number of possibilities before buying something
9	scare away	make someone leave by frightening them
10	pass away	walk past
11	fool around	cause damage
12	fade away	gradually disappear

B Complete the crossword with verbs from the box above, using the clues provided.

Across:

1 Be careful you don't _____ away all your savings at the casino.

4 I'm afraid the doctors say his cousin is about to _____ away.

6 I'm in no hurry. I'll _____ around here until you're ready.

8 I can't stand cats! _____ it away!

10 We heard the last few notes of the concerto _____ away in the evening air.

11 If you don't need that plastic bag, just _____ it away.

14 The driver just managed to _____ away as the traffic warden approached.

15 The film's message didn't _____ across very clearly.

16 The shop hasn't got the batteries in stock. They'll have to _____ away for them.

17 You needn't rush. I'll _____ around the museum while I'm waiting.

18 Two famous players have decided to _____ away from the International Chess Association.

Down:

1 Jack Hobbs, the millionaire, wants to _____ away all his money to the poor.

2 The gunners began to _____ away at the target, the moment the signal was given.

3 Could you _____ away the dirty plates, please?

5 How did the boy get to New York? Did he _____ away on a plane?

7 I'm not sure I managed to _____ across the urgency of the situation.

9 She's fainted! Don't _____ around! Give her air!

12 If you talk loudly in the woods, you'll _____ away the wild animals.

13 I can't understand how the police let the robbers _____ away.

14 All the toys must be _____ away at once.

16 We're going to _____ around and compare prices before we decide.

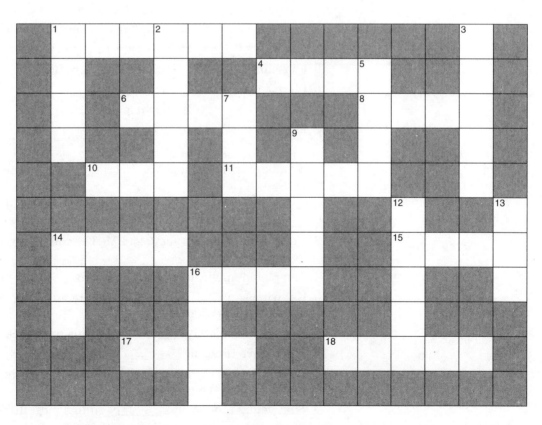

Phrasal verbs with *in* and *into*

---

in
barge   break   burst   butt   call   check   drop   fill   fit
get   give   hand   join   move   pay   phase   plug   pop
pull   send   settle   show   sink   stay   take   tune

into
break   bump   burst   come   dig   fool   look   run   rush
talk   turn

In/Into often have the meaning of including, or of an inward movement.

A Match each phrasal verb with the correct definition. (There may be other possible definitions.)

1	take in	A	meet accidentally
2	butt in	B	pay an unexpected visit
3	bump into	C	persuade to do
4	look into	D	start to occupy a house, office, etc.
5	drop in	E	deposit (money)
6	talk into	F	introduce (a system) in easy stages
7	turn into	G	complete (a form)
8	pay in	H	interrupt rudely
9	phase in	I	change into, become
10	fill in	J	investigate
11	move in	K	participate
12	join in	L	deceive

B Complete each sentence with the correct form of a phrasal verb from the box above.

1 By an amazing coincidence, George _____ into his long-lost brother in Berlin.

2 It was some time before the enormity of what had happened _____ in.

3 No wonder you can't get Jazz FM. The radio's not properly _____ in.

4 Completed application forms should be _____ in by Friday.

5 Katarina can _____ her father into anything. She twists him round her little finger!

6 We were completely _____ in by his hard-luck story.

7 If you have time, do _____ in for coffee.

8 We'll give the newcomers a chance to _____ in, then invite them round to meet the neighbours.

9 That young tomboy has _____ into a most attractive woman.

10 Lucy will have to _____ into her savings to pay for the operation.

11 Don't just _____ in like that, without knocking!

12 The manager asked his secretary to _____ the visitors in.

13 The local authorities have decided to _____ in the new taxes over a five-year period.

14 If you give us your bank details, your salary will be _____ in on the 28th of every month.

C Add **it** where necessary to the following sentences, and say what **it** means or might mean.

1 Here's the hairdryer. You can plug in over there.

2 The door was flung open and Gloria burst in.

3 I'll probably stay in tonight, as I've got a cold.

4 Have you finished the report? Hand in tomorrow, please.

5 Rolf pulled in for petrol at the motorway services.

6 The new clerk needs to be the right sort of person to fit in here.

7 I don't think poor Mrs Gates can take all in.

8 Well, I give in! I'll do whatever you like!

9 That horse is completely wild. You'll have to break in.

10 If you'd like a lift, get in.

11 If you feel energetic enough, why not join in? The dance steps are quite easy.

12 When you receive the application form, you must fill in and return to our central office immediately.

D Complete each sentence with a phrase from box A followed by a phrase from box B. Do not use any phrase more than once.

A	B
moving in	the isolated house.
came into	as she waved goodbye.
have broken into	anything.
rush into	before we have dinner?
fool me into	soon?
burst into tears	believing you!
check in	a fortune.

1 On her aunt's death Karin _____

_____

2 Burglars _____

_____

3 Daisy _____

_____

4 It's no good. You can't _____

_____

5 Don't you think we should _____

_____

6 Is your sister _____

_____

7 Think about it. Don't _____

_____

UNIT 38

Three-part phrasal verbs

carry on with	face up to	get up to	look down on
catch up with	feel up to	go ahead with	look up to
come down with	get along with	go along with	miss out on
come in for	get away with	go on with	put up with
come out in	get down to	go through with	run out of
come up against	get on with	grow out of	send away/off for
come up with	get out of	hold on to	settle up with
cut down on	get rid of	keep up with	walk out on
do away with	get round to	live up to	write away/off for

A Decide whether the definitions are true (T) or false (F). Give the correct definition(s) if necessary.

1 put up with — tolerate
2 get away with — avoid punishment
3 come in for — receive, be the object of
4 do away with — restore, decorate
5 come up with — produce (an idea, solution etc)
6 get round to — appear on stage
7 look down on — consider another person superior
8 grow out of — move upwards
9 face up to — confront, tackle (a problem, etc)
10 get along with — have a good relationship with
11 go through with — accompany
12 run out of — use up completely

B Rewrite the sentences, using a phrasal verb from the box above, to produce the opposite meaning of the words in italics.

1 Bernadette *is very contemptuous of* certain groups of people.
2 The company decided to *stop work on* the project.
3 I would find it very difficult to *oppose* the committee's proposals.
4 The doctor advised Luciano to *eat more* carbohydrates for the sake of his health.

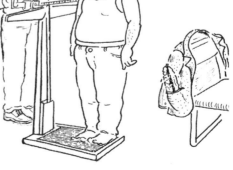

5 During his holiday he *lost touch with* current events.

6 Trevor has *volunteered to do* the work.

7 The guests *didn't pay their hotel bill* before leaving.

8 After their many arguments, Bryan *stayed with* his wife.

9 I wish we'd *kept* those old mirrors when we moved house.

10 Jacqui makes a point of *ignoring* the latest fashions.

C Complete each sentence with the correct form of a phrasal verb from the box opposite.

1 I don't think I can _____ with his behaviour any longer.

2 If you're interested, why don't you _____ for details of the job?

3 Carolina has always _____ very well with her colleagues.

4 Are you sure you _____ to coming out tonight?

5 I'm sorry I didn't _____ to replying earlier.

6 On last year's expedition the team _____ against terrible difficulties.

7 Anna won't be at work today. She's _____ with flu.

8 I think I'd better _____ to some work now.

9 Sadly, the boy couldn't _____ to his father's expectations.

10 I wonder what mischief the children are _____ to this morning?

11 I'm afraid we've _____ of coffee, so would you like tea?

12 Most problems in life just have to be _____ to.

D Complete each sentence with a phrase from box A followed by a phrase from box B. Do not use any phrase more than once.

A	B
do away with	those stamps. They're valuable.
go through with	the monarchy.
hang on to	the wedding.
get away with	spots yesterday.
missing out on	a great deal of criticism lately.
came out in	such a good opportunity.
come in for	murder!

1 Sarah was disappointed at _____

_____

2 The boss always lets Fred _____

_____

3 The President has _____

_____

4 Many people would like to _____

_____

5 The baby's ill: she _____

_____

6 You should _____

_____

7 Rachel decided she couldn't _____

_____

Phrasal verbs as nouns

breakdown	dropout	hold-up	onlooker	stand-in
break-in	getaway	knockout	onset	stopover
breakthrough	get-together	lay-by	outbreak	stowaway
breakup	go-ahead	lay-off	outburst	take-off
castaway	goings-on	layout	outlook	takeover
check-in	grown-up	let-down	sell-out	turnout
comedown	handout	let-up	setback	upbringing
cutback	hangover	lookout	standby	

A Complete each sentence with the correct noun from the box above.

1 Tony's been demoted to Assistant Manager. What a _____ for him!

2 Customs officers were on the _____ for illegal drugs.

3 The tourist office has a free _____ on cheap accommodation in London.

4 Patricia suffered a nervous _____ when she lost her job.

5 Miguel's devotion to the company contributed to the _____ of his marriage.

6 If you were a _____ on a desert island, how would you cope?

7 Scientists have made an important _____ in the field of genetic engineering.

8 The planning authorities gave the school the _____ for an extension.

9 At South London University, there were several _____ from the Computer Science course this year.

10 Tommy, ask a _____ to help you next time you want to do some painting.

11 Keith has always had a rather narrow _____ on life. I put it down to his strict _____.

12 It poured down all day without any _____.

13 The whole room was stunned into silence by Gordon's angry _____.

14 The robbers made an incredibly quick _____ in a waiting car.

15 The _____s in the building trade are a direct result of the _____s in government spending.

16 The advantage of flying Air Canada is that the fare includes a free _____ in Vancouver.

17 Whenever Mrs Khan chairs the meeting, we get a much better _____.

18 To the delight of the _____s, the Princess posed on the steps for photographs.

B Complete the crossword with words from the box opposite, using the clues provided.

Across:

3 Can be relied on in an emergency

5 The act of assuming power

7 A commercial success (e.g. a concert)

10 See 1 Down

11 See 17 Down

12 A person who hides aboard a ship or plane to gain free passage

13 & 9 Down   An armed robbery

14 Arrangement of written material on a page

19 A sudden occurrence (of disease or war)

20 A hindrance to a plan

21 See 18 Down

23 Delayed after-effects of drinking too much alcohol

Down:

1 & 10 Across   A person substituting for an actor

2 A disappointment

4 & 10 Across   The illegal entering of a building

6 A blow rendering an opponent unconscious

8 A place for drivers to stop, off the main road

9 See 13 Across

15 The beginning (of something bad)

16 & 22   To register (at a hotel)

17 & 11 Across   Happenings, events

18 & 21 Across   Informal meeting or social gathering

22 See 16 Down

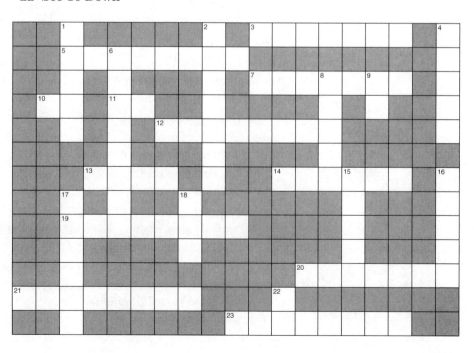

Recycling

A Choose the correct word or phrase to complete each sentence. Write the letter in the space.

1 The speaker failed to get his message _____ to his audience.

  a) around b) in c) across d) out

2 The reporter announced solemnly that the President had _____ in his sleep.

  a) passed away b) died away c) passed out d) dropped off

3 He's been to the USA, Australia and India this year. He certainly gets _____!

  a) on b) around c) out d) away

4 Look, I'm sorry to _____ in, but I think I can help you.

  a) move b) plug c) butt d) pop

5 The elaborate bridal costumes of the coastal Indians are _____ from mother to daughter.

  a) taken after b) put by c) parted with d) handed down

6 Politicians frequently _____ a lot of criticism.

  a) come out in b) catch up with c) come in for d) get up to

7 I was disappointed when I saw the film. It was a real _____.

  a) let-down b) breakdown c) turnout d) dropout

8 You'll lose marks if you don't _____ in all the gaps.

  a) send b) fill c) fit d) join

9 He gambled _____ his life's savings before starting on his wife's.

  a) across b) around c) out d) away

10 Did you notice Bob trying to _____ doing the washing-up?

  a) get up to b) break out of c) get out of d) get along with

11 To beat the holiday traffic, we'll have to _____ out at dawn.

  a) set b) go c) move d) drive

12 I could probably _____ out the answer if I had a pencil, some paper and a calculator.

  a) think b) study c) hand d) work

13 Delilah wasn't at all hungry, and could only _____ with the food on her plate.

  a) finger b) toy c) snack d) side

14 I know it's a pretty boring routine, but you'll just have to _____ on for the moment, I'm afraid.

  a) count b) live c) soldier d) move

15 As the years passed, Joe's memories of his terrible experience _____ away, and he began to lead a normal life again.

  a) faded b) backed c) passed d) got

16 This is a big decision to make. Think it _____ before you give me your final word tomorrow.

  a) over b) upon c) carefully d) on

B Read the text, and underline the twelve phrasal verbs. Give a definition for each one, according to its meaning in the text.

Unfortunately, the department store ruled Laura out, as she had no relevant experience. So she went on waitressing part-time at Tasty Bites, until the day she arrived at work to find that the place had been closed down by the authorities for reasons of hygiene.

When she had got over her initial surprise, she decided to look around for another, more secure job. Eventually she was taken on at the local airport, where she worked at the checkout in the duty-free shop. The hours were long and the other staff rather unfriendly, but Laura was determined to put up with the job. At least she was able to spend her breaks watching the planes take off and land, and join in the general feeling of excitement that pervades a bustling international airport. But her university studies were beginning to suffer and so, when she was laid off at the end of the busy summer season, she gave up any further ideas of trying to earn money, and went back to her books.

C Complete each sentence with a phrase from box A followed by a phrase from box B. Do not use any phrase more than once.

A	B
are the result of	at the student hostel.
made their getaway	his upbringing.
was blamed on	in a stolen car.
allows them a stopover	ready for take-off.
the goings-on	government cutbacks.
an impressive turnout	in Hong Kong.
your seat belts	for the by-election.

1 There was _____

2 Police investigated _____

3 The culprits _____

4 Please fasten _____

5 The hospital closures _____

6 Their ticket to Sydney _____

7 The accused's antisocial behaviour _____

D Follow the instructions for Exercise C.

A	B
came across	completely out of control.
owned up	pretty fast.
talk him into	to having started the rumour.
will get around	giving up golf.
blazed away,	outside the star's home.
hung around	a rare coin among her loose change.

1 The plain-clothes policeman _____

2 Josephine _____

3 The fire _____

4 Eventually he _____

5 News of their affair _____

6 She'll never _____

UNIT 41

E-mail and the internet

A Choose the correct word from the pair in brackets to complete these sentences about using the internet and your computer.

1 All you need to get connected to the internet is a fairly modern (PC/RAM), a modem and a (mobile phone/phone line).

2 Once you're online, you may want to find out information by using a (search engine/reference file), see what people are discussing by accessing the messages in a(n) (outbox/newsgroup), or simply join a (cybercafe/chat room) for a real-time conversation.

3 Have you heard someone say, 'I lost all my work because my computer (crashed/downloaded)'? They should have remembered to (back up/cut and paste) before switching off.

4 To open a folder or a document, just move your (cursor/finger) on to its (toolbar/icon) and (double-click/single-switch).

5 If someone you don't know sends you an (attachment/application) with an e-mail, don't open it, in case it contains (an infection/a virus).

B Read the passage, then decide which word from A, B, C or D is most appropriate for each space.

PENICILLIN BEFORE PENTIUMS FOR THE POOR

One of the hottest topics on the international development agenda is how to harness the power of 1) _____ for the benefit of developing countries. What is sometimes called 'the death of distance', brought about by the 2) _____, allows professional services such as 3) _____, education and training to be provided easily and quickly to 4) _____ areas. Some of the gains can be seen in countries as diverse as India and Morocco, where innovations range from 5) _____ government announcements to local craftsmen selling their wares to a 6) _____ market. But already a huge and expanding 7) _____ divide is opening up between developed and developing nations. The major task facing world leaders at present is to 8) _____ everybody on the planet with clean water, basic education and the drugs needed to fight preventable diseases. Installing a 9) _____ in every classroom and linking us all to 10) _____ must be a lesser 11) _____, for the time being at least.

	A	B	C	D
1	ISP	ICT	IMF	IOU
2	computer	telephone	modem	internet
3	stationery	software	hardware	equipment
4	far	uninhabited	remote	secluded
5	online	broadcast	recorded	programmed
6	global	technical	village	shrinking
7	physical	digital	electrical	economical
8	supply	give	donate	administer
9	plug	video	mobile phone	modem
10	the real world	cyberspace	virtual reality	outer space
11	priority	advantage	importance	criteria

C Read this e-mail sent to an office colleague. Then use the information to complete the formal letter which follows. Use either **one** or **two** words for each gap. The words you will need do not occur in the e-mail.

From: Jason <jasong@postit.com>
To: David <daveh@postit.com>
Sent: Thurs, 24 June 2002, 10.23 am
Subject: ISP complaint

Can you do a formal letter to Castle, to let them know we are not too pleased with the service they're giving us? Mention:
– connecting has been difficult lately
– it's been taking ages to send and receive e-mails
– when we ring up Castle's engineers for help, they just don't seem to have a clue! according to Jackie and Ross in Accounts
– Castle did nothing to stop all that spam we were deluged with last week.
If they don't do something about all this, tell them we'll stop paying them, and find another ISP. We want a snappy answer.
Thanks.
Jason

Dear Sir or Madam,

I am writing to 1) _____ you that we are 2) _____ with the level of service you are 3) _____. On several occasions we have not been able to 4) _____ easily. In addition, sending and receiving e-mails has become a 5) _____, and some of our staff have complained that the Help Desk 6) _____ who answer calls have not been able to 7) _____ their problems. You were also 8) _____ when we found ourselves the 9) _____ for huge quantities of 10) _____ e-mail recently.

11) _____ you take steps to address these points, we shall be forced to 12) _____ our subscription to you. I look forward to your 13) _____ reply.

Yours faithfully,

David Heath
IT Manager

D Answer these questions as fully as you can, in conversation or in writing.

1 What are the advantages and disadvantages of e-mail over traditional letter writing?

2 Do you feel the internet performs a useful function in connecting people with each other? Do you feel it enriches our existence? Or do you think it is a waste of time, and merely encourages us to make virtual relationships instead of real ones?

UNIT 42

The media and the arts

A Complete the passage with these words and phrases. There is one more than you need.

press	jingles	subliminal	commercials
disseminate	slogans	hoardings	advertising agency
pressure groups	posters	brand	

Advertising on television is big business. Advertising 1) _____ and 2) _____, if they are catchy enough, often become part of our culture. However little attention we pay to 3) _____, we cannot avoid being influenced by the constant repetition of a 4) _____ name or image. The message we receive may even be 5) _____, so that we are not aware of it. Not all advertisements are purely financially motivated, however. Political parties and 6) _____ aim to 7) _____ their views more widely by putting up 8) _____ on street 9) _____ and by buying space in the 10) _____ and time on the small screen.

B Match the words on the left, connected with newspapers, with the correct definitions.

1	obituary	A	critical assessment of a book, film etc.
2	leader	B	leading editorial article
3	horoscope	C	regular article about celebrities
4	review	D	announcement of a death, with a short biography
5	gossip column	E	phrase or title at the top of an article
6	headline	F	humorous or satirical drawing
7	deadline	G	time limit for reporting news
8	cartoon	H	prediction of someone's future according to his/her sign of the zodiac

C Complete each sentence with a word formed from one of these verbs.

catch	censor	circulate	commentate	cover	criticise

1 The new gallery was given the seal of approval by *The Observer's* art _____, who wrote several enthusiastic articles about it.

2 Former champion John McEnroe has now made a name as a tennis _____.

3 Under the government's wartime _____ rules, all newspaper articles had to be checked by officials before being printed.

4 The tabloids have excellent _____ of scandal and sport: the quality papers deal with everything else.

5 The local newspaper's _____ fell dramatically when the editor was sacked.

6 That jingle from the teabag ad is so _____ that I can't get it out of my head.

D Choose the correct word or phrase from the pair in brackets to complete each sentence.

1 The actors have been _____ the play all this week. (rehearsing/repeating)

2 The audience applauded wildly when the director appeared on the _____ to take his bow. (scene/stage)

3 I've been watching a fascinating new _____ of art programmes. (serie/series)

4 Although the play has a large number of _____, it is comparatively easy to follow the plot. (characters/persons)

5 If you don't like that programme, you can always switch over to a different _____. (channel/canal)

6 The latest television dramatisation was filmed entirely _____ in a country village not far from here. (in the wild/on location)

7 Which _____ did Marlene Dietrich play in her last film? (role/performance)

8 There's a wonderful _____ of 'A Midsummer Night's Dream' in *The Evening Herald*. (critic/review)

E Complete the sentences with these words and phrases.

| standing ovation | soap opera | supporting roles | low-budget |
| prime-time | box-office success | subtitles | final curtain |

1 Despite being a critical disaster, the film was a huge _____.

2 The orchestra and their conductor were given a _____ at the end of the concert.

3 People who are addicted to a particular _____ seldom miss an episode.

4 It wasn't until the _____ fell that the audience voiced their disapproval by hissing and booing.

5 At the local arts cinema, foreign films are usually shown with _____, and only occasionally dubbed.

6 Compared with most American blockbusters, it was a _____ film, as very little funding was available.

7 Programmes on _____ television attract the greatest number of viewers.

8 Although the lead actor and actress were excellent, the _____ were very well acted too.

F Answer these questions as fully as you can, in conversation or in writing.

1 Which medium do you find
a) most informative? b) most sensational? c) most biased?

2 How can we avoid being brainwashed by prejudiced views or propaganda?

3 Is there a gap in the media market? What kind of new magazine, newspaper, TV or radio programme would you launch if you had adequate funds and a creative team behind you?

4 How important is the image or presentation of an organisation or public figure? Is employing a public relations firm a good way of improving this?

Success and fame

A Complete the passage with these words. There are two more than you need.

public	reap	market	fame	wealth	ambition
	respected	jet set	whizz-kid	success	
	best-seller	rising	achieve	rocketed	
		expanding	potential		

What is success? Achieving a long-held 1) _____? Earning a million by the time you're twenty-five? Joining the 2) _____? 3) _____ to the top of your chosen profession? Writing a 4) _____? 5) _____ means different things to different people, but one man has managed to 6) _____ all this in a very short space of time.

Jeff Packham was still at university when he realised the 7) _____ profits to be made from the sale of posters to an eager public. The poster stall he manned every Saturday was regularly surrounded by enthusiasts keen to snap up a bargain. So after graduating, he took out a loan, rented office space, and acquired a stock of posters. Soon his business was 8) _____ rapidly, and he was able to rent a warehouse, which he renovated and used as a centre for his operations. Other shops were opened in other parts of the country, and sales 9) _____.

Hard-headed businessmen flocked to buy shares in this 10) _____'s company when it went public, and Jeff was able to 11) _____ the rewards of his hard work by taking time off to buy a house and get married.

He is still only in his mid-twenties, a father of two, and a 12) _____ businessman with a product which is a 13) _____ leader. To admirers of his achievements he points out that he has had to make sacrifices. 'It's difficult to maintain one's privacy,' he says. 'Once you are successful, you have to live in the 14) _____ eye, to a certain extent.'

B Make adjectives from these nouns, and check their meanings in a dictionary.

1 prodigy _____
2 dedication _____
3 ruthlessness _____
4 skill _____
5 notoriety _____
6 success _____

7 ephemera _____
8 stress _____
9 celebrity _____
10 legend _____
11 renown _____
12 talent _____

C Choose the correct word or phrase from the pair in brackets to complete each sentence.

1 The life of a child _____ can be fraught with difficulties. (prodigy/idol)

2 Garth left his small home town in the Midwest, lured by the bright _____ of New York.   (lights/stars)

3 The rock group shot to _____ after appointing a new manager. (publicity/stardom)

4 The _____ Dr Crippen, who was executed for poisoning his wife, was the first criminal to be apprehended by the use of radio-telegraphy. (infamous/famous)

5 Ayrton Senna had already been world motor-racing _____ several times before his tragic death on the Imola circuit. (champion/winner)

6 An ambitious person is committed to improving his or her _____ at work. (status/rank)

7 The fans all waited excitedly at the stage door to get the singer's _____. (signature/autograph)

8 The _____ of my neighbour's business was largely due to the world recession. (failing/failure)

9 Princess Diana found the _____ of her privacy intolerable. (intrusion/invasion)

10 Mr Sampson enjoys an excellent _____ as a heart specialist. (reputation/fame)

11 Many great geniuses receive only _____ recognition of their talents. (posthumous/post-mortem)

12 Isabel's _____ came when her designs were spotted by a Paris fashion house. (big break/window display)

13 People connected to the rich and famous often write diaries and memoirs for _____. (longevity/posterity)

14 Sir Alfred Marks made his great fortune by identifying a(n) _____ in the market. (gap/opportunity)

15 When Guy went back to the casino, he gambled his previous night's _____ on one turn of the roulette wheel, and lost them all. (earnings/winnings)

16 Many _____ these days are famous merely for being famous. (celebrities/gurus)

D Answer these questions as fully as you can, in conversation or in writing.

1 What are the advantages and disadvantages of maintaining a high profile in public life?

2 Do you think that people in the public eye are entitled to privacy, or should their privileged role expose them to public scrutiny at all times?

3 How would you define success? What area would you like to be successful in?

4 Do you think a person can become successful purely on his/her own merits, or is there always an element of influence or corruption?

5 Do you think the current cult of success, with massive salaries for company directors, and megastar status for singers, footballers and media personalities, reflects the achievements or the failures of our society? Are there other ways of rewarding high achievers, and what, in your opinion, should be rewarded?

Animals and their rights

A Complete the passage with these words and phrases.

widespread	tested	experiments	livestock	climate
vivisection	consumers	factory farming		entertainment
activists	free-range		blood sports	opposition
	animal rights	cruelty	battery hens	

People's attitudes to animals have changed considerably in the last two decades. Using animals in scientific 1) _____ and as a primary food source, once considered a human prerogative, is now being questioned by 2) _____ campaigners. There is also a 3) _____ revulsion against 4) _____ such as fox-hunting, and 5) _____ often endanger their own lives in an attempt to stop what Oscar Wilde called 'the unspeakable in pursuit of the uneatable'. Several cosmetics companies now claim that their products are not 6) _____ on animals, a policy which has been found to be popular with 7) _____.

Although the medical and scientific professions still maintain that 8) _____ is necessary for research purposes, there is more public 9) _____ to this than ever before. This change in the 10) _____ of public opinion means that using animals for 11) _____ is also frowned on. Zoos and circuses are sometimes accused of 12) _____, and are losing their popularity. Even in agriculture, changes are slowly being introduced in response to public concern about animal welfare. Many supermarkets now offer 13) _____ eggs to their customers, as well as eggs from 14) _____, and although 15) _____ is still widespread, farmers are aware that consumers are increasingly interested in the living conditions and even the feelings of 16) _____.

B Match the words in the lists to make compound nouns or well-known phrases, some of which may need a hyphen. Check their meanings in a dictionary.

1	book	A	fat
2	stag	B	crossing
3	dark	C	hole
4	puppy	D	party
5	zebra	E	tears
6	pigeon	F	eyes
7	crocodile	G	whistle
8	dog	H	worm
9	wolf	I	collar
10	cat's	J	horse

C Put these animal names into the correct sentences. You may have to change the form of the word, and/or add a hyphen.

whale	sardine	rat	wolf	horse	parrot	wild goose
	butterfly	fly	frog	bird	dog	

1 Wouldn't you just love to be a _____ on the wall when Sarah tells him it's all over?

2 Could I have some water, please? I've got a _____ in my throat.

3 Even the great cellist, Dmitri Radovic, admitted to having _____ in his stomach before a concert.

4 From the helicopter the police had a _____ eye view of the accident.

5 Unfortunately Donald doesn't try to understand grammar rules. He just learns sentences _____ fashion.

6 Roger is extraordinarily selfish and possessive – a real _____ in the manger.

7 The old man led us all over town on a _____ chase, and so we never found the house we were looking for.

8 I'm afraid you're flogging a dead _____, Rupert. The boss will never agree to your proposal.

9 Caroline has cried _____ so many times before that people just don't believe her any more.

10 There's something strange about that plan of Mary's. I smell a _____!

11 Jane was having a _____ of a time at the party, and could hardly be dragged away.

12 When the train doors closed, we were packed like _____ and could not move an inch.

D Match each verb with the correct definition.

1 beaver away	A	move the head or body quickly downwards
2 duck	B	play or meddle (with something)
3 monkey about	C	confuse (someone)
4 worm your way	D	trouble, plague, bother (someone)
5 dog	E	work industriously
6 fox	F	insinuate yourself

E Answer these questions as fully as you can, in conversation or in writing.

1 If new medicines and cosmetics are not tested on animals, we will have to use humans as guinea pigs. What are your views on this?

2 How cruel do you think zoos and circuses really are? Animals kept in cages are certainly not free, but at least they are fed regularly and protected from danger and extinction. Do you think it is right for us to use animals for our entertainment?

3 What are the possible grounds for becoming a vegetarian, and which of them most appeals to you?

4 Why do you think people's attitudes towards animal rights have changed so radically, as described in Exercise A? Are the reasons historical, financial or sociological? Why do we not consider the rights of other species, like insects, plants or bacteria?

Language

A Complete the passage with these words. There are two more than you need.

literal	translation	nuances	dialect	metaphor
evoking	colloquial	original		authors
allusions	translators	interpreting		

At the recent World Congress of the International Federation of Translators in Brighton, selected 1) _____ shared a platform with their translators. 2) _____ is generally agreed to be the rendering of meaning from one language or 3) _____ to another. However, there is a central dilemma which all 4) _____ have to face, and which was discussed at length at the congress. How can readers of other nationalities understand all the 5) _____ and linguistic 6) _____ of particular writers? The translators' answer to this is to aim to capture the tone of the 7) _____, without translating it into 8) _____ language or slang. 9) _____ the flavour or atmosphere of the text is considered far more important than giving a(n) 10) _____ translation.

B Match the words on the left with the correct definitions.

1	pidgin	A	a word or phrase which reads the same backwards or forwards
2	jargon	B	non-standard, informal language
3	spoonerism	C	using the same letter to start each word in a sentence or a line of verse
4	onomatopoeia	D	unintentional confusion of two words
5	palindrome	E	a phrase or sentence difficult to say quickly
6	limerick	F	a simple language made up of elements of two or more languages
7	alliteration	G	five lines of comic verse
8	tongue-twister	H	using words whose sound imitates their meaning
9	malapropism	I	specialised language for e.g. a profession
10	slang	J	transposing the initial consonants of a pair of words

C Now match the terms in Exercise B with these examples.

1 You have deliberately tasted two worms and you can leave Oxford by the town drain.
2 Lend me five quid till tomorrow, will you?
3 Five miles meandering with a mazy motion
4 In the warm sunshine the bees buzzed round the hive.
5 Madam, I'm Adam.
6 The tractor feed is the part of the printer designed for handling continuous stationery.

7 Trespassers will be executed.

8 Peter Piper picked a peck of pickled pepper.

9 Me go house big-feller.

10 There was an old lady called Jane,

Who feared she was terribly plain,

But because she had wealth,

And, sadly, poor health,

She was proposed to again and again!

D Choose the correct word from the pair in brackets to complete each sentence.

1 The hall was packed for the visiting professor's _____ on eighteenth-century poetry.   (lecture/conference)

2 It was warm in the church, and some of the congregation found themselves dozing off as the vicar came to the end of his _____. (sermon/speech)

3 My aunt had a terrible _____ with her neighbour, which turned into a ten-year feud.   (argue/quarrel)

4 The mayor made a _____ in Italian, to welcome the delegates from Rome.   (speech/talk)

5 Wayne speaks English with a noticeable Canadian _____. (accent/dialect)

6 The two politicians had a heated _____ about capital punishment in front of the studio audience.   (debate/row)

7 The _____ of the word 'watch' is different from 'wash'. (accent/pronunciation)

8 The two old soldiers kept interrupting as each tried to finish his _____. 'No, no, it didn't happen like that!' they said, correcting each other.   (anecdote/history)

9 Every English _____ must have a working verb in it. (phrase/sentence)

10 Children often enjoy asking each other a _____, like 'When is a witch not a witch? When it's a sandwich!'   (puzzle/riddle)

E Answer these questions as fully as you can, in conversation or in writing.

1 How important do you think it is to learn standard English, or Received Pronunciation? Should regional accents and dialects be retained in any language, and taught to foreigners? Is there a social stigma attached to a non-standard accent in your country?

2 How different is written English from spoken English? Give examples. What differences are there in your language, spoken and written?

3 Does a language reflect the climate or location of the country where it is spoken? Does it reflect the character of people in that country? Give examples.

4 In what ways does learning a foreign language help to create international understanding?

5 What are the best ways of learning a foreign language?

Medicine and health

A Complete the passage with these words and phrases.

transplants	heavy smokers	National Health Service
policy emergency patient medical bypass collapses		
cardiac addicts surgery consultants treatment interim		

Wythenshawe Hospital in Manchester maintains a 1) _____ of refusing to carry out heart 2) _____ operations on smokers. It is important to be clear about the views of the hospital 3) _____. They are happy to treat any smoker who 4) _____ and needs 5) _____ treatment, but they draw the line at carrying out expensive, non-urgent, preventive 6) _____ surgery on patients who refuse to stop smoking. There is a high risk of complications for 7) _____ during and after heart 8) _____, so many clinicians prefer to provide 9) _____ medical treatment, while encouraging the 10) _____ to give up smoking.

The death of a Manchester 25-cigarettes-a-day man, who died after being refused tests at Wythenshawe, has given rise to furious debate in 11) _____ circles. If this argument is taken further, drunken drivers could be denied emergency 12) _____, drug 13) _____ HIV treatment, and drinkers liver 14) _____. In other words, should any individual who can be shown to have contributed to his own medical problems be refused help on the 15) _____?

B Choose the correct word or phrase from the pair in brackets to complete each sentence.

1 John's been off work for a week with flu, and he still feels rather _____. (under the weather/full of beans)

2 Chickenpox is a children's infectious _____, but adults can catch it too. (disease/sickness)

3 The _____ who performed the operation visited the patient soon after she came round. (physician/surgeon)

4 Don't worry, I can assure you that this medicine produces no _____ at all. (side effects/results)

5 I'd like to visit Patricia, now that she's out of intensive care, but I'm not sure which _____ she's in. (ward/cell)

6 Your state of health must be good before you can become a blood _____. (giver/donor)

7 Although Bob recovered fairly quickly from the accident, he had to have plastic _____ to remove facial scars. (operation/surgery)

8 Mrs Wright took her son to the weekly baby _____, to have him weighed and to check that he was making good progress. (hospital/clinic)

9 If someone collapses in the street, it may be necessary to give them _____ aid until the ambulance arrives.   (emergency/first)

10 Most food experts now criticise the use of drastic slimming _____. Instead, they recommend a programme of exercise and balanced eating.   (regimes/diets)

11 Medical students are usually encouraged to watch operations in the operating _____, as part of their training.   (room/theatre)

12 You'll need to take your _____ to the chemist's, Mrs Hall. (prescription/recipe)

13 When Jayne cut her hand, we had to drive ten miles to Bristol, as our local hospital has no _____ department.   (acute/casualty)

14 Have you ever had to have a blood _____? (transference/transfusion)

15 Trying to dress yourself with your arm in a _____ is almost impossible.   (bandage/sling)

C Decide whether the definitions are true (T) or false (F). Give the correct definition if necessary.

1 *Bacteria* are a group of micro-organisms, many of which cause disease.

2 *Organically* grown food is food grown without artificial pesticides or fertilisers.

3 Someone who is *vulnerable* to infection can resist infection well.

4 A *paediatrician* specialises in elderly people's health problems.

5 An *epidemic* is a widespread occurrence of a disease.

6 *Obesity* means having extremely low blood pressure.

7 An *injection* is a means of giving food to patients who cannot swallow.

8 *Antibiotics* are drugs used to fight infections.

9 *Homeopathy* involves treating people's joints and muscles with exercise and massage.

10 An *X-ray* is a photograph taken with special equipment which can show if bones are broken or internal organs damaged.

D Answer these questions as fully as you can, in conversation or in writing.

1 What are your views on the ethical problems raised in the text in Exercise A?

2 Do we all have a right to free medical treatment, provided by the state, or should we make our own provision for health care, using private health insurance?

3 How can we reconcile the fact that the demand for health care these days is unlimited, whereas health budgets are limited? What priorities would you set if you were Health Minister? How important is health education?

4 What do you expect, and what do you get, from your family doctor? Which do you think is more important, the consultation or the prescription?

5 What factors have the greatest effect on our health?

6 What do you think of alternative medicine? Is it just a fashionable fad that will not last long, or might it replace orthodox medicine in the end?

Danger and risk

A Match the words or phrases to make common expressions connected with danger and risk. Use each word or phrase only once.

1	a narrow	A	the risk
2	raise	B	folly
3	the odds are	C	of mind
4	a false sense	D	overboard
5	risk life	E	escape
6	run	F	and sound
7	take	G	a charmed life
8	peace	H	the alarm
9	bear	I	and limb
10	safe	J	heavily stacked against
11	be swept	K	sensible precautions
12	sheer	L	of security

B Now use the phrases from Exercise A in their correct form in these sentences.

1 I had a very _____ on my way to work this morning. I was just crossing the road when I was nearly mown down by a car jumping the lights.

2 If you choose to drink and drive, you _____ of being arrested and sent to prison.

3 Mrs Geeson was very relieved to see her sons come home _____ from their canoeing trip on the River Ardèche.

4 Two men are still missing from their yacht in the Indian Ocean. It is feared they may have _____ by a freak wave and drowned.

5 Douglas should never have attempted to climb Mont Blanc. With his heart condition, it was _____.

6 You will only have complete _____ if you insure yourself carefully against every possible disaster.

7 Tony seems to _____. He's already been involved in a shipwreck, two car accidents, a helicopter crash and a supermarket fire, and has come out of all of them without a scratch.

8 If you are going mountain climbing in winter, you are advised to _____, such as wearing the right clothing, and taking the correct equipment with you.

9 I can't believe that Sabina is going to _____ on that parachute jump. Of course, she's doing it for charity.

10 As there had never been an accident at that pit before, the miners were lulled into _____, and became careless.

11 When one of the walkers was injured, two of the group stayed with him, while another boy set off down the mountain to _____.

12 The _____ the missing fishermen, but the search for them will be resumed at first light, if weather conditions allow.

C Match the words on the left with the correct definitions.

1	intrepid	A	dangerous
2	hazardous	B	difficult living conditions
3	survivor	C	food and other necessities
4	hardships	D	extremely brave
5	endurance	E	someone still alive after an accident or a disaster
6	foolhardy	F	to put someone or something in danger
7	sponsor	G	(providing) the money needed
8	provisions	H	having a fixed aim, being single-minded
9	jeopardise	I	being able to put up with difficult conditions
10	funding	J	someone who is hurt or killed, e.g. in an accident
11	determination	K	someone who provides money for a venture
12	casualty	L	carelessly, rashly adventurous

D Now complete the text with the words from Exercise C, in their correct form.

The small team of scientists who have recently been exploring the Brazilian rainforest endured many 1) _____ before they reached home. Some commentators felt that it was 2) _____ of them to set out without proper 3) _____ from government or commercial 4) _____. They had very little equipment, and ran short of 5) _____ after six weeks, so that extra food and supplies had to be airlifted to them. At one point, the team admitted later, they all began to think that there would be no 6) _____ from this extremely 7) _____ and poorly planned expedition. Their leader, Professor Ralph Blackwood, has since been criticised for 8) _____ his colleagues' lives in the name of science. Fortunately, however, they were clearly 9) _____ and resourceful men, with the necessary grit and 10) _____ to succeed in their undertaking. 'We needed all our stamina and 11) _____ ,' one of them told our reporter, 'to get out of that jungle alive.' They returned home last week, with no 12) _____.

E Answer these questions as fully as you can, in conversation or in writing.

1 Statistics show that people are more likely to have a road accident near their home than when they are further away. Why do you think this might be so?

2 What is the greatest danger you are aware of in your daily life? Do you do anything to protect yourself from it? How likely is it to happen?

3 Make a list of what you consider to be dangerous sports. Should these be banned? Should people have to pay for their own medical care if they are injured in sports?

4 Do you enjoy taking risks? What kind of risks do you deliberately run?

5 What types of danger should we warn small children about? What is the best way of preparing school-age children for potentially dangerous situations?

The environment

A Complete the passage with these words. There are two more than you need.

damage	obliterated	irrigation	developing	resources
drought	environmental	tribal	environmentalists	
source	construction	conservation	rugged	scale

Problems arose in the 1990s over the Indian government's giant dam project in the 1) _____ Narmada Valley, where many of Rudyard Kipling's stories are set. The Narmada River rises in the heart of central India and flows westwards to the Arabian sea. According to officials, the planned 2) _____ of a huge dam and 3) _____ canals would provide water for drinking and agriculture in an area worryingly prone to 4) _____. The Narmada dam would also offer a major 5) _____ of electricity to power-starved regions. As part of its commitment to 6) _____ countries, the World Bank originally gave India a $450 million loan for this vast project. However, critics argued that the dam project represented 7) _____ and cultural destruction on a 8) _____ so massive that the benefits would pale in comparison to the 9) _____ it would cause. They pointed out that more than 200,000 people would be uprooted and rehoused, and ancient 10) _____ cultures would be 11) _____. The World Bank subsequently halted funding as a result of intense pressure from 12) _____, following an unfavourable independent review of the project.

B Choose the correct word or phrase from the pair in brackets to complete each sentence.

1 There are very few unexplored areas left in the _____. (world/cosmos)

2 Barnaby spent all his life working on the _____, like his father and grandfather before him. (earth/land)

3 After a long day in the town, you really appreciate the fresh air of the _____. (nature/countryside)

4 Some market gardens find labour costs for casual workers so high that they allow the public to _____ the produce themselves. (pick/pick up)

5 The children watched open-mouthed as the meteor blazed across the evening _____. (heavens/sky)

6 From the helicopter the navigator could see the red cliffs of the Devon _____. (coast/shore)

7 It is hoped that recent advances in medical research will enable us to _____ many of the diseases which currently kill a large number of people in developing countries. (devastate/eradicate)

8 The travellers gazed in awe at the _____, a beautiful stretch of clear, fresh water surrounded by snow-capped peaks. (lake/sea)

9 South Africa is a country of great beauty and immense natural _____. (sources/resources)

10 The travellers gazed in awe at the _____, a beautiful stretch of clear, fresh water surrounded by snow-capped peaks.   (lake/sea)

C Find adjectives connected with these nouns and verbs, and check their meanings in a dictionary.

1 tropics	9 region	17 disposal
2 globe	10 protect	18 biodegrade
3 town	11 congestion	19 solve
4 countryside	12 conifer	20 produce
5 nature	13 pollute	21 problem
6 scenery	14 climate	22 pole
7 mountain	15 disaster	
8 coast	16 replace	

D Match the words to make common expressions connected with the environment. Use each word only once.

1 health	A waste
2 fossil	B bank
3 unleaded	C effect
4 ozone	D fuels
5 acid	E balance
6 ecological	F hazard
7 greenhouse	G rain
8 pressure	H layer
9 sea	I petrol
10 chemical	J group
11 sewage	K levels
12 bottle	L disposal

E Answer these questions as fully as you can, in conversation or in writing.

1 What is your greatest environmental concern, and why?

2 What can the individual do to reduce pollution of the environment?

3 What should governments do to tackle pollution?

4 Are you optimistic or pessimistic about the future of our planet? Explain why.

5 What sources of energy are most environmentally friendly? Discuss their pros and cons.

6 Is there a need for a world population policy and, if so, what would you like to see included in it?

Right and wrong

A Match the words or phrases to make common expressions connected with right and wrong. Use each word or phrase only once.

1	pangs	A	crime
2	a point	B	stricken
3	gross professional	C	values
4	conscience-	D	of civilised society
5	standards	E	problem
6	cook	F	of honour
7	family	G	abiding
8	law-	H	of conscience
9	a heinous	I	misconduct
10	an ethical	J	the books

B Complete the passage with these words.

> devious   corrupt   rival   loyalty   integrity   accused
> blame   bribed   reproached   disgrace   hoodwinked
> espionage   conscience   traitor

Rupert worked as a food scientist with Mixo, a large company producing packet cake-mixes and instant desserts. His wife, Josie, had a similar job with a 1) _____ company, Whizzo. So when both companies almost simultaneously produced a new instant strawberry mousse, Rupert's boss hit the roof and 2) _____ him of selling industrial secrets.

'You've 3) _____ us all!' he shouted furiously. 'How much did Whizzo pay you to give the details of Strawberry Dream to your wife? It's industrial 4) _____!'

'Sir,' stammered Rupert in reply, 'I don't know how it happened. It's true that Josie and I were talking about mousse some time ago – perhaps that gave her the idea. I promise you, my commitment and 5) _____ to Mixo have always been one hundred per cent!'

'Get out of my sight, you 6) _____ little worm!' growled his boss.

Although Rupert was sure in his own mind that he was not to 7) _____ , he was upset that his professional 8) _____ had been called into question, and he felt that his colleagues considered him a 9) _____. At home, when he 10) _____ his wife for getting him into such hot water, she flew into a temper. 'I'm in 11) _____ at work too!' she cried. 'Whizzo think *I* was 12) _____ to reveal the secret mousse recipe. Just because we had the same idea at the same time, they assume we're both 13) _____ . Well, Rupert, we're both going to carry on working with a clear 14) _____!'

C Now complete the sentences with words from the box in Exercise B.

1 Judge Clark is renowned for his _____ and high principles.

2 Guy Trilby passed state secrets to a foreign power, and is therefore regarded as a _____ by most people.

3 Hugh is entirely trustworthy. His _____ to the organisation cannot be questioned.

4 Fortunately, James's _____ little plan to discredit the manager and gain promotion for himself did not succeed.

5 Sarah _____ herself for not confessing the truth earlier.

6 That man must have _____ you completely. Didn't you see through his story?

D Make adjectives from these nouns and verbs, and check their meanings in a dictionary.

1	honour	7	fraud
2	ethics	8	deceive
3	suspect	9	vice
4	pettiness	10	sin
5	bankruptcy	11	sacrifice
6	scandal	12	betray

E Choose the correct word or phrase from the pair in brackets to complete each sentence.

1 If you make a false statement to the Inland Revenue, you may be accused of _____.   (tax evasion/tax avoiding)

2 During the earthquake, gangs of youths _____ the electrical goods stores in the centre of town.   (stole/looted)

3 Dropping litter in the street is not a crime, but a(n) _____.   (misdeed/offence)

4 Big Ed tried to avoid arrest by _____ the policemen who came to take him away.   (bribing/corrupting)

5 Whoever stole the money must come forward. If the _____ does not own up by the end of the day, the whole school will be punished. (wrongdoer/culprit)

6 As a family man, Terry has many _____. He never takes the kids out to the park, or helps with the housework.   (vices/shortcomings)

7 Julie seems to have no moral standards at all. She is completely _____.   (amoral/immoral)

8 I'm afraid your assistant has _____ the trust you placed in him, and leaked the whole story to the press.   (betrayed/deceived)

F Discuss the following ethical questions, in conversation or in writing.

1 Is shoplifting a serious crime?

2 Should euthanasia, or mercy killing, be allowed under any circumstances?

3 What is your definition of dishonesty? Should we always tell the complete truth?

4 To whom should your first loyalty be? To your family, friends, country, religion? Or to something or someone else?

5 What should be the criteria for selecting families to adopt or foster children?

6 Who should teach children the difference between right and wrong?

Money and finance

A Complete the passage with these words.

factors	expenditure	increase	wealth	poverty	income
	material	economists	level	satisfaction	

Surveys show that, contrary to public expectation, 1) _____ does not always bring happiness. At 2) _____ level – that is, for the poorest fifth of the population in advanced economies – there is of course an 3) _____ in well-being for every £1000 increase in 4) _____. Beyond that, however, there is almost no improvement in people's 5) _____ with their lives relative to any rise in their 6) _____ of income. Strangely, market 7) _____ maintain that the purpose of the market is to maximise the satisfaction of 8) _____ wants, largely by encouraging personal 9) _____. However, according to most recent studies, there is little connection between the 10) _____ contributing most to people's happiness, such as a good family life or friendships, and their incomes.

B Match the words to make common expressions connected with money or finance. Use each word only once.

1	spending	A	card
2	profit	B	economy
3	credit	C	tax
4	market	D	test
5	per capita	E	margin
6	income	F	instalment
7	monthly	G	GNP (gross national product)
8	pocket	H	account
9	means	I	power
10	current	J	money

C Decide whether the definitions are true (T) or false (F). Give the correct definition if necessary.

1 A *hallmark* is a sign of quality or excellence.
2 A *wholesaler* buys from a retailer and sells to the public.
3 *Gross* profits are calculated after tax.
4 *Yuppies* is a word for loose change.
5 If you have a bank account, you normally receive a *statement* at regular intervals.
6 People who are very well-off could be called *impecunious*.
7 A *stockbroker* handles clients' financial investments.
8 Running up an *overdraft* means spending more than you have in your bank account.
9 A *bargain* is a purchase obtained at a surprisingly low price.

10 If you take out a *loan*, you are lending money to someone.

11 If an item is *under guarantee*, the manufacturer is obliged to replace or repair it free of charge.

12 A *bonus* is an extra charge added to your hotel or restaurant bill.

D Choose the correct word or phrase from the pair in brackets to complete each sentence.

1 It's easier to pay electricity and gas bills by _____. (direct debit/mail order)

2 The Robinsons are having difficulty in meeting the _____ repayments on their house. (hire purchase/mortgage)

3 Sandra's uncle left her £10,000 in his _____. (will/testament)

4 I'm afraid you are already three months _____ with your rent, Miss Hughes. (in arrears/in debt)

5 Mr Micawber owed money to so many people that his _____ used to crowd round his house, demanding satisfaction. (creditors/debtors)

6 The spirit of _____ helps private enterprise to thrive. (concurrence/competition)

7 The property developer was obliged to declare his annual _____ to the Inland Revenue for tax purposes. (profit/gain)

8 When the customer's cheque _____, the store manager refused to deliver the goods. (rebounded/bounced)

9 No _____ has been spared on the grandiose public buildings which continue to rise in the new capital city. (cost/expense)

10 We don't accept credit cards, I'm afraid. Please pay in _____. (cheque/cash)

11 Remember to keep the _____ in case you need to ask for a refund or replacement. (recipe/receipt)

12 If you show your student card, you may qualify for a _____. (decrease/discount)

13 Please make sure you have the correct change for the _____ before boarding the bus. (fee/fare)

14 Mrs Maitland has some _____ Picasso sketches in her private collection. The insurance premiums she has to pay are astronomical. (worthy/priceless)

15 People on a limited budget have to try to live _____, even if it means going without luxuries. (by all means/within their means)

16 The _____ from the village fair are earmarked for a local charity. (funds/proceeds)

E Answer these questions as fully as you can, in conversation or in writing.

1 What difference would it make to your life if you won a large sum of money – in a national lottery, for example?

2 Do you have a budget? Do you wait until you have enough cash to buy something, or do you use credit? What are the advantages and disadvantages of using credit?

3 Do you think 'telephone-number' salaries for young City stockbrokers are justifiable?

Recycling

Choose the correct word or phrase to complete each sentence.

1 I presume you declare any private _____ to the appropriate authorities.
a) income   b) revenue   c) interest   d) allowance

2 Derek had no experience of white-water canoeing, so it was extremely _____ of him to try and shoot the rapids.
a) hazardous   b) intrepid   c) perilous   d) foolhardy

3 Meg had a _____ escape when she was hang-gliding yesterday.
a) narrow   b) close   c) near   d) slender

4 The five-hour _____ which was performed on Mrs Brown's hip was expensive but effective.
a) treatment   b) operation   c) medicine   d) therapy

5 Peregrine Thorpe _____ the rewards of his hard work when he was given the chair of classics.
a) got   b) obtained   c) reaped   d) collected

6 I can't understand Juan's Spanish, because he speaks a regional _____.
a) dialect   b) jargon   c) accent   d) slang

7 When the lift finally started moving, we were all packed inside like _____.
a) fish   b) anchovies   c) sardines   d) dates

8 Mrs Taylor decided to buy a new coat by _____ order, as she didn't have time to look round the shops.
a) postal   b) mail   c) banker's   d) standing

9 I usually switch off the television when the _____ come on.
a) commercials   b) posters   c) slogans   d) advertising

10 'When do you have to hand in that report?' 'The _____ is Thursday 12th April.'
a) lifeline   b) byline   c) headline   d) deadline

11 The police accused the bank employee of _____, after financial irregularities were uncovered in his department's accounts.
a) fraud   b) hoodwink   c) swindle   d) cheating

12 When the accused was found guilty of reckless driving, he asked for five other _____ to be taken into consideration.
a) crimes   b) offences   c) shortcomings   d) misdeeds

13 *The Gloucester Gazette* wanted to boost its _____ by targeting a younger market.
a) circulation   b) readers   c) coverage   d) market

14 The soldier who saved the lives of three of his comrades was given a _____ award.
a) prenatal   b) posthumous   c) postprandial   d) predicted

15 You never quite know what Ken is up to – he's rather a dark _____.
a) dog   b) fox   c) wolf   d) horse

16 Tina took her four-year-old daughter to the children's hospital for an appointment with a _____.
a) paediatrician   b) pedestrian   c) philologist   d) philatelist

17 For my _____ of mind, promise you'll wear a life jacket in the boat.
a) satisfaction   b) contentment   c) peace   d) calmness

18 The burglar suffered _____ of conscience when he realised he had unwittingly stolen the little girl's teddy bear.
a) pains   b) aches   c) stabs   d) pangs

19 In attacking the old lady, the youth committed a _____ crime.
a) heinous   b) naughty   c) bad   d) evil

20 The World Health Organisation has stated that smallpox has been almost completely _____.
a) uprooted   b) eradicated   c) obliterated   d) extinguished

21 John's amateur dramatic group are _____ 'My Fair Lady' this weekend. The first performance is on Wednesday.
a) rehearsing   b) repeating   c) playing   d) practising

22 Once the new Marketing Manager's ideas were implemented, sales _____ and the company made huge profits.
a) plunged   b) lifted   c) rocketed   d) achieved

23 I can't possibly make the announcement now – I've got a _____ in my throat!
a) fish   b) toad   c) bird   d) frog

24 Cosmetics companies who claim not to _____ their products on animals are gaining a large share of the market.
a) test   b) try   c) experiment   d) practise

25 Looking at old photos in family albums often _____ happy memories of the past.
a) creates   b) evokes   c) makes   d) reminds

26 The week of exams left Miranda exhausted, and she's still rather _____.
a) low down   b) full of beans   c) under the weather
d) in worse condition

27 It was a complicated, subtle text, and the translator was not sure he had captured all its _____ of meaning.
a) allusions   b) tones   c) shadows   d) nuances

28 What a mad thing to do! You could all have been killed! It was _____ folly!
a) merely   b) only   c) sheer   d) wild

29 The President, flanked by his bodyguards, made a powerful _____ on the steps of the White House.
a) speech   b) talk   c) lecture   d) sermon

30 Because Trevor had started a fight in the playground, he was in _____ for the rest of that day.
a) punishment   b) exile   c) dishonour   d) disgrace

31 Blood _____ are needed urgently, as the national blood bank reserves are getting low.
a) volunteers   b) donors   c) givers   d) offers

32 Those who live on the _____ tend to have a less sentimental view of nature than city dwellers.
a) country   b) soil   c) earth   d) land

UK government

A Read the passage, then decide which word from A, B, C or D is most appropriate for each space.

The full name of the UK is the United Kingdom of Great Britain and Northern Ireland. Great Britain, strictly speaking, is the island comprising England, Wales and Scotland. Ireland, to the west of Great Britain, is the island made up of Northern Ireland, which is part of 1) _____, and the 2) _____ of Ireland (known in Irish as Eire).

Great Britain and Ireland belong to the whole group of islands known as the 3) _____ Isles, which includes all the Scottish islands such as the Hebrides, the Orkneys and the Shetlands, plus others such as Anglesey and the Scilly Isles. Most of these smaller islands are part of the UK and are 4) _____ from the mainland, although the Isle of Man (in the Irish Sea) and the Channel Islands (between England and France) are largely 5) _____. In fact, the Isle of Man's 6) _____, the Tynwald, was established more than 1000 years ago, and is thought to be the oldest legislature in continuous existence in the world.

Until 1999, all parts of the UK were governed from London. However, following 'yes' votes in the Scottish, Welsh and Northern Irish 7) _____, the British government set up a new Scottish Parliament and Welsh and Northern Irish Assemblies, 8) _____ many of its powers to these bodies.

For economic purposes, England is divided into nine large 9) _____; development agencies exist to improve their economic performance and to tailor national 10) _____ to regional needs. However, most individuals feel a much stronger attachment to their 11) _____, which in most cases represents a historical link with the past. There are over forty of these in England, of varying 12) _____, from tiny Berkshire to enormous North Yorkshire.

The citizens of the United Kingdom have British 13) _____. In addition, they are citizens of the European 14) _____, because the UK is a 15) _____ state.

	A	B	C	D
1	the UK	England	Great Britain	Scotland
2	Kingdom	State	Homeland	Republic
3	English	Scottish	British	United
4	legislated	administered	accounted	enforced
5	self-governing	democratic	self-elected	tolerant
6	monarch	chamber	regime	parliament
7	referendums	elections	polls	surveys
8	depositing	deliberating	devolving	deratifying

	A	B	C	D
9	provinces	regions	states	localities
10	ideas	ambitions	policies	suits
11	region	town	village	county
12	beauty	sizes	shapes	age
13	identity	rights	statehood	nationality
14	Union	Club	Charter	Parliament
15	member	participant	voting	partner

B Match the words and phrases on the left, connected with UK politics, with the correct definitions.

1	a constituency	A	all qualified voters
2	a candidate	B	when all MPs are replaced or re-elected
3	a Member of Parliament	C	someone who offers him/herself for election as an MP
4	the electorate	D	the container in which you put your vote
5	a by-election	E	someone elected to represent his/her constituents
6	a general election	F	the building where you go to cast your vote
7	a ballot box	G	a district that sends an MP to Parliament (or its residents)
8	a polling station	H	the largest party in Parliament which is not part of the Government
9	the Opposition	I	when one particular constituency votes for a new MP
10	a majority	J	the number of votes/seats by which a candidate/party wins an election

C Use words or phrases from Exercise B to complete these sentences.

1 The government's currently trying to woo the _____ by promising huge tax cuts. Supposedly, these would kick in after the _____, so they represent an attractive lure for the man or woman in the street.

2 Even my cousin is rather dismissive of the party's tactics, and she's standing as their _____ for her local _____!

3 She takes her politics very seriously, and says she wants to become a(n) _____ so that she can improve the way the country's governed.

4 The Leader of the _____ joined with the Prime Minister in condemning the latest terrorist outrages.

D Answer these questions as fully as you can, in conversation or in writing.

1 What is the difference between the United Kingdom, Great Britain and the British Isles?

2 What do you think of the largely symbolic role played by the sovereign in the British parliamentary system? What effect, if any, do you think the monarch has on British politics?

3 What are the pros and cons of a written versus an unwritten constitution?

4 Who should hold more power, local or central bodies? Which should take precedence, regional or national interests?

UNIT 53

Conflict and revenge

A Match the words or phrases to make common expressions connected with revenge or forgiveness. Use each word or phrase only once.

1	settle	A	into your own hands
2	a fit	B	a grudge
3	take the law	C	your just deserts
4	turn	D	feud
5	an eye	E	old scores
6	get your own	F	of jealousy
7	get no more than	G	amends
8	make	H	and forget
9	forgive	I	for an eye
10	a family	J	back
11	bear	K	the hatchet
12	bury	L	the other cheek

B Choose the correct word from the pair in brackets to complete each sentence.

1 The two secretaries kept up their _____ for six months, and did not speak to each other unless they had to. (feud/argument)

2 Don't _____ him by pointing out his mistakes. (antagonise/exacerbate)

3 What was the Minister's _____ for giving his assistant the sack? (cause/motive)

4 When they heard of the atrocities committed by the occupying army, the exiled government vowed to _____ a terrible revenge if they ever regained power. (wield/wreak)

5 Throughout world history, countries have engaged in _____ for reasons of territorial aggression, or religious or racial hatred. (warfare/rioting)

6 The marriage guidance counsellor is hoping to bring about a _____ of both parties, to prevent a divorce. (redress/reconciliation)

7 Three villagers were shot in _____ for the killing of three soldiers. (reprieve/reprisal)

8 'Good! I'm glad you're hurt!' said Gloria _____. (enviously/vindictively)

9 Callers jammed the switchboard after a request was broadcast for information from _____ of burglary. (casualties/victims)

10 Max's feelings of _____ persisted, even though the company made every effort to placate him. (rancour/apprehension)

11 When Julian criticised her dress sense, Jacky _____ by commenting on his bald spot. (reprimanded/retaliated)

12 I wish you could have a discussion without getting _____! (aggressive/assertive)

C Complete the missing answers or clues in the crossword. All the answers can be found in Exercise B, but you may have to change the form of the word.

A	_____	revenge
B	_____	bitterness
C	14 across	a long-standing quarrel
D	15 across	people who suffer harm or injury
E	1 down	a feeling of wanting revenge
F	_____	the state of competing with other people
G	7 across	a reason for doing something
H	_____	punishment or compensation
I	_____	a private family feud
J	_____	to repay an injury, fight back
K	_____	to put right a wrong
L	4 down	to re-establish friendly relations after a quarrel
M	11 down	to inflict (revenge)
N	3 across	to make someone hostile
O	6 down	the process of waging war
P	9 across	deep bitterness or hostility

D Answer these questions as fully as you can, in conversation or in writing.

1 Can you think of occasions when you have tried to get your own back? Has it always worked?

2 Have you any personal experience of long-harboured resentment or family feuds? How can these problems be resolved?

3 How can the desire for revenge affect a) negotiation of disputed national boundaries? b) arrangements for a couple's divorce?

4 Should the desire for revenge play any part in the legal system or the punishment of criminals? How can an innocent victim be helped to come to terms with the effects of a crime committed against him/herself?

Technology and progress

A Match the words to make common expressions connected with technology or progress. Use each word only once.

1	digital	A	crops
2	DNA	B	television
3	optimum	C	efficiency
4	remote	D	testing
5	cable	E	facility
6	market	F	control
7	solar	G	aerial
8	security	H	dish
9	satellite	I	tag
10	mobile	J	dispenser
11	playback	K	energy
12	indoor	L	leader
13	cash	M	highway
14	GM	N	phone

B Complete the passage with these words. There is one more than you need.

integrated	monopoly	digital	initiative
encoded	revenues	investing	market
spreadsheet	system	PCs	compatible
lucrative	rivals	consumers	growth

Microsoft is the giant of the computer software market, and its quarterly 1) _____ regularly exceed one billion dollars. It originally supplied the operating 2) _____ adopted by IBM for its 3) _____, and now sells its own phenomenally popular system, Windows. Building on the latter's success, the company developed carefully 4) _____ software products designed to be thoroughly 5) _____ with each other, but not necessarily with those of all other companies. Microsoft's business strategy has been widely criticised by its 6) _____, who have accused it of attempting to create a 7) _____, thus stifling healthy competition as well as harming the interests of 8) _____. Although it is currently the 9) _____ leader, the company cannot assume that the unprecedented 10) _____ in software sales will last for ever. Therefore, in order to maintain its market position, it has joined the telecommunications industry in 11) _____ heavily in cable technology, in order to create a so-called 12) _____ highway capable of delivering digitally 13) _____ video, the internet and other services to the home. This concept may turn out to be a very 14) _____ one for Microsoft and any other companies associated with the 15) _____.

C Complete the sentences with these words and phrases. Use each expression only once.

robot	electromagnetic field	closed-circuit
security tags	microchip	remote control	streamline
solar	white goods	optimum efficiency	anti-nuclear
	central locking	programme	

1 When a man with a shotgun took his girlfriend hostage, the Maryland police decided to send a _____, operated by_____, into the building to disarm him.

2 Parents of a 13-year-old leukaemia victim are suing their local electricity company on the grounds that the _____ in their son's bedroom contributed to his death.

3 Police attempted to hold back the _____ protesters as they surged towards the parliament building.

4 Contrary to popular belief, _____ energy can still be collected and stored even on a cloudy or misty day.

5 Most supermarkets and department stores have a system of _____ television in operation twenty-four hours a day.

6 Customers are requested to ensure that all _____ are removed from garments at the time of purchase.

7 The board of directors is currently seeking to _____ the decision-making process at management level.

8 Hoover, Zanussi and Bosch are all well-known manufacturers of _____.

9 The electronics and computer industries have been revolutionised by the development of the _____.

10 The _____ of a centrifugal pump is related to its speed of rotation.

11 Many cars these days have a _____ system, enabling all doors to be locked by turning just one key.

12 You can _____ the central heating to come on at set times, using a time switch connected to the boiler.

D Decide whether the definitions are true (T) or false (F). Give the correct definition if necessary.

1 A *catalyst* is a person or thing that causes a change.

2 A *gadget* is a large electrical appliance.

3 *Data* is another word for information.

4 A *trolley* is a two-wheeled cart for carrying shopping.

5 *Radiation* is the emission of energy in the form of rays.

6 A *sophisticated* machine is a complex one.

7 A *socket* is a device attached to a flex, used to make an electrical connection.

8 A *vehicle* is a means of transport with wheels.

E Answer these questions as fully as you can, in conversation or in writing.

1 What, in your opinion, was the greatest technological achievement of the twentieth century?

2 Which area of technology do you think deserves further research and development, and why?

3 Name three gadgets or other pieces of equipment which you feel are indispensable to your comfort, and explain why.

Work and study

A Match the words to make common expressions connected with employment. Use each word only once.

1	trade	A	salary
2	curriculum	B	pay
3	aptitude	C	retirement
4	sick	D	action
5	industrial	E	prospects
6	promotion	F	union
7	probationary	G	test
8	short	H	period
9	monthly	I	vitae
10	early	J	list

B Choose the correct word or phrase from the pair in brackets to complete each sentence.

1 If you work longer than your contract stipulates, you will be paid _____. (flexitime/overtime)

2 Every year there are at least 50,000 _____ for that particular examination. (applicants/candidates)

3 People who are unable to find work may be eligible for unemployment _____. (payment/benefit)

4 Dr Brewer decided to spend his _____ year on research into comparative religions. (secondment/sabbatical)

5 As the shipyard had run out of orders, all the workers were made _____. (redundant/sacked)

6 Chris really is very talented, but he can't possibly expect to make a _____ from his painting. (profession/living)

7 University students who take out a _____ to pay for their studies may be seriously in debt when they graduate. (loan/mortgage)

8 I hope *Jane Eyre* will be on the _____ again next year. (studies/syllabus)

C Choose the correct word to complete each sentence.

1 When Lucinda graduated, she had no idea which _____ to choose.
a) living   b) business   c) career   d) work

2 The sales manager failed to negotiate a suitable _____ with his Japanese counterpart.
a) deal   b) transaction   c) business   d) accord

3 The job you've applied for isn't _____. It's only temporary, I'm afraid.
a) long-lasting   b) permanent   c) eternal   d) durable

4 Pete has a well-paid position with a local _____.
a) firm   b) association   c) house   d) society

5 When you send in your application, remember to supply the names of two _____.
a) umpires   b) judges   c) supporters   d) referees

6 The day-to-day running of the school is handled by the headteacher, who is responsible to the _____ of governors.
   a) board   b) table   c) committee   d) meeting

7 Silvio was the first member of staff ever to be _____ for gross professional misconduct.
   a) dispatched   b) sacked   c) released   d) shot

8 Employers are often less interested in an applicant's academic _____ than in his or her experience.
   a) papers   b) certificates   c) qualifications   d) degrees

9 Gary accepted the job in Lisbon, although he would only be _____ half his previous salary.
   a) winning   b) gaining   c) deserving   d) earning

10 Depending on their circumstances, university students live on a _____ from the bank, an allowance from their parents or income from part-time jobs.
   a) loan   b) pension   c) fund   d) purse

D Complete the sentences with these expressions. There is one more than you need.

on-the-job training   achieve his potential
enter the labour market   off sick   on the dole
on leave   wage dispute   picket line

1 Peter lost his job in 1998 and has been _____ ever since.

2 Kirsty feels this is an inopportune moment to _____, so she is planning to continue her studies instead.

3 We attach very little importance to the fact that you have no experience of computers, because you will be given the necessary _____.

4 When we took on Craig Henderson a couple of years ago, we hoped he would become a high-flyer. But I'm afraid he has completely failed to _____.

5 Staff morale is at an all-time low, largely owing to the recent _____.

6 During the strike, the union organised a 24-hour _____ outside the gates, to discourage people from entering the factory.

E Answer these questions as fully as you can, in conversation or in writing.

1 How much freedom and choice should children be given at school? How important do you think rules and discipline are?

2 Suggest ways of improving a country's education system.

3 How would you balance work and leisure, if you had a free choice?

4 How important is it to have high educational qualifications when looking for a job?

5 What qualities would you look for in
   a) a boss?   b) a colleague?   c) a subordinate?

6 What are the advantages and disadvantages of
   a) single-sex education?   b) boarding schools?
   c) freelance work?   d) early retirement?

Different lifestyles

A Match the words to make common expressions connected with different lifestyles. Use each word only once.

1	fast	A	tension
2	standard	B	image
3	poverty	C	of living
4	child	D	durables
5	welfare	E	level
6	nuclear	F	state
7	working	G	flyer
8	disposable	H	parent
9	consumer	I	benefit
10	single	J	family
11	subsistence	K	class
12	racial	L	income
13	self	M	pace
14	high	N	trap

B Complete the passage with these words. There is one more than you need.

> renovation   habitation   bare necessities   polarised   threats
> brave   victimising   plight   support   demolish
> sympathise   cottage   belongs   survival   evict

A Welsh district council has refused to pay for the 1) _____ of a tiny two-room stone 2) _____ , and has declared it unfit for human 3) _____. The cottage 4) _____ to Miss Heather Morton, who has lived there since her childhood. She manages with only the 5) _____ of life, as there is no electricity or piped water. She wants to stay in the 150-year-old cottage, but the council is determined to 6) _____ her and 7) _____ the building. Her 8) _____ has 9) _____ the community. A few of her neighbours 10) _____ the council's decision, but most 11) _____ with Miss Morton and accuse the council of 12) _____ an elderly lady. Despite the council's 13) _____, Miss Morton intends to 14) _____ out the winter in her home, with her five dogs for company.

C Decide whether the definitions are true (T) or false (F). Give the correct definition if necessary.

1 *Materialism* is an excessive interest in money and material possessions.
2 A *status symbol* is a possession which is regarded as proof of the owner's social position.
3 An *acquisitive* person is someone who asks too many questions.
4 *Affluence* is the power exerted by one person over another.
5 *Slums* are squalid, overcrowded areas of a city.

6 *Squatters* are people who illegally occupy houses or land.

7 The *metropolis* is the capital or main city of a country.

8 *Tramps* are people who travel around on foot, with no permanent home.

9 *Priorities* are young couples who are buying their first home.

10 An *au-pair* is a person who insists on equal opportunities.

11 A *busker* is someone who plays an instrument in a public place and asks passers-by for money.

12 A *New Age traveller* is a person who travels around the country, camping wherever he/she feels like it.

D Choose the correct word or phrase from the pair in brackets to complete each sentence.

1 Many housing estates and blocks of flats were put up in the building _____ of the 1980s. (surge/boom)

2 People are encouraged to live _____ these days, by making excessive use of credit facilities. (in the red/beyond their means)

3 Residents of the _____ enjoy good social amenities without the noise and bustle of living in the town centre. (downtown/suburbs)

4 It is becoming fashionable to dress in _____ clothes snapped up from junk shops and jumble sales. (second-hand/antique)

5 Some people opt out of the _____ and take early retirement. (rat race/grindstone)

6 A house can be seen as a comfortable dwelling to bring the family up in, or as a lucrative _____. (investment/profit)

7 While some householders have open-plan gardens, others feel the need for high fences, guard dogs and _____ lights. (privacy/security)

8 Tastes in interior decoration vary from the plain, simple, farmhouse style to the _____, expensive decor you find in many town houses. (tasty/sophisticated)

9 If a marriage does not work out, the couple often split up, share out their assets, and live _____. (separated/apart)

10 So many celebrities have a private life which is quite different from their public _____. (picture/image)

11 In certain countries, _____ visitors is always done in hotels or restaurants, while in others it is considered more hospitable to invite guests to the home. (entertaining/greeting)

12 It is difficult for people in serious _____ to get out of the spiral of borrowing and paying interest on ever-increasing loans. (credit/debt)

E Answer these questions as fully as you can, in conversation or in writing.

1 What factors make a lifestyle challenging or rewarding?

2 How do you account for the current interest in the material aspects of life, rather than the spiritual? Do you think this is a temporary aberration, or purely a more realistic approach which will last?

3 Can you give reasons for the widening gap between rich and poor in developed countries as well as the Third World? Is there a long-term solution to this problem?

4 What would your ideal lifestyle be, if you had no financial considerations or family responsibilities to take into account?

UNIT 57

Belief and superstition

A Match the words or phrases to make common expressions connected with belief or superstition.

1	dabble	A	account
2	mind	B	pokery
3	extra-sensory	C	telling
4	sleight	D	in the occult
5	jiggery-	E	magic
6	far-	F	perception
7	burden	G	of proof
8	unidentified	H	illusion
9	fortune	I	of hand
10	black	J	over matter
11	optical	K	fetched
12	eyewitness	L	flying object

B Decide whether the definitions are true (T) or false (F). Give the correct definition if necessary.

1 A *premonition* is an intuition of a future happy event.

2 A *charlatan* is someone who pretends to have knowledge he or she does not possess, especially in medicine.

3 To *levitate* means rising or causing to rise and float in the air.

4 A *seance* is a meeting where spiritualists try to receive messages from the spirits of the dead.

5 *Astrology* is the study of the planets and stars.

6 A *poltergeist* is a spirit which makes noises and moves objects.

7 *Telepathy* means being able to understand, and communicate with, people's thoughts.

8 A *clairvoyant* is someone who knows exactly what happened in the past.

9 To *haunt* means to visit a person or a place regularly. (used of ghosts)

10 A *sceptic* is someone who does not believe a person or an idea.

11 To *dowse for water* is to hunt for water by holding a forked stick over the ground.

12 *Fringe medicine* refers to alternative treatments, many of which are not generally recognised by the traditional medical establishment.

13 A *cult* is a sect devoted to the practices of a particular religion or set of theories.

14 An *atheist* is someone who believes in God.

15 *The evil eye* is a look or glance superstitiously supposed to have the power of inflicting harm.

16 *Old wives' tales* are superstitious beliefs passed on by word of mouth.

17 *Witchcraft* is the art of using magic to make certain, usually evil, things happen.

18 A *totem pole* is a carved post set up by certain Native Americans as a tribal symbol.

C Fill in the missing words, all beginning with **m.**

1 People sometimes see a ☐☐☐☐.☐☐ , of an oasis or water, in the desert. It recedes as they approach it.

2 A ☐☐☐☐☐☐ is a person who claims to carry messages between the dead and the living.

3 The unicorn is a ☐☐☐☐☐☐☐☐ beast.

4 Do you believe the Loch Ness ☐☐☐☐☐☐☐ exists?

5 ☐☐☐☐☐☐ is the art which supposedly influences events by the use of spells.

6 A ☐☐☐☐☐☐☐ is a surprising event attributed to a supernatural cause.

7 The cult members were ☐☐☐☐☐☐☐☐☐☐☐ by their fascinating but manipulative leader, and agreed to do whatever he wanted.

D Choose the correct word to complete each sentence.

1 His story appeared completely _____ at the time, and we were all taken in.
a) gullible   b) believable   c) credulous   d) honest

2 When the police found her, she was living under a(n) _____ name.
a) assumed   b) fraudulent   c) bogus   d) fake

3 Adam was only able to pass the entry test by _____.
a) duping   b) fooling   c) cheating   d) deceiving

4 I am afraid I cannot give _____ to Humphrey's account of what happened.
a) truth   b) belief   c) faith   d) credence

5 The journalists asked the Prime Minister to _____ the date of the next election.
a) predict   b) foretell   c) presage   d) prevaricate

E Answer these questions as fully as you can, in conversation or in writing.

1 What superstitious habits are common in your country?

2 Do you need proof before you can believe anything, or do you take some things on trust? Give examples.

3 Discuss whether you think the following situations are supposed to bring good or bad luck:

a) a black cat crossing your path

b) walking under a ladder

c) arranging something for Friday the 13th

d) driving a green car

e) breaking a mirror

f) taking the last sandwich on a plate

g) catching the bride's bouquet as she leaves for her honeymoon

h) treading in a cowpat or dog mess, or being hit by bird droppings.

4 Astrology, palmistry and reading tea leaves or tarot cards are all ways of trying to predict the future. Do you believe in any of them?

Time and memory

A Match the words on the left with the correct definitions.

1	decade	A	a hundred years
2	diary	B	a chart showing the days and months of a year
3	epoch	C	a clock in a tall wooden case
4	century	D	ten years
5	calendar	E	a personal record of daily events
6	stopwatch	F	a watch used for timing sporting events
7	timer	G	a person descended from someone
8	grandfather clock	H	a device which can be set to ring after a period of time or to switch on a system
9	ancestor	I	a period of time in history
10	descendant	J	a person from whom someone is descended

B Choose the correct word or phrase from the pair in brackets to complete each sentence.

1 The old man often used to _____ happily about the past. (reminisce/recollect)

2 When Allen was asked the all-important question, his mind was _____. (a total blank/total recall)

3 At least the photos are a _____ reminder of that wonderful holiday. (durable/lasting)

4 Eleanor brought back several interesting _____ of her trip to South America. (memorials/souvenirs)

5 When the boy was asked for an explanation, he _____, making up a story about a long-lost uncle. (procrastinated/prevaricated)

6 Too many people indulge in unnecessary _____ for the past. (recall/nostalgia)

7 My aunt has taken the wrong keys again. She's so _____. (absent-minded/open-minded)

8 The memory of the beggar's face _____ Sam for a long time. (hampered/haunted)

9 Any event recorded by history is a(n) _____ event. (historic/historical)

10 The village church dates back to _____ times. (ancient/antique)

11 Aya spent a whole week _____ facts and figures for her statistics exam. (memorising/remembering)

12 Olga Berkov has furnished her London flat in striking _____ style. (contemporary/day-to-day)

13 I expect you'll receive a reply from the Education Department _____. (at last/sooner or later)

14 Please make sure you arrive at eight _____. (on the dot/on the spot)

15 Have you seen the long-range weather _____? They say there'll be gales this weekend. (prediction/forecast)

16 Please note that Theatre Royal performances always start _____. Latecomers will not be admitted until the interval. (in time/on time)

17 Of course the hero marries the heroine _____ of the story, and they live happily ever after. (in the end/at the end)

18 I used to be able to reel off my French irregular verbs just like that, but I'll have to _____ my memory before next week's test. (arouse/refresh)

19 I only met her briefly, but I'm sure I would _____ her again. (recognise/memorise)

20 The young boy politely gave up his seat to the _____ lady who had just hobbled on to the bus. (elder/elderly)

C Fill in the missing words. The first letter of each is given.

1 I can't remember his name. It's on the [T | |] of my tongue.

2 You must remember! Think! [R | | |] your brains!

3 Warren never remembers anything. He's got a memory like a [S | | | |] .

4 The cathedral was built in the Middle [A | |] .

5 The new President took over immediately from his [P | | | | | | | | | |] .

6 The standing stones at Woodhenge date back to [P | | | | | | | | |] times.

7 It's [H | | |] time you told him the truth.

8 Rosemary thought she would never get over Colin's death, but with the [P | | | | | |] of time she began to come to terms with it.

9 Time [F | | | |] when you're enjoying yourself.

10 Much of our information on the mediaeval way of life has come from [D | | | | | | | |] originally written by monks.

11 Only [P | | | | | | | |] will be able to judge whether the Prime Minister made the right decision or not.

12 With [H | | | | | | | |] the Government realised they had blundered, but it was too late to rectify the situation.

D Answer these questions as fully as you can, in conversation or in writing.

1 Describe any historic events which occurred in the year of your birth. Which events that have happened since then are the most important, in your opinion?

2 Choose the three dates that you consider the most important historically, and give reasons for your choice.

3 What different systems are there for improving memory? Do these work, and if so, why?

4 Find out as much as you can about the life and achievements of a historical figure, and write an essay or give a talk about him or her. Could this person have achieved as much in a different historical period or not?

5 Describe your first memory, your most embarrassing memory, and your happiest memory.

Travelling and transport

A Match the words to make common expressions connected with travelling. Use each word only once.

1	steering	A	reservation
2	off-	B	shoulder
3	central	C	hour
4	Highway	D	calming
5	hard	E	carriageway
6	rush	F	peak
7	high	G	crossing
8	dual	H	wheel
9	pedestrian	I	season
10	filling	J	Code
11	traffic	K	holiday
12	package	L	station

B Decide whether the definitions are true (T) or false (F). Give the correct definition if necessary.

1 The *flight recorder* is a plane's co-pilot.
2 A *traffic jam* occurs when heavy traffic moves slowly, if at all.
3 *Commuters* travel considerable distances from home to work.
4 *Off the beaten track* is used to describe an isolated, relatively unknown place.
5 A *berth* is a type of camp bed.
6 You put coins into a *parking meter*, to pay for time to park there.
7 A *tachograph* measures a vehicle's fuel consumption.
8 An *itinerary* is a plane or train timetable.

C Complete the passage with these words. Use each word only once. There is one more than you need.

resort	luxury	picturesque	lounging	cuisine	facilities
	range	cruise	brochure	self-catering	spectacular
	overseas	excursions	accommodation	inclusive	

Welcome to the wonderful world of Portland Holidays! In our latest 1) _____ we are sure you'll find the widest 2) _____ of holidays on the market. You can pamper yourself at the five-star Portland Sheraton in the well-known 3) _____ of Los Reyes, where 4) _____ for sports and nightlife are second to none. Or you can 5) _____ around the island on a 6) _____ yacht, 7) _____ on deck in the warm Mediterranean sunshine, and admiring the 8) _____ scenery. Alternatively you might prefer to take a 9) _____ apartment in one of the 10) _____ fishing villages. Here you can sample the authentic local 11) _____, with its famous seafood specialities, and go on a variety of 12) _____ to places of cultural and archaeological interest. Our prices are 13) _____ of all flights and 14) _____ , and represent excellent value. Book now!

D Complete the missing answers or clues in the crossword.

A _____ a long, difficult journey, often on foot
B 11 down a road around a town, not through it
C 15 across a house in the country or at the seaside
D _____ a fee to be paid when using a bridge or motorway
E 9 across a central island with traffic moving round it
F 8 down a small room on a ship
G _____ a small house in the mountains, usually of wood
H 2 down a holiday where everything is included in the price
I 3 across an overland or hunting expedition, especially in Africa
J 14 down passing through
K _____ the place where a train or bus ends its journey
L 4 across a piece of paper showing you have paid to travel
M 5 across a booklet advertising holidays
N 6 down (travelling) across a country
O _____ sections of a train (e.g. 1st class)
P 13 across 'You must be tired after your long _____.'
Q 12 down the London Underground
R _____ a cheap flight booked by a package tour company
S 1 down state of complete tiredness

E Answer these questions as fully as you can, in conversation or in writing.

1 What are the advantages and disadvantages of travelling in remote areas? What preparations would you make for a holiday trekking in the foothills of the Himalayas, or exploring the Brazilian rainforests, or crossing the Sahara Desert by jeep?

2 What traffic control or traffic calming measures can you suggest to improve life for pedestrians in towns?

3 What do you think the best means of transport is

a) for a short journey across town to work every day?

b) for an evening at the cinema or theatre?

c) for a touring holiday in Europe?

Books and reading

A Choose the correct word from the pair in brackets to complete each sentence.

1 All Shakespeare's plays are out of _____, as he has been dead for over seventy years. (copyright/playwright)

2 Before publication, an author usually checks the _____ sent by the publishers. (manuscript/proofs)

3 If you go on holiday to a country where you don't speak the language, you probably need a _____. (phrasebook/guidebook)

4 I'm afraid I lost interest in the book. The _____ was too complicated. (plot/theme)

5 I probably won't buy anything from the bookshop. I'll just _____ . (peruse/browse)

6 You'll get an idea of what the book is about by glancing at the _____. (dedication/dust-jacket)

7 Is this the latest _____ of *The Evening Herald*? (volume/edition)

8 To appreciate historical novels you need a good _____. (imagination/fantasy)

9 Have you done the exercises? Look the answers up in the _____. (key/bibliography)

10 The information should be clearly presented in well-planned _____. (sectors/paragraphs)

11 Most modern poetry doesn't _____. (verse/rhyme)

12 Some of the best writers can be interpreted both _____ and metaphorically. (laterally/literally)

13 'Is that the end of the story, Mummy?' 'Let's turn over the _____ and see.' (page/sheet)

14 I really enjoyed the suspense. It's one of the best _____ I've ever read. (romances/thrillers)

15 The new biography of Gandhi is rather expensive, so I think I'll order it from the _____, rather than buying it. (bookshop/library)

B Fill in the missing words. The first letter of each is given.

1 I never buy H☐☐☐☐☐☐☐ books, as they're so expensive. I just wait till they come out in paperback.

2 Karl Marx's works have been T☐☐☐☐☐☐☐☐☐ into most of the world languages.

3 It was impossible to attract Mike's attention. He was so E☐☐☐☐☐☐☐☐ in his book.

4 *Never Look Back* has already sold 100,000 copies and is going to be another B☐☐☐-☐☐☐☐☐☐ for Alexander Fleming.

5 In the opening C☐☐☐☐☐☐ of the novel, the young boy has a terrifying experience which will haunt him throughout his life.

6 Many people have a favourite A☐☐☐☐☐ and read all his or her books avidly.

7 Thomas Hardy is better known for his [P____] than for his poetry.

8 Yet another [B_____] of D.H. Lawrence has just been published, with some new insights into his unhappy adolescence.

9 Could I borrow your [C____] of *Macbeth* for this afternoon's lesson? I seem to have left mine at home.

10 Children's books are often lavishly [I_____] by accomplished artists.

C Match the words on the left, connected with books or reading, with the correct definitions.

1	a whodunnit	A	a book from which information may be obtained
2	an atlas	B	an alphabetical list of names or topics referred to in a book
3	a reference book	C	a section at the end of a literary work, in the form of a commentary
4	an index	D	imaginative writing based on recent or future scientific discoveries
5	a satire	E	a passage taken from a book, play etc.
6	plagiarism	F	a crime novel
7	an epilogue	G	a collection of poems or literary passages
8	an extract	H	the act of taking ideas, passages etc. from another writer
9	science fiction	I	a complete list of items (e.g. for sale)
10	a catalogue	J	a work in which topical issues, politics etc. are ridiculed
11	non-fiction	K	a book of maps
12	an anthology	L	factual writing

D Answer these questions as fully as you can, in conversation or in writing.

1 What, for you, are the ingredients of a good book? How would you set about writing a best-seller?

2 Will reading become a thing of the past, as more people watch videos and use computers in their spare time?

3 How do a country's history, customs, economic situation, climate and language development affect the literature it produces? Give examples.

4 Write a review of a book you have read recently. Either recommend it, or say why, in your opinion, it is not worth reading.

5 People read for various reasons: for relaxation, to acquire information, for escapism, to help further their studies or career, for fun, to keep up with current events.

Decide which of the above are true for you. If you do not read much, explain why reading does not appeal to you.

Law and order

A Match the words or phrases to make common expressions connected with law and order.

1	tackle	A	police
2	riot	B	sentence
3	open	C	oath
4	prison	D	custody
5	under	E	the problem
6	take into	F	hooligans
7	commit	G	concern
8	soccer	H	bail
9	public	I	a crime
10	release on	J	prison

B Complete the passage with these words and phrases. Use each word or phrase only once.

reach a verdict	deterrent	charged	court
criminologists	evidence	plead	sum up	lawyers
offenders	jury	acquitted	pass sentence
committed	offence	witnesses	stand	defendant

A person who is 1) _____ with a serious 2) _____ in Britain has to 3) _____ trial, and 4) _____ guilty or not guilty in 5) _____. During the case the judge and 6) _____ will examine all the 7) _____ presented by both sides, and listen to the cross-examination of any 8) _____ called by the defence and prosecution 9) _____. Finally the judge will 10) _____ the case in legal terms, and the jury will retire to 11) _____. If the 12) _____ is found guilty, the judge will 13) _____ on him, but if he is found not guilty, he will be 14) _____. His sentence will be heavier if he has 15) _____ the same offence previously, though some 16) _____ argue that the number of persistent 17) _____ suggests that prison is not necessarily the most effective 18) _____.

C Complete the missing answers or clues in the crossword. You will find some of the answers in Exercise B.

A	2 down	the place where trials are conducted
B	14 down	Handcuffs go on these!
C	_____	a policeman's rubber weapon
D	18 across	a reason or apology for doing or not doing something
E	8 down	a judge in a lower-level court
F	12 across	a violent public protest
G	_____	a theory or system of fairness for everybody
H	_____	a young person whose behaviour is uncontrolled and destructive or violent
I	15 across	something which puts people off committing a crime

J 3 down   The accused was found innocent and was _____.

K 10 across   'I have no option but to report this incident to the _____.'

L _____   repeated relapse into crime

M 11 across   another word for prison

N 13 across   the person who listens to evidence in court and decides on a punishment

O 5 down   A juvenile _____ is a young person who commits minor crime.

P 4 across   a lawyer who represents his/her clients in court

Q _____   someone in prison

R _____   a formal accusation of an offence or crime

S 16 across   money paid as a punishment for an offence

T 19 across   to attack and rob violently in the street

D Answer these questions as fully as you can, in conversation or in writing.

1 How could law and order be improved in your town? Is it a question of investment in police training and manpower, or should ordinary citizens become more involved (as in neighbourhood watch, patrolling or vigilante schemes)?

2 What is the worst miscarriage of justice you can remember in recent times? Does this make you sceptical about the fairness of the legal system and the courts?

3 Do you see prison as a means of punishment, or rehabilitation, or a cross between the two?

Recycling

A Choose the correct word or phrase to complete each sentence.

1 Jane was full of _____ towards her stepmother.
 a) retribution b) resentment c) reprisal d) vengeance

2 Factories are having to _____ all production processes and, in some cases, the workforce too.
 a) slim b) simplify c) streamline d) train

3 Digitally _____ messages can be delivered via cable direct into our homes.
 a) numbered b) dialled c) encoded d) deciphered

4 Josie makes a good _____ from her freelance work.
 a) profession b) job c) living d) earnings

5 When Wilson's company was hit by the recession, he decided to take early _____.
 a) redundancy b) retirement c) resignation d) redeployment

6 Who needs more than the _____ necessities of life?
 a) naked b) pure c) bare d) sole

7 The _____ of the abandoned orphans in Romania has aroused the world's pity.
 a) sadness b) trouble c) case d) plight

8 I'm afraid Jennifer's very _____. She believes everything she's told.
 a) gullible b) trustworthy c) credible d) honest

9 People can make themselves walk on nails or through fire. It's a question of mind over _____.
 a) body b) material c) matter d) facts

10 If you aren't sure what day the 24th is, look it up on the _____.
 a) calendar b) diary c) agenda d) dairy

11 With _____, it's easy to see that a mistake has been made.
 a) rear view b) overlook c) retrospect d) hindsight

12 In August we always go to this wonderful little Greek village, miles from anywhere and really off the beaten _____.
 a) road b) track c) path d) lane

13 The woman accused of shoplifting was found not guilty and was _____.
 a) acquitted b) liberated c) excused d) interned

14 You're not supposed to park on the hard _____ except in an emergency.
 a) lane b) shoulder c) leg d) area

15 While the yacht sailed on, I went to my _____ and changed my clothes.
 a) deck b) cabin c) bunk d) cockpit

16 Some people prefer to watch a film first, and then read the _____ in the paper.
 a) critic b) revue c) review d) criticism

17 We can always find out what books the author consulted by referring to the _____.
 a) index b) bibliography c) key d) dust jacket

18 The old man did not notice it had begun to rain. He was so _____ in feeding the pigeons.
    a) concentrated   b) obsessed   c) engrossed   d) fascinated

19 Several influential pressure _____ are campaigning for a reduction in the current prison population.
    a) groups   b) charities   c) points   d) members

20 Burglar alarms on cars and houses may act as a _____ to the casual thief.
    a) prevention   b) deterrent   c) stopper   d) precaution

21 A lot of old _____ were settled in the New York gangland killings of the 1960s.
    a) quarrels   b) criminals   c) scores   d) feuds

22 I had a strong _____ that a disaster would occur, and it did.
    a) premonition   b) prediction   c) forethought   d) anticipation

23 Don't worry if you run out of money at the weekend. You can always get some from the cash _____.
    a) desk   b) dispenser   c) counter   d) card

24 We should never have quarrelled like that. Let's bury the _____ and forget all about it.
    a) axe   b) argument   c) hatchet   d) subject

25 It is often difficult for a householder to _____ squatters and regain possession of his or her property.
    a) eliminate   b) withdraw   c) evict   d) vacate

26 When the teacher asked Amanda what the chemical formula was, her mind was a total _____.
    a) void   b) empty   c) nothing   d) blank

27 If you have a(n) _____ control handset, you don't even need to get out of your chair to change TV channels!
    a) distant   b) electronic   c) far   d) remote

28 As a result of the recent rise in the divorce rate, there are far more _____ parents than there used to be.
    a) single   b) only   c) unique   d) separate

29 I was really hoping to get the job, as they'd put me on the _____ list, but in the end they appointed someone else.
    a) interview   b) short   c) top   d) good

30 Geraldine always brings back beautiful little _____ from her African trips.
    a) memorials   b) reminders   c) souvenirs   d) memories

31 The Shorter Cambridge Dictionary consists of two _____, A – L and M – Z.
    a) volumes   b) editions   c) tomes   d) issues

32 When Delia's brother Mike pulled her hair, she got her own _____ by kicking him under the table.
    a) back   b) fun   c) revenge   d) retaliation

33 Some of the villagers thought the old woman had the _____ eye.
    a) black   b) evil   c) magic   d) wicked

B Read the passage, then decide which word from A, B, C or D is most appropriate for each space.

E-STYLE!

Remember all that advice people used to give you about how to lay out a 1) _____? Well, the good thing about 2) _____ is that you don't need to worry about most of that. No need to put your 3) _____ in the top right-hand corner or wherever. No need to say 'Dear Dan' if you don't want to. Some people do, however, add a 4) _____ at the bottom of their 5) _____ – it usually contains all their 6) _____ details.

In 7) _____ of general style, though, it's a good idea to keep it short and sweet. 8) _____ that people are paying to 9) _____ your mail, so try not to add to their 10) _____. You'll find your e-mail style tends to be much more 11) _____ than in conventional correspondence, as most people see it as an extended form of conversation. Of course, your mail won't look at all 12) _____ if it's so ungrammatical or badly spelt that no one can understand it!

Most 13) _____ mail features headings and text that scream at you in capitals. This is 14) _____ as the equivalent of shouting, and looks rather rude, so it's better not to annoy people by doing it.

	A	B	C	D
1	telegram	fax	heading	letter
2	communication	electronics	e-mail	websites
3	address	surname	phone number	file number
4	dedication	signature	autograph	postscript
5	message	memo	folder	report
6	contract	private	contact	factual
7	matter	terms	course	regard
8	Remind	Bear	Remember	Recall
9	store	send	forward	download
10	receipts	bills	invoices	accounts
11	stylish	looser	lazy	informal
12	impressive	impressed	impressing	impressively
13	rubbish	junk	recycled	direct
14	thought	considered	looked	regarded

C Think of **one** word only which can be used appropriately in all three sentences in each group.

1 I should have _____ that document I was working on today.
She _____ all her old love letters in case she wanted to re-read them.
Toby fell overboard, but his friends _____ him from drowning.

2 My brother has no idea of the problems his arrival will _____.
It makes no difference to me whether I _____ for the photos or not.
The detective decided to _____ as a social worker in order to gain the suspect's confidence.

3 A man is being _____ by the police in connection with the assault.

The elections were _____ in the first week of May, according to custom.

Fortunately for me, my good luck _____, and I managed to get the job.

4 Deborah must _____ an excellent chance of passing the exam if she revises properly.

Our MP has made the decision not to _____ for re-election.

If there's trouble, you'll have to _____ your ground and defend yourselves.

5 I cautiously _____ the car into the last space in the car park.

When it came to signing the contract, the buyers _____ out of the deal.

As he did every evening, Dick _____ up all his files on disk.

D Choose from the list A–I the best phrase to fill each gap. Use each correct phrase only once. There are more answers than you need.

SIGN OF THE TIMES

The pen-and-paper signature is dying. In fact, it may soon be dead. There is a current rash of laws being passed worldwide 1) _____ to digital signatures on digital documents as to pen signatures on paper ones. A digital signature can be one of many things. It may mean a unique physical attribute, for example, your face, iris or fingerprint, 2) _____ at the entrance to a secure building before you are allowed access. But where financial affairs are concerned, it generally means a string of numbers 3) _____. Eventually, once the right background checks have been carried out, and 4) _____, we will all be able to 'sign' electronic forms and correspondence with our personal digital signature.

But the real death blow to the manual signature is likely to come 5) _____ with cards that carry built-in digital signatures. In future, your signature will no longer be held in your brain but in your pocket. It will be a signature invented by a computer, and lent to you for use only 6) _____ and no longer.

A while you are creditworthy
B with the help of the appropriate software
C which give the same legal status
D while they check your bank details
E when banks start replacing the old-style plastic cards
F with the arrival of the paperless office
G which are allocated exclusively to you
H which is a modern invention
I which is electronically scanned

Humour, puns and jokes

Humour is notoriously difficult to understand in a foreign language. Many **jokes** in English are based on lexical ambiguity and therefore require an in-depth knowledge of advanced vocabulary. A **pun** is the use of a word or phrase which exploits such ambiguity, usually for humorous effect, and is a play on words. In order to understand puns in English, watch out for the different meanings a word can have.

The **punchline** is the culminating point of a joke or funny story, that gives it its humour. It often gives a different answer from what might normally be expected.

A Think of **two** different meanings for each of these words. Then choose the correct word to complete each joke.

pride	spring	skate	dressing	trunk	spotted
spirits	branch	scales	hailing	refuse	crane

1 What would you do if someone offered you a bag of rubbish? _____.

2 If you met an arrogant lion with a troublesome family, what would you say to him? *Watch that _____ of yours!*

3 What bird is good at lifting weights? *A _____.*

4 What's worse than raining cats and dogs? _____ *taxis.*

5 Waiter, there's a twig on my plate. *All right, sir, I'll get the _____ manager.*

6 Why doesn't anybody with a watch go thirsty in the desert? *Because a watch has a _____ in it.*

7 Why did the lobster blush? *Because it saw the salad _____.*

8 What kind of fish is most useful on ice? *A _____.*

9 What did the guard say to the elderly elephant getting off the train? *I'll help you with your _____.*

10 Why do leopards never manage to escape from the zoo? *Because they're always _____.*

11 What did the barman say when the ghost asked for a drink? *Sorry, sir, we don't serve _____.*

12 Which part of a fish weighs the most? *The _____.*

B Look at the first lines of these jokes and think what answer you would expect. Then match them with the correct punch lines.

1 I feel like a banana.

2 Waiter, will the pancakes be long?

3 What's the best thing to buy as a parting gift?

4 How did you find your steak, sir?

5 When is a door not a door?

A When it's ajar.

B Really? Which platform?

C To keep up the conversation.

D Extremely tired.

E A comb.

6 Why do they put telephone wires so high?

7 What are you growing in your garden?

8 One of my ancestors died at Waterloo.

9 Why do birds fly south in winter?

10 Waiter, do you serve shellfish?

F Quite by accident. I moved a few peas, and there it was.

G You don't look like one.

H Because it's too far to walk.

I No problem, sir. We serve anybody.

J No sir. Round.

> Most jokes are designed to be told, not written down, so the **sound** is more important than the spelling. Don't worry if you don't immediately see the joke when you read it. If you say it out loud, the meaning is more likely to become clear.

C What is the key word in each of these jokes, and how can it be spelt or spoken differently to acquire a different meaning?

1 What's black and white and red all over? *A newspaper.*

2 What runs around forests making animals yawn? *A wild boar.*

3 Why do you always lose if you play cards in the jungle? *Because there are so many cheetahs.*

4 Where does Dracula get all his jokes? *From his crypt-writer.*

5 Why is the theatre such a sad place? *Because the seats are always in tiers.*

6 How do you make a gold pie? *Put fourteen carrots in it.*

7 What animal do you eat for dessert? *A moose.*

8 Why is getting up at 4 am like a pig's tail? *Because it's twirly.*

9 What did the ram say to his girlfriend? *I love ewe.*

D Read the first line of each joke. Then think up a punchline, using one of the phrases in the box and making changes to it if necessary. Sometimes there is a clue in brackets to help you.

> no time like the present
> here today, gone tomorrow   make a clean getaway
> drop me a line   take a dim view of things   to make ends meet
> unidentified flying object   Morse code

1 What did the barber say to the client as he finished shaving his head? (hair)

2 What did the astronomer see in his frying pan?

3 How did the Vikings send secret messages? (Norse)

4 What did the boss say when deciding when to hand over a clock as a farewell gift to a member of staff?

5 What's the best way to communicate with a fish?

6 Why does a poverty-stricken dog chase its tail?

7 Why did the thief take a bath?

8 Have you heard the one about the man who always wore sunglasses?

E Use the words in capitals to make longer words that fit the spaces in this text about a particular type of recurring joke. (There will always be at least one word which needs a prefix in this type of exercise.)

Responding to 1) _____ insults that have been thrown at you is a 2) _____ way of honing your sense of humour. The great 3) _____ George Bernard Shaw was a contemporary of Winston Churchill's. GBS 4) _____ invited Churchill to the first night of one of his plays, 5) _____ two tickets with a note which said, 'One for yourself and one for a friend – if you have one.' Churchill lost no time in writing back, saying that 6) _____, due to pressure of work, he would be 7) _____ to come, but could he have tickets for the second night – 'if there is one.'

This joke was 8) _____ more recently by a prominent 9) _____ in the Labour Party, when speaking to a colleague and 10) _____ rival of his. The two men found themselves in the same meeting, despite being 11) _____ enemies. The colleague 12) _____ rose to excuse himself, saying that he had arranged to phone some friends, 13) _____ the statesman immediately handed him a small coin (enough for a brief local call) and said 14) _____, 'There you are. Go 15) _____ and phone them all!'

PROVOKE
WONDER
PLAY

THOUGHT
CLOSE

FORTUNATE
ABLE

DATE
POLITICS
TERM

SWEAR
APPEAR
UPON

WIT
HEAD

F Match these jokes with their punchlines, and explain why people might find them funny.

1 Who invented the 5-day week?

2 What happened to the piglet who wanted to act in a Shakespeare play?

3 What kind of boats do vampires like?

4 How do ghosts pass through a locked door?

5 What did the sea say to the sand?

6 What's the difference between a nightwatchman and a butcher?

7 Where do astronauts leave their spaceships, when in town?

A Blood vessels.

B One stays awake and the other weighs a steak.

C At parking meteors.

D Nothing. It just waved.

E He ended up as Hamlet.

F Robinson Crusoe. He had all his work done by Friday.

G They use a skeleton key.

Idioms

> **An idiom** is an expression whose sense is not easily deduced from the meanings of the individual words that form it. Verb tenses and pronouns can be changed but otherwise an idiom must be treated as a unit of language. For example, *kick the bucket* is an idiom which means *die*. Another word for *bucket* is *pail*, but this cannot be used instead of *bucket* in the idiom.
>
> An idiom must be used accurately and in an appropriate situation.

A Complete the sentences with these idioms, in the correct form. There are two more than you need.

> watch your step   give someone the cold shoulder
> take the biscuit   have a bone to pick with someone
> give someone the slip   take someone/something for granted
> on the tip of your tongue   tongue in cheek
> make a mountain out of a molehill   pull someone's leg
> out of the question   get your own back
> down in the mouth   play second fiddle

1 Look, the party's going to be quite easy to arrange.
  Don't _____.

2 You live next door to Julia Roberts? No! You must be
  _____.

3 We can't possibly stop for a snack on the way home. Sorry, it's
  _____.

4 Send Max into my office when he arrives, will you? I've got
  _____ with him.

5 Sally, you're looking rather _____. Has anything
  happened?

6 You know Stuart borrowed my stapler yesterday and didn't return
  it? Well, I've just seen my calculator on his desk! That really
  _____!

7 Although police were watching all the ports, the escaped convict
  managed to _____ and stow away on a cross-channel
  ferry to France.

8 I don't think Nigel meant what he said. His remark was rather
  _____.

9 When smoke from Mr Reeve's bonfire dirtied Mrs Ward's washing,
  she _____ by throwing the contents of her dustbin over
  the fence into his garden.

10 I'll remember his name in a moment. It's _____.

11 If you're going to see the Head today, _____. She's in a
   really foul mood, for some reason.

12 I'm afraid Derek doesn't really appreciate all his sister does for him.
   He just _____.

B Match the idioms on the left with their meanings.

1	get (hold of) the wrong end of the stick	A	specify exactly
2	put your finger on	B	make an embarrassing mistake
3	go like a bomb	C	go out of control, work erratically
4	come to terms with	D	look serious, avoid smiling
5	put your foot in it	E	terrify you
6	keep a straight face	F	eventually accept
7	go haywire	G	boast about yourself
8	keep your head	H	misunderstand
9	make your hair stand on end	I	have a very good relationship
10	blow your own trumpet	J	be nervous
11	have butterflies in your stomach	K	not panic
12	get on like a house on fire	L	be very successful, sell well

C Idioms often include animal images. Choose the correct animal idioms to complete the sentences. Use each idiom only once.

---

red herring   bee in his bonnet   dark horse   lame duck

barking up the wrong tree   whale of a time

get the lion's share   sort out the sheep from the goats

flogging a dead horse   let the cat out of the bag

dog-eared   putting the cart before the horse

---

1 That's the third time Trevor's put forward that suggestion. He's got a _____ about it.

2 There are lots of good candidates, but the three-day selection process is bound to _____.

3 You'll never persuade Simon to change his views on smoking. You're _____, I'm afraid.

4 Areas with high unemployment often _____ of EU subsidies.

5 Don't, for heaven's sake, _____! Elise mustn't even guess at the truth!

6 Strangely enough, the boss had organised the new training programme before he even interviewed the first applicant, rather _____, if you ask me.

7 Nobody knows anything about Gerry's past. He's a bit of a _____.

8 I'm afraid we've got a _____ for a leader. She's lost three elections so far, and looks like losing the next.

9 The class spent twenty minutes discussing school lunches before the teacher realised it was a _____, and insisted they return to the main topic.

10 It certainly wasn't my sister you saw in the cafe. You're _____ there!

11 'Did you enjoy the party?' 'Oh, I had a _____! I couldn't drag myself away!'

12 Here's my copy of *Pride and Prejudice*. I've read it so often I'm afraid it's rather _____.

D Match the idioms on the left, all connected with colour, with their meanings.

1 a red-letter day
2 black and blue all over
3 out of the blue
4 white-collar (worker)
5 in the red
6 green-eyed monster
7 white elephant
8 the green light
9 see red
10 yellow streak

A owing money
B jealousy
C non-manual, clerical
D an important day
E signal to go ahead
F badly bruised
G cowardly characteristic
H become very angry
I unwanted, useless possession
J unexpectedly

E Choose the correct word from the pair in brackets to complete each sentence.

1 Nicole smokes continuously. She's a real _____ smoker. (chain/ring)

2 We'll go _____, shall we, and each pay for our own drinks? (French/Dutch)

3 You can't see a thing in the attic. It's _____ dark up there. (pitch/coal)

4 The window cleaner lost his balance and nearly fell off his ladder. It was a _____ shave. (narrow/close)

5 You'll never persuade Sam to help you decorate the house – he's _____ idle. (bone/wood)

6 You like that china cabinet? I was so lucky, I bought it for a _____ at a jumble sale. (tune/song)

7 I'm sorry, I can't understand this leaflet at all. I can't make head or _____ of it. (tail/foot)

8 Are you two still talking _____? I know your work's fascinating, but can't you find something more relaxing to talk about?! (job/shop)

9 I just want to say a big thank you to all my wonderful customers. Drinks on the _____ for everyone! (table/house)

10 Vincent Ryan? Do you know, that name rings a _____. I'm sure I've heard of him before. (bell/buzzer)

11 It's 6.30. Shall we call it a _____, and go and get a bite to eat? We can finish off the report tomorrow. (stop/day)

12 Kathy and Dee have been at _____ ever since they started sharing an office. They don't even speak to each other now! (deadlock/loggerheads)

13 I'd love to be a fly on the _____ when Mary hands in her resignation. (ceiling/wall)

14 We thought we might have trouble finding the house in the dark but it was a piece of _____, thanks to Paul's directions. (cake/cheese)

15 Since our argument, I've been having second _____ about going on holiday with Isabel. (thoughts/worries)

Proverbs and similes

> **A proverb** is a common saying. It may be a famous quotation, a practical tip or the result of bitter experience! Often people only say the first half of a proverb, and the second half is understood. Proverbs are surprisingly frequent in everyday conversation, so it is useful to be able to recognise and use them.

A Match these beginnings and endings of proverbs, and then say what each proverb means.

1	Too many cooks	A	is another man's poison.
2	One man's meat	B	keeps the doctor away.
3	The early bird	C	calls the tune.
4	Don't count your chickens	D	while the sun shines.
5	An apple a day	E	is worth two in the bush.
6	Marry in haste,	F	before they're hatched.
7	He who pays the piper	G	catches the worm.
8	A bird in the hand	H	saves nine.
9	Make hay	I	repent at leisure.
10	A stitch in time	J	spoil the broth.

B Decide which of these proverbs is suitable for each situation. There is one more than you need.

> A You can't judge a book by its cover.   B The more the merrier.
> C It never rains but it pours.   D Every cloud has a silver lining.
> E Waste not, want not.   F There are plenty more fish in the sea.

1 You are trying to persuade your parents to invite a large number of friends to your 21st birthday party.

2 You broke your leg skiing, but in your three months' sick leave from work you had time to teach yourself conversational Italian.

3 You are encouraging a friend to save water and not leave taps running.

4 You are discussing a neighbour's problems. Not only has the poor woman lost her job, but now her eldest son has been sent to prison.

5 You are surprised to hear that Samantha at work, who looks so quiet and shy, drives a red Porsche and is often seen at nightclubs.

C Choose the correct word to complete each proverb.

1 Don't look a gift horse in the _____. (mouth/eyes/stable)

2 A rolling _____ gathers no moss. (snowball/pin/stone)

3 Let sleeping _____ lie. (cats/dogs/babies)

4 A little learning is a _____ thing. (dangerous/wonderful/useful)

5 _____ news is good news. (Some/Recent/No)

6 _____ was not built in a day. (Paris/Rome/London)

7 One swallow does not make a _____. (summer/drink/nest)

8 A leopard cannot change his _____. (skin/spots/hide)

9 You can't teach an old _____ new tricks. (dog/peasant/monkey)

10 It's no use crying over spilt _____. (blood/wine/milk)

D Match these beginnings and endings of proverbs, and then say what each proverb means.

1	While the cat's away,	A	shouldn't throw stones.
2	People who live in glasshouses	B	'twixt cup and lip.
3	There's many a slip	C	that blows nobody any good.
4	It's an ill wind	D	less speed.
5	Nothing venture,	E	flock together.
6	More haste,	F	without fire.
7	There's no smoke	G	make light work.
8	It's the last straw	H	nothing gain.
9	Birds of a feather	I	the mice will play.
10	Many hands	J	that breaks the camel's back.

> **A simile** is a comparison of two things, usually introduced by **like** or **as**, and is used to emphasise or illustrate an idea.

E Match each of these adjectives or adjective phrases with one of the twelve similes.

> healthy   unflappable   very pale   tough   well-behaved
> hard of hearing   extremely short-sighted   crazy
> without shame   obvious   ancient   defunct

1 as cool as a cucumber _____

2 as good as gold _____

3 as bold as brass _____

4 as white as a sheet _____

5 as hard as nails _____

6 as dead as a doornail _____

7 as blind as a bat _____

8 as fit as a fiddle _____

9 as deaf as a post _____

10 as mad as a hatter _____

11 as plain as the nose on your face _____

12 as old as the hills _____

F Form correct similes to complete the sentences, using *as* or *like*, the word in brackets, and a word or phrase from the box. There is one more than you need.

two short planks	out of water	bull	thin	rock
bell	red	judge	mule	

1 You won't need another check-up for a while, Mr Ferguson. Your chest is _____. (sound)

2 She was so embarrassed! She went _____. (beetroot)

3 Do you know, Andy barged right in without a by-your-leave! He's just _____. (china shop)

4 Mandy hasn't got used to being a student again. She misses her job, and hasn't made any new friends yet. At the moment she feels _____. (fish)

5 That lad doesn't understand a thing you say to him. He must be _____. (thick)

6 At least you don't need to think about losing weight! You're _____! (rake)

7 I didn't mind the police breathalysing me at all, because luckily I was _____. (sober)

8 You simply cannot make her change her mind. Once she's decided something, that's it. She's _____. (stubborn)

G Match the two halves of the sentences correctly. They all contain similes with *like*, some involving idiomatic usage.

1 The photographers clustered round the actress

2 They treated me very kindly,

3 He avoids family holidays

4 In a very short time the rumour spread

5 Jeff's new board game is selling

6 I've got absolutely soaked. I look

7 He can't put a foot wrong, or Janet comes down on him

A just like one of the family.

B like wildfire.

C like a ton of bricks.

D like hot cakes.

E like a drowned rat!

F like the plague.

G like bees round a honeypot.

H Match each of these similes with the appropriate situation.

A as brown as a berry   B as pleased as Punch   C as safe as houses
D as large as life   E as thick as thieves   F as strong as an ox
G as quick as a flash   H as like as two peas in a pod
I as light as a feather   J as right as rain

1 being completely out of danger _____

2 being big and strong _____

3 feeling delighted _____

4 doing something extremely fast _____

5 being completely recovered after an illness _____

6 seeing two very similar-looking people _____

7 having a good suntan _____

8 seeing someone you thought was dead or missing _____

9 picking up something weighing very little _____

10 seeing two people co-operating closely _____

Newspaper language

Newspaper headlines often use the present simple to describe an action that has already taken place: • *France wins World Cup*
the passive with the verb **to be** omitted: • *President re-elected*
and the infinitive with **to** to refer to a future action: • *Star to wed dustman*
To keep the headline as short and snappy as possible, no unnecessary words (e.g. auxiliary verbs, articles) are used.

Nouns are frequently piled up in headlines to make compound nouns: • *Government bribe scandal.* There is often a play on words to catch and hold the reader's interest.

A Match these verbs used in headlines with their definitions, using a dictionary if necessary.

clash	top	woo	wed	flee	rock	axe	dog
name	go	up	net	clear	cut		

1 be higher than
2 marry
3 shock severely
4 disagree
5 sack, dismiss
6 reveal the identity of
7 raise, increase
8 try to persuade
9 reduce
10 gain, win
11 acquit
12 be a source of worry to
13 resign, leave, disappear
14 run away from

B Explain these headlines in your own words.

1 TRIO SAVED IN CLIFFTOP DRAMA
2 MOTORWAY CRASH TOLL RISES
3 PM'S PLEDGE ON JOBS
4 POLICE BAN ON LONG HAIR
5 FISH SHOP BLAST RIDDLE
6 RAILMEN'S BID SET TO FAIL
7 DRUGS HAUL AT HEATHROW
8 BRIBES CASE SHAKES CABINET
9 AID FOR QUAKE VICTIMS
10 PIT PERIL LIKELY

C Look at the headlines and choose the correct synonym from the box for each word in italics.

disappointment	election	weapons	angry outburst
hurried visit	ambassador	employment	negotiations

1 *Arms* haul in attic
2 Anglo-French *talks* off
3 November *jobs* rise
4 Madrid *envoy* to resign
5 *Blow* for English cricket
6 High *poll* turnout expected
7 Education chiefs in *storm*
8 Pope's *dash* to Poland

Borrowed words

> **A borrowed word** has originally come from another language. When it is assimilated into English, it may keep its original meaning, or acquire an alternative or additional meaning. It may also be pronounced differently from the original.

A Complete the sentences with these borrowed words or phrases.

faux pas	vice versa	bona fide	ad lib
post-mortem		persona non grata	
blasé	non sequitur	spiel	contretemps
alibi	curriculum vitae	coup d'état	née

1 We could go first to Rome, and then to Florence, or _____, if you have urgent business in Florence.

2 A _____ appears to have taken place in the province of Murumba, where an army general is now reported to be in control.

3 He can easily prove he's a _____ resident, just by showing his passport.

4 When you apply for that job, don't forget to enclose a _____ with your letter of application.

5 I'm afraid I made an awful _____ the other day. I asked Marianne how her husband was, quite forgetting he died last year!

6 Nobody likes the new accountant in Jack's office. He's _____ as far as we're concerned.

7 A _____ was carried out on the victim, to establish the exact cause of death.

8 You looked so confident and _____ about it all that I thought you must have parachuted before!

9 What he said had very little connection with what we were discussing – it was a complete _____, in fact.

10 Dick had a bit of a _____ with a traffic warden this morning – that's why he's late.

11 Fellow graduates will be pleased to hear that Caroline Parrott, _____ Neill, has become a director of Pelco Insecticides Ltd.

12 Yet another double-glazing salesman rang up last night, but at least his _____ was short and to the point!

13 If you forget your lines, you'll just have to _____. The audience won't notice a thing!

14 The police were unable to charge Jefferson, as he had an unshakeable _____ for the time when the robbery had been committed.

B Match the borrowed words on the left with their definitions.

1	cuisine	A	hiding place or hidden store
2	siesta	B	ahead of fashion, daring
3	wanderlust	C	summary
4	paparazzi	D	type (literary or artistic)
5	cache	E	relationship or understanding
6	forte	F	prestige
7	avant garde	G	urge to travel
8	rapport	H	afternoon sleep
9	genre	I	photographers desperate for photos of celebrities
10	vigilante	J	style of cooking
11	kudos	K	strong point
12	résumé	L	self-appointed guard

C Complete the sentences with these borrowed words or phrases.

alfresco	tête-à-tête	incognito	quid pro quo	macho
verbatim	carte blanche	kamikaze	ad infinitum	
aplomb	entrepreneur	in camera		

1 I was delighted when Mrs Starr asked me to furnish her house for her. She gave me _____ to order whatever I needed.

2 We could go on _____ considering the various options, but I think it's time we made a decision.

3 It was such a warm evening we decided to have a little _____ supper in the garden.

4 The two of them were enjoying a quiet _____, over coffee.

5 The judge decided to hold the hearing _____ , as it was important to protect the children from unnecessary publicity.

6 John recovered quickly from the shock of seeing his sister, and said with great _____, 'Wonderful to see you back so soon, Denise!'

7 The photographer made an almost _____ attempt to retrieve his camera from under the wheels of the double-decker.

8 'I think I owe you a _____ ,' smiled the manager. 'If you take on the extra responsibility now, I'll make sure you get promotion next year.'

9 My neighbour is an up-and-coming _____. He owns several shops, and is always on the lookout for a new business opportunity.

10 Jane's husband seems a big, tough, _____ type. Yet you should see him changing the baby's nappies!

11 I think that man looks just like Mel Gibson. It *could* be him, travelling _____. He wouldn't want to be bothered by autograph-hunters.

12 At the public meeting, the discussion was recorded _____ by the council secretary, although some of the protesters did not express their points very clearly.

Words with two or more meanings

A Complete the sentences with these words.

degree	initial	pound	coach	trip
common	surgery	very	suit	plot

1 Sadly, beggars have become a _____ sight in many of our cities.

2 There were some _____ teething troubles when the no-smoking rule was first introduced, but most people have accepted it now.

3 Please come to the _____ to consult the doctor if at all possible. He only makes house calls in cases of serious illness.

4 My heart began to _____ as I cowered behind the door, watching the handle turn slowly.

5 Maria had arranged to see the specialist on Monday. That _____ morning the letter arrived from the clinic, with her blood test results.

6 In his spare time Sam used to _____ the under-14 football team.

7 I suppose I'll have to wear a _____ and tie for the interview.

8 Be careful not to _____ over the children's toys in the hall.

9 I wish I'd bought a programme. Then I might have been able to follow the _____! Who was it who died in Act 1?

10 On graduation day, Mohamed's parents turned up to see their son receive his _____.

B The words you used in Exercise A have more than one meaning. Match each one with one of these definitions.

1 a long-distance bus _____

2 unfenced land which anyone may use _____

3 operations on hospital patients _____

4 a British monetary unit (=100p) _____

5 extremely _____

6 a short journey _____

7 to conspire (against someone) _____

8 the first letter of a name _____

9 to be appropriate for _____

10 a measurement of heat or angle _____

C Think of a word that has both meanings, and write it in the box.

1 a company [＿＿＿＿＿] unyielding, strict

2 limbs [＿＿＿＿＿] weapons

3 a written message [＿＿＿＿＿] a part of the alphabet

4 a stick used in golf [＿＿＿＿＿] a group of members who share an interest

5 magic words [＿＿＿＿＿] to write a word correctly

6 part of a tree [＿＿＿＿＿] a large suitcase

7 used for smoothing metal or manicuring nails [＿＿＿＿＿] a collection of papers under a name or heading

8 a bird's mouth ⬚ this tells you what you have to pay

9 a living green thing ⬚ a factory

10 new ⬚ a book (fiction)

11 similar to ⬚ to enjoy

12 to reserve ⬚ pages bound together for reading

13 completely ⬚ rather, fairly, not very

14 a white fish ⬚ only

D Think of **one** word only which can be used appropriately in all three sentences in each group.

1 The government's overthrow should _____ as a reminder of the transience of power.

Despite serious misgivings, Delia continued to _____ on the board for a further five years.

Make sure you toss the salad in the dressing before you _____ it to your guests.

2 If you buy a new car from an established dealer, it should _____ a twelve-month guarantee.

Unfortunately the ice wasn't thick enough to _____ the boy's weight, so he fell into the lake.

If you _____ that argument to its logical conclusion, you'll need to buy bigger premises.

3 There was a deafening _____ of thunder just over our heads.

You can ring up the town hall to check that you're on the electoral _____.

I bought a cheese and tomato _____ and ate it in the park.

4 The summer is our busy period, so it's difficult for me to _____ time off then.

It is expected that government forces will _____ the city by the end of the week.

I decided to _____ Peter's advice if I was made redundant again.

5 Sally doesn't _____ any interest at all in her work.

Don't bother to get up, I can _____ myself out.

Even relatively unknown artists will be able to _____ their work in the new gallery.

6 I had almost finished the exam, when the drilling began again outside the window and _____ my train of thought.

Tourists started leaving the resort when the warm weather _____ at the end of August.

I'm not sure which newspaper first _____ the story, but now it's common knowledge.

7 There is great public _____ over the addition of unnecessary chemicals to our food supply.

As it's just a small family-run _____, I don't suppose we'll ever float it on the stock exchange.

What happens when the new policy is implemented is of no _____ to me.

Confusing words

A Choose the correct word from the pair in brackets to complete each sentence.

1 I think we could improve this dish with a _____ use of seasonings. (judicious/judicial)

2 Sharon, who's seven, _____ bickers with her little sister Anne. They're always fighting! (continually/continuously)

3 Mrs Hodge was sent to _____ for shoplifting, as it was her third offence. (goal/gaol)

4 It was very _____ of Trevor to refuse to co-operate with us. (childish/childlike)

5 By improving the interview process, we are hoping to achieve more _____ treatment of immigrants into this country. (human/humane)

6 Did you notice the _____ your remarks had on Gregory? He was quite shocked! (effect/affect)

7 Many businesses have suffered as a result of the world-wide _____ recession. (economic/economical)

8 The examiner decided that he could not mark the paper, as the candidate's handwriting was _____. (eligible/illegible)

9 What would you _____ me to do in my situation? (advice/advise)

10 That new hairstyle seems to _____ you – it looks just right on you. (suit/suite)

11 When the police frogmen came to the surface, they reported that they had discovered the _____ on the river bed. (corps/corpse)

12 Katie has always written up her _____ every night, ever since she was a schoolgirl. (diary/dairy)

13 The _____ of the story is 'Look before you leap'! (moral/morale)

14 My _____ reason for moving to the Lake District was to be nearer my family. (principle/principal)

B If the word in italics in each sentence is correct, put a tick. If not, write the correct word.

1 Stephen has always preferred *classic* music to pop.

2 My neighbour is a very *practicable* man – always repairing or making something.

3 Can you believe it? The bus was *stationery* for twenty minutes, while we all sat there fuming!

4 Tim and Mick went to India and Australia *respectfully*.

5 The President's New Year banquet is one of the capital's most important *social* gatherings.

6 *Loathe* though I am to criticise, I must say I thought the bread was rather stale.

7 It was extremely *official* of the policeman to demand to see our passports, and quite unnecessary.

8 I believed everything he told me. But then my friends always say I'm far too *credible*.

9 The marines disembarked from the *troupe* carrier onto the beach.

10 Add one *desert* spoon of sugar to the mixture.

11 From what you say I *imply* that you are not satisfied with your current job.

12 Vivienne is attending an *intensive* secretarial course.

C There are many pairs of confusing words which sound the same (called homophones), but which have different spellings and meanings. Match each word in the box with the correct definition. (Other definitions may also be possible.)

pier/peer	medal/meddle	wave/waive	core/corps
pare/pair	gambol/gamble	course/coarse	horse/hoarse
ore/oar	fare/fair	tears/tiers	beer/bier	guilt/gilt
sweet/suite	canvass/canvas	aisle/isle	

1 to peel (fruit, vegetables etc.) _____

2 untreated metal _____

3 gold paint _____

4 to bet money _____

5 an award for service given _____

6 to greet by lifting a hand _____

7 a series of lessons or medical treatments _____

8 a group of soldiers _____

9 water from your eyes _____

10 an artist paints on this _____

11 to interfere _____

12 an equal _____

13 two of something _____

14 awareness of having done wrong _____

15 an alcoholic drink made with hops _____

16 a passage between rows of seats _____

17 the centre of an apple _____

18 rough, common _____

19 an island _____

20 just, right _____

21 a set (chairs, rooms) _____

22 a jetty _____

23 an animal you ride _____

24 to ask for votes _____

25 to jump around playfully _____

26 used for rowing _____

27 money you pay for transport _____

28 rows placed above each other _____

29 to not insist on/enforce _____

30 used for carrying a dead body _____

31 having a sore throat _____

32 with a sugary taste _____

Spelling and punctuation

Notice how these words ending in **-y** change:
- *hurry~hurries, penny~pennies, worry~worried, obey~obeyed, play~plays*
Exceptions are: • *say~said, pay~paid*

Remember that most adjectives add **-ly** to become adverbs, but if the adjective ends in **-y**, this is replaced by **-ily**, and if it ends in **-le**, the final **-e** is replaced by **-y**. But note: • *whole~wholly* (See **Unit 14, Adverbs**.)

When adding the suffixes **-ed** and **-ing** to words, remember that

a one-syllable words ending with one vowel and one consonant (except **x** and **w**) double the final consonant: *drip~dripping*

b most words ending in silent **-e** lose the **-e**: • *rate~rating*

c longer words ending with one vowel and one consonant usually double the consonant if the stress is on the final syllable: • *begin~beginning*
There are a few exceptions, e.g. *travelling, kidnapping*.

A useful spelling rule is '**i before e except after c**'. This is used for /iː/ sounds where there is **ei/ie** confusion, e.g. *believe*. There are some exceptions, e.g. *seize, counterfeit*.

A Tick the words which are spelt correctly, and correct any which are not.

1 hurrys	6 chief	11 happening	16 bowwing
2 happily	7 flaping	12 ruinning	17 comfortabley
3 wholy	8 married	13 taxing	18 friendily
4 instaling	9 separateing	14 plaied	19 becoming
5 ageing	10 deceit	15 rolling	20 siege

B Choose the correctly spelt word or phrase from the pair in brackets to complete each sentence.

1 Although Tina and Matt are married, they keep their money in _____ accounts. (seperate/separate)

2 During the incubation period, the female bird is totally _____ on the male for food. (dependant/dependent)

3 Daphne has always been _____ in collecting antiques. (interessted/interested)

4 It's a pity I didn't _____ this information earlier. (receive/recieve)

5 Don't _____ your nerve! I know it's dangerous, but you can do it. (loose/lose)

6 Pete is having his films _____ at the photographic shop on the corner. (developed/developped)

7 It's the hospital's _____ to ensure that proper precautions are taken to protect patients from infection. (responsability/responsibility)

8 Unemployed actors often make good money by doing voice-overs for television _____. (advertisments/advertisements)

9 Now that my uncle has retired, he won't have to commute to Brussels _____. (anymore/any more)

10 Our plans for the summer are not _____ yet, but we'll let you know as soon as we've decided. (definite/definate)

11 No sooner had the helicopter landed _____ it was ordered to take off again. (then/than)

12 Young children have the habit of saying the most _____ things in public. (embarassing/embarrassing)

C In **most** lines of the text there is a spelling mistake. Write the correct spelling next to the number on the right. Tick any lines that are correct.

British universities are currently gearing up for there new   1 _____

intake of students. 'It's bean complete chaos this year,' one   2 _____

registrar told me. 'Because of problems with the computerised   3 _____

application system, we still don't no how many new students   4 _____

we'll be getting.' It now appears that, far from having to many   5 _____

first-year students, universities will not have enough, and it is   6 _____

doubtful weather full government funding will be available to   7 _____

university departments witch have not met predicted targets.   8 _____

As a result, both students and officials are calling for a revue   9 _____

of the hole university entrance procedure, from application to   10 _____

acceptance. It is generally felt that confusion has rained for   11 _____

far too long.   12 _____

> **Capital letters** are used for the first letters of people's titles and names, geographical names, historical periods and events, languages and nationality nouns or adjectives, days of the week, months, festivals, planets and stars (but not *the sun* or *the moon*), named buildings, titles of creative works, organisations and political parties, and at the beginning of every sentence.

D Correct this passage by rewriting it with capital letters where necessary.

plans for a spectacular pop concert in falmer park, just outside portsmouth, have been submitted to hampshire county council. the open-air event, featuring the singer neil silver and his backing group the raiders, is planned for wednesday 6th july and friday 8th july, to coincide with portsmouth arts festival as well as the tour de france. the organisers, gigs unlimited, say the show will have a french theme to fit in with the cycle race. the proposal will be considered at a special meeting on thursday 12th may.

local people are divided on the issue. while some welcome the influx of visitors and the increase in trade that the concert will bring to portsmouth, others are predicting an invasion of new age travellers. hampshire's chief constable edward lang-jones is, however, confident that he has adequate manpower to deal with any disturbance that might occur.

The apostrophe is used

a to show that a letter or letters have been omitted:
- *Who's there?* • *I'd like some help.* • *It's Monday today.*

b to show possession: • *my wife's birthday*

c to indicate plural forms with dates and letters of the alphabet: • *the 1980's*
- *How many t's are there in 'getting'?*

It is not correct to use the apostrophe for any other plurals, or for the possessive pronouns *its, hers, ours, theirs*.

Note also that **s'** is used for the possessive of plural nouns. But irregular plurals like *men* add **'s**: • *my parents' house* • *the men's uniforms*

E Rewrite the sentences to include apostrophes where necessary, and say which of the above uses (**a**, **b** or **c**) is involved in each case.

1 Her aunts been in hospital for years. ____
2 It isnt easy to create new jobs in a recession. ____
3 Would you take Mr Browns file to the teachers room, please? ____
4 His is a family company, which was founded in the 1920s. ____
5 Hes so meticulous. He always dots his is and crosses his ts. ____
6 Has anyone seen Jamess pen? ____
7 The childrens toys are all over the floor. ____
8 Celias friends cant come next week. ____
9 The Bennets house is far larger than the Joneses. ____
10 Toms plan wont work as well as his fathers. ____

Commas are used

a to separate items in a list (but not usually before *and*): • *cows, sheep and pigs*

b to divide clauses or phrases: • *If he had seen you, he would have said hello.*

c to show a difference in meaning in relative clauses (see **Unit 13**).

F Say which of the above uses of the comma (**a**, **b** or **c**) is involved in each of these sentences.

1 The manager explained that, if he had known we were coming, he would have made other arrangements. ____
2 Unless I hear from you by tomorrow, I shall assume the meeting is off. ____
3 You can sail any kind of dinghy, cruiser, yacht or surfboard in the harbour. ____
4 The rescuers, who had no extra provisions with them, had to be rescued themselves. ____
5 I decided to go to Paris with my cousin, who lives in Cornwall. ____
6 Who's been invited? Let's see – John, Angie, Brett and Simon. ____
7 The Sales Manager has been all over Europe, except to Austria. ____
8 Louise's mother, who is almost 92, has never left her home town. ____

Recycling

A Tick any of the sentences which are correct. Rewrite any in which the idiom or proverb is not in its usual form.

1 I did most of the work, so I should get the bear's share of the money!
2 Many hands need washing.
3 Nothing venture, nothing gamble.
4 The entry test is bound to sort out the wolves from the lambs.
5 Sorry, I thought *you* were getting married next week, not Janice. I often get the wrong end of the stick.
6 Waste not, if you want to save the world.
7 A stitch in time is a very good idea.
8 Rafael couldn't make head or tail of the instructions, so he had to ask Paco to put up the tent.
9 The early bird calls the tune.
10 Make hay in the sunshine.
11 The lorry whizzed past me but luckily didn't touch me. It was a narrow shave.
12 Don't count your chickens before they lay eggs.
13 If you don't blow your own trombone, nobody else will.
14 Birds of a feather make nests in spring.
15 You're looking rather down in the face these days. Is life really that bad?
16 An apple a day is worth two on the bush.
17 Guess who turned up yesterday out of the sky?
18 Every cloak has a silken lining.
19 Poor old Mrs Hyde kicked the basket last week, and was buried yesterday.
20 The children took it for granted that they would be allowed to watch the late film.

B Fill in the boxes with a suitable word or phrase to complete each sentence. In each case, a letter is given to help you.

1 As the weather was so wonderful, we decided to eat [| | | | | | |O|], on the patio.
2 The whole cast noticed the immediate [| |P| | | |] between the director and his leading lady.
3 If you think I'm going to go on working for you [| |] [I | | | | | | | |], think again! I'm leaving tomorrow!
4 At the Red Lion Hotel you will be able to sample the delights of our local [| U | | | | |], with dishes such as fresh salmon, wild rabbit and roast pheasant.
5 You will have to supply full details of your financial background if you wish to be considered [E | | | | | | |] for a scholarship.
6 Considering that he had just been made to look a complete fool, I thought he carried it off with amazing [| | | | |B|].

7 Bodyguards surrounded the royal limousine, trying in vain to protect the princess from the attentions of the ⬚⬚⬚⬚⬚⬚Z⬚ , who were crowding round with their cameras.

8 As we wish to encourage more mature students to take the course, we are prepared to W⬚⬚⬚ the fees in your case, so you'll only have your accommodation to pay for.

9 Medical experts recommend us to have a short S⬚⬚⬚⬚ in the afternoon. Apparently a nap after lunch helps our digestion and our concentration.

10 Robbers stashed gold bullion away in a garden shed five years ago. Today their ⬚⬚⬚H⬚ was discovered by a small boy.

C Think of a word that has both meanings, and write it in the box.

1 smart matching business clothes ⬚⬚⬚⬚ to look good on

2 to fall (over something) ⬚⬚⬚ a journey

3 to conspire ⬚⬚⬚ the story of a play or film

4 the first letter of a name ⬚⬚⬚⬚⬚⬚ early, at the beginning (adj)

5 a doctor's office ⬚⬚⬚⬚⬚⬚ hospital operations

6 unfenced land for general use ⬚⬚⬚⬚⬚ usual

7 a unit of British currency ⬚⬚⬚⬚ to beat or thump

8 to train (students or sportsmen) ⬚⬚⬚⬚⬚ a type of bus

9 extremely ⬚⬚⬚ particular, exactly that one

10 a unit of temperature ⬚⬚⬚⬚⬚ university studies diploma

11 weapons ⬚⬚⬚ limbs

12 only ⬚⬚⬚ a white fish

13 a large suitcase ⬚⬚⬚⬚ main part of a tree

14 a nation or people ⬚⬚⬚⬚ a speed contest

D Tick any of the sentences which are correct. Rewrite any similes which are incorrect.

1 Louisa was so frightened she looked as white as a daisy.

2 The grandchildren behaved extremely well. They were as good as gold.

3 Do you know, Gerry came to work in his slippers the other day! He's as mad as a monkey!

4 She doesn't really feel happy here, does she? She's like a fish on the beach.

5 The judge could not tell the difference between the pair of twins. They were as like as two eggs in a basket.

6 I thought the manageress would panic when she saw the mess the hooligans had left but, no, she was as calm as a cucumber.

7 Without his glasses, Uncle Jock is as blind as a bat. He can't see a thing.

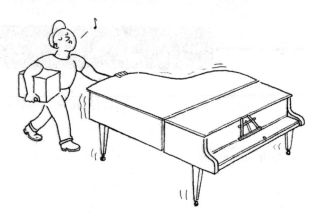

8 He had no trouble moving the piano, all on his own. He must be as strong as a bull!

9 Christine marched into her boss's office, as bold as a brick, and demanded a pay rise.

10 I've heard that joke dozens of times before. It's as old as the mountains.

11 You'll never be able to bring Vincent round to your point of view. He's as stubborn as a mule!

12 The new model Ford have brought out is selling like a bomb.

13 When the student nurse realised her mistake, her face went as red as a postbox.

14 Don't worry about your money. It'll be as safe as houses in my keeping.

E In **most** lines of the text there is either a spelling or a punctuation mistake. Write the correct spelling or punctuation next to the number on the right. Tick any lines that are correct.

The city of Cambridge has made great efforts to solve it's	1 _____
traffic problems in recent years. Congestion has been eased	2 _____
in the centre by closeing the main thoroughfare to motorists	3 _____
during the daytime. This means that these days if you	4 _____
attempt to drive into cambridge, you'll find your route	5 _____
blocked by bollards, wich can only be unlocked by the	6 _____
emergency services. Pedestrians and cyclists are unanimous	7 _____
in praising this change, and it certainly makes window-	8 _____
shoping much pleasanter. On the other hand, it may	9 _____
encourage the growth off large, out-of-town supermarkets,	10 _____
were customers can more easily park and shop for bulky	11 _____
products town councils are currently being urged by the	12 _____
government not to give planning permission for these huge	13 _____
developments, which encroach on our shrinking green belt,	14 _____
but as most people are now used to stocking up fore long	15 _____
periods at large supermarkets, they will definately not take	16 _____
kindly to an enforced change in there routine.	17 _____
Another interesting developpment in Cambridge was the	18 _____
introduction of free bicycles, available at certain point's for	19 _____
locals or visitors to borrow an return to the same or a	20 _____
different place. Unfortunately all 350 bikes were stolen	21 _____
within weaks.	22 _____

UNIT 72

Collocations

Collocations are combinations of words which are frequently used together in a way that sounds natural and correct. These words 'collocate' with each other, and approximate synonyms are very often unacceptable:
- *a hard frost* (NOT *strong* or *rigid*) • *a sorry state of affairs* (NOT *apologetic*)
- *catch a cold* (NOT *take* or *capture*) • *come to a standstill* (NOT *approach* or *go*)

Strong collocations are ones which are extremely common or instantly recognisable. They may be **fixed collocations**, where no other words collocate to produce the same meaning:
- *for the time being, a breach of the peace, power of attorney*

Many **idioms** are, in fact, fixed collocations, but the broad difference between idioms and collocations is that the component parts of idioms, which may refer to animals, colours, objects etc, make their meaning much less predictable. (See **Unit 64** on Idioms.)

There are also **open collocations**, where a number of different words may be used to complete the word group. Sometimes there seems little difference between the alternatives:
- *keep to/stick to a diet, do your best/utmost to persuade him, have/hold/bear a grudge*
but in other collocations a different word can change the meaning:
- *gather/lose momentum, lingering/serious scruples, call for/offer up a sacrifice*

A Choose the correct word from the pair in brackets to complete each sentence. All the collocations include the verb **call**.

1 I paid for this week's petrol and you paid for last week's, so we don't need to settle up. We can call it _____. (quits/evens)

2 Poor Ruth had to accept her father's decision to cancel her trip. She's not earning yet, so he calls the _____. Perhaps she can go when she's paid off her overdraft! (melody/tune)

3 I can't quite call to _____ the incident you mention. Late 1980s, did you say? I expect it'll come back to me. (memory/mind)

4 You two are getting married? Wonderful news! This calls for a _____! (ceremony/celebration)

5 The fact that he was prepared to falsify documents calls into _____ his fitness to carry out his professional duties. (discussion/question)

6 I'm simply exhausted! Let's call it a _____! We can always finish tomorrow. (day/night)

7 When several of the demonstrators were arrested, the organisers called _____ to the protest. (an ending/a halt)

8 I thought Josh would lose his temper with his little brother Harry and call him _____, but he managed to stay surprisingly calm. (names/insults)

9 If Ross tells me one more time about his Porsche, I'll call his _____ and ask him to take me for a drive in it! That'll teach him a lesson! (game/bluff)

B Choose the correct word from the box to complete the collocations, all connected with the word *light*. There are two more words than you need.

	set	years	by	face	travelling	
first	make	shed	let	come	reading	in

1 I set my alarm so that I could wake up at _____ light, before anyone else was stirring.

2 It is hoped that the current research will _____ light on the hitherto unknown causes of this terrible disease.

3 Clara always makes a point of _____ light, with just a change of clothes rolled up in a small backpack.

4 The principal announced that the culprit would be _____ off lightly, as long as he or she owned up immediately.

5 The full story didn't _____ to light until a fifty-year-old diary was unearthed in an attic.

6 The cut was bleeding quite badly, but Nicki was determined to _____ light of it, and said it was just a scratch.

7 Will's _____ lit up as he entered the room and saw the long table groaning with food. He suddenly realised how ravenous he was.

8 Well, I got my first job soon after leaving school. It seems light _____ away now, but I can still remember how excited I was.

9 _____ the light of recent events, the government will shortly be making an announcement on the action it plans to take.

10 With mounting rage, Daisy tore up the letter, threw the pieces into the grate, and _____ light to them with a match.

C Choose the correct expression from the box to complete the collocations, all connected with *heat*.

hot off the press		hot under the collar
get into hot water	hotting up	piping hot
in the heat of the moment		blowing hot and cold
a heated discussion		take the heat off you
just so much hot air		a hot potato

1 Hazel regretted what she had said _____.

2 When I entered the house, I could hear _____ going on in the kitchen.

3 I'm not sure the project will be going ahead – the boss is _____.

4 Make sure that meat pie's _____ before you eat it.

5 If Neil resigns, at least it'll _____ for a while.

6 Things are _____ at work now we're approaching the peak tourist season.

7 I got all _____ when they asked to see my driving licence.

8 You'll _____ if your mother finds out.

9 Immigration is such _____ that few politicians can agree on it.

10 I didn't pay any attention to what he said – it's _____.

11 Here's the council's list of sports centres, _____.

D Read the passage, then decide which word from A, B, C or D is most appropriate for each space.

A BLAST FROM THE PAST

In recent years, museums around the world have 1) _____ a campaign to tell us as much about extinct species like dinosaurs as possible. They have been 2) _____ and abetted in their endeavours by film directors like Steven Spielberg and by the public's passion for prehistoric creatures. Now the Natural History Museum in London has 3) _____ delivery of a Tyrannosaurus rex, which is the most sophisticated model of a dinosaur ever built. It draws on a 4) _____ of information gleaned from important finds over the last thirty years, and is a 5) _____ cry from the dry-as-dust fossils and skeletons that used to be the best a museum could offer – this creature looks, sounds and even smells like a dinosaur. It incorporates state-of-the- 6) _____ movement sensors, so that it can respond to the approach of a 7) _____ being by lunging terrifyingly with its hideous mouth 8) _____ open. Its first victims were a class of primary school pupils, 9) _____ into the prehistory section by their teacher. When Tyrannosaurus rex became 10) _____ of their movements, it lashed its three-metre tail, threw up its great head and bellowed. This stopped the school children in their 11) _____, and they gazed up at the huge animal, transfixed.

The model took a team of Japanese engineers three months to construct, and cost in the 12) _____ of £220,000. This dinosaur was known to be a messy eater; it probably flattened its prey under a massive foot, then ripped it to 13) _____ with its teeth and claws. Because of the decaying food that would have lodged between its teeth, it must have had truly revolting breath, but the museum curators 14) _____ the line at allowing their model to stink of rotting flesh. Instead, they arranged for it to give off a swampy smell, like badly cooked spinach.

	A	B	C	D
1	authorised	pioneered	validated	spearheaded
2	aided	helped	assisted	supported
3	ordered	announced	taken	completed
4	treasure	heap	harvest	wealth
5	distant	far	remote	prolonged
6	art	science	method	technology
7	whole	human	hated	hesitant
8	broad	all	wide	right
9	shepherded	manhandled	hoodwinked	mollycoddled
10	sensible	aware	alert	acquainted
11	path	steps	shoes	tracks
12	region	lines	area	roundabout
13	fragments	shreds	morsels	chunks
14	toed	ruled	drew	measured

New language

> Many **new words or phrases** are connected with people's work or lifestyle. They reflect current social trends, political movements, technological and scientific developments, and popular interests. The most frequently used expressions are called *buzz words*.

A Complete the passage with these words and phrases. There are two more than you need.

proactive	dotcom	cutting edge

proactive   dotcom   cutting edge
keyhole surgery   text messages
user-friendly   biodiversity   latte
counsellor   grassroots   name of the game
healthcare   asylum seeker   body piercing
sell-by dates   number cruncher   raves

MOVING SWIFTLY ON

Modern society is made up of all kinds of people, doing all kinds of things. You might be a computer whizz-kid, at the 1) _____ of technology, doing your best to make soft- and hardware 2) _____ for the consumer. Or you might be a senior hospital consultant, pioneering techniques such as 3) _____ while bemoaning the inadequacies of 4) _____ funding. You might be a 5) _____, a financial expert, assessing the risks of investing in hi-tech 6) _____ companies. Perhaps you're a teenager, campaigning to protect the 7) _____ of the natural world; or you might be into having fun at weekend 8) _____, with 9) _____ from your friends constantly appearing on your mobile. You could be an 10) _____, hoping against hope that you will be accepted into a new community, or a 11) _____, working hard to mend relationships and heal psychological wounds. You may be a parent, providing the best you can for your family by buying organic food and religiously checking 12) _____ on supermarket products, or a 13) _____ politician, nostalgic for the values of the past, or a student, struggling to get by on a student loan and seeing your debts spiralling out of control.

Whoever you are, you probably accept the need to be 14) _____ rather than reactive, in today's socio-economic climate. Our work and lifestyles are constantly evolving. Innovation is the 15) _____, and although the speed of change can be quite alarming, most of us realise it is necessary for progress.

There are many new words which are **abbreviations**, formed from the initial letters of a group of words:
• *GM* (genetically modified), *TLC* (tender loving care)
If the new word is pronounced as a word, and not as separate initials, it is an **acronym**:
• *AIDS* (Acquired Immune Deficiency Syndrome)

B Complete the sentences with these items. What do they mean in full? Which one is the true acronym?

BSE	aka	PIN	RSI	asap	PC	TLC	OTT

1 You'd better not write your _____ number down anywhere, in case someone sees it.

2 Rolf's been looking really down in the dumps lately. What he needs is some _____.

3 Chris has been off work for ages. Apparently she's suffering from _____ and is planning to sue the company.

4 'Have you heard? Doug in Sales has been sacked for sending in his reports late!' 'That's a bit _____, isn't it?'

5 'Who's your sister's getting married to?' 'Oh, he's a local radio DJ. Terry Murphy, _____ the Prince of Cool!'

6 Pete, can you e-mail me the invoice reference _____? Then I can arrange immediate payment.

7 I don't think Rhona likes being called an actress. She says 'actor' is more _____.

8 The incurable brain condition found in cattle, _____, is commonly known as mad cow disease.

When a new gadget is invented or a new phenomenon develops, a name is sometimes created for it by telescoping two existing words together to form a new one:
• *brunch* (a meal between breakfast and lunch), *smog* (a combination of smoke and fog)
These new words are known as **portmanteau words** and they are often first seen on shop signs, in advertisements for products, or in media reviews.

C Which portmanteau words are the names for these objects or concepts?

1 a video camera which also records sound

2 a film about the life of a particular person

3 a documentary filmed like a soap opera

4 the jargon or 'babble' used by psychotherapists

5 a TV programme in a series focusing on situational comedy

6 an airport for helicopters

7 an estimate which is based largely on guesswork

8 banking by telephone

D Complete the text with these informal expressions. There are two more than you need.

big time	the full monty	vegging out
a bad hair day	been there, done that
a couch potato	gobsmacked	crying foul
cherry-picked	to die for
drop-dead gorgeous	get a life

Fed up with work? Having 1) _____? Don't worry, you've always got the next episode of *I'll Be There For You* to look forward to when you get home from the office. *IBTFY*, the Aussie version of the American smash-hit sitcom, *Friends*, is all set to clean up 2) _____, so that's good news for the ATV production company, who 3) _____ the best locations from an admittedly stunning range on offer. Oh, 4) _____, I hear you say, with *Neighbours*, *Home and Away* and so on. Ah, but this is different. For a start, you'll be 5) _____ by the stunning leading actor, George Rooney, who's guaranteed to get the girls swooning. He's supported by a great cast, including the 6) _____ Fran Jacobs, whose clothes are 7) _____. The plotlines are inventive, the jokes come thick and fast, and as the credits roll, you're left wanting more. *IBTFY* is 8) _____, all right. So don't feel bad about being 9) _____ and 10) _____ in front of the TV – just switch on and enjoy!

SHORT OF FUNDS

You see, I started the job with the highest of hopes. I mean, I'd never really thought of fund-raising as a career, but 1) _____ it's a job, isn't it? It pays the bills. Well, it would have done 2) _____. That was the trouble. First they wanted me to phone their *previous* sponsors, then they said I should forget them and concentrate on attracting *new* donors. And of course, I was having to input everything 3) _____ – you wouldn't believe the things it could do! I wasn't getting on well with my boss either – you could tell 4) _____. Who knows why? I must have done something to upset her. But when she discovered I hadn't raised any money at all in the whole three months I'd been there, 5) _____ and I found myself out on my ear.

Well, I never liked it much there anyway. Being unemployed 6) _____. I've got enough money to tide me over till about September. I'm still looking around for something else, but if there's absolutely nothing and 7) _____, I might try and set up my own business on the internet. It can't be that difficult, can it?

E Choose from the list A–J the best phrase to fill each gap. Use each phrase only once. There are more answers than you need.

A push comes to shove
B it all went pear-shaped
C on this all-singing, all-dancing computer
D in your face
E I just wasn't her flavour of the month

F it took off
G isn't the end of the world
H if they hadn't kept moving the goalposts
I on a level playing field
J at the end of the day

Plural and feminine forms

Plurals of the majority of nouns are formed by adding **-s** or **-es**. In nouns ending in **-o**, both forms are occasionally possible. Nouns ending in **-f** or **-fe** normally change to **-ves** in the plural, although there are some exceptions.

There are a number of **irregular plural forms**: • *child~children, man~men, woman~women, foot~feet, mouse~mice,* etc.
Certain nouns do not change at all in the plural: • *deer, sheep, fish, salmon*

A Give the correct plural form of these nouns, using your dictionary if necessary.

1 mosquito	6 casino	11 echo	16 video
2 piano	7 shampoo	12 potato	17 kangaroo
3 avocado	8 ghetto	13 hero	18 radio
4 volcano	9 rodeo	14 studio	19 biro
5 motto	10 tomato	15 concerto	20 solo

B Follow the instructions for Exercise A.

1 leaf	6 child	11 hoof	16 sheep
2 goose	7 house	12 postman	17 life
3 deer	8 mouse	13 belief	18 louse
4 foot	9 roof	14 half	19 knife
5 wife	10 tooth	15 wolf	20 self

Some plural nouns look singular, e.g. *police, people,* and some singular nouns look plural, e.g. *a means, a crossroads.* Some singular nouns referring to groups of people can be used with either a singular or a plural verb, e.g. *army, government, orchestra, team.* Uncountable nouns, e.g. *information, furniture,* have no plural form.

C Decide whether you should use a singular (S) or plural (P) verb after these nouns. In some cases both are possible.

1 family	6 jury	11 accommodation	16 means
2 news	7 scenery	12 people	17 army
3 staff	8 cattle	13 police	18 knowledge
4 series	9 crossroads	14 information	19 advice
5 air	10 water	15 sand	20 training

D Match each of the twelve nouns with one of these collective nouns. Some of them can be used twice.

flight	bunch	flock	gang	swarm	shoal	pack	herd

1 keys	4 criminals	7 bees	10 geese
2 steps	5 sheep	8 cows	11 carrots
3 cards	6 fish	9 wild dogs	12 ants

There are three categories of plurals for **words of classical origin** in English.

1 Anglicised plurals, adding **-s** or **-es**: • *bonuses, circuses, operas, viruses*

2 Classical plurals, retaining Greek or Latin forms: • *criterion~criteria, automaton~automata, diagnosis~diagnoses, larva~larvae, nucleus~nuclei, stimulus~stimuli, appendix~appendices, curriculum~curricula*

3 Classical plurals in formal contexts, but Anglicised plurals for general use:
• *cactus~cacti/cactuses, formula~formulae/formulas, referendum~referenda/referendums*

Compound nouns either form plurals in the usual way by adding **-s**:
• *girlfriends, sit-ins*
or by pluralising the first element: • *sisters-in-law, passers-by*

E Give the correct plural(s) of these nouns. Use your dictionary if necessary.

1	nucleus	6	aquarium	11	circus	16	virus
2	formula	7	brother-in-law	12	cactus	17	appendix
3	boyfriend	8	bonus	13	breadwinner	18	larva
4	press-up	9	stimulus	14	opera	19	bacterium
5	take-off	10	criterion	15	diagnosis	20	automaton

Although most nouns in English do not have separate **masculine or feminine forms**, there are a number of exceptions. A common feminine ending is **-ess**, although with some words, e.g. *poet, priest, murderer*, the **-ess** ending is becoming less common.

F Give the feminine form of these nouns, if there is one. Use your dictionary if necessary.

1	heir	6	actor	11	doctor	16	uncle
2	fiancé	7	sculptor	12	manager	17	landlord
3	masseur	8	emperor	13	host	18	cousin
4	monk	9	hero	14	barman	19	headmaster
5	nephew	10	widower	15	bridegroom	20	steward

G Match the group nouns on the left with the appropriate nouns on the right.

1	congregation	A	sportsmen
2	cattle	B	computer programmes
3	orchestra	C	cows
4	cutlery	D	worshippers
5	crockery	E	paper and pens
6	team	F	tools, machines
7	stationery	G	cups, plates and bowls
8	fuel	H	petrol
9	equipment	I	musicians
10	software	J	knives, forks and spoons

UNIT 75

Prefixes and suffixes

A **prefix** is added to the beginning of a word. The most common use for a prefix is to make an adjective, adverb or verb negative, or to give it the opposite meaning.

A Form the opposite of these adjectives by adding the correct prefix. Choose from **un-**, **im-**, **il-**, **in-**, **ir-**, **dis-**, **non-**.

1 attainable	7 aware	13 satisfied	19 legible
2 existent	8 expensive	14 patient	20 rational
3 legitimate	9 conscious	15 complicated	21 perfect
4 resistible	10 tolerant	16 able	22 resident
5 accessible	11 likely	17 capable	
6 prepared	12 probable	18 enthusiastic	

B Form the opposite of these words by adding the correct prefix. Choose from **anti-**, **un-**, **dis-**, **mis-**, **de-**.

1 do	7 cast	13 classify	19 employment
2 approve	8 wrap	14 incentive	20 personalise
3 clockwise	9 embark	15 confirmed	21 fire (*verb*)
4 understand	10 centralise	16 mount	22 cyclone
5 used	11 climax	17 damaged	
6 briefing	12 prove	18 common	

C Match the prefixes **counter-**, **over-** and **co-** with these words.

1 worker	7 attack	13 espionage
2 balance	8 estimate	14 board
3 pilot	9 react	15 simplify
4 claim	10 director	16 educational
5 author	11 operate	17 due
6 priced	12 anxious	18 dose

D Match the prefixes **out-**, **ex-**, **re-** and **under-** with these words.

1 pouring	6 cooked	11 size	16 unite
2 wife	7 organise	12 distribute	17 assure
3 last	8 boyfriend	13 exposure	18 clothes
4 vote	9 elect	14 stay	19 achiever
5 direct	10 mine	15 claim	20 integrate

E Match the prefixes **a-**, **hyper-**, **mal-**, **mono-** and **neo-** with these words.

1 active	6 political	11 function
2 moral	7 sensitive	12 symmetrical
3 nutrition	8 syllable	13 adjusted
4 Nazi	9 classical	14 market
5 formation	10 critical	15 tone

A **suffix** is added to the end of a word, to make it into an adjective, noun or verb.

F Make adjectives from these verbs and nouns by using the suffixes **-able**, **-al**, **-ful**, **-ic**, **-ish**, **-ive**, **-less**, **-ous**, **-proof**, **-some**, **-ly** and **-y**. Make any necessary spelling changes.

1 fog	6 child	11 home	16 hope
2 help	7 tragedy	12 wash	17 imagination
3 destroy	8 fire	13 nostalgia	18 rely
4 befriend	9 humour	14 quarrel	19 drama
5 hate	10 magic	15 grace	20 reality

G Make nouns from these verbs and adjectives by using the suffixes **-al**, **-ance**, **-ence**, **-ety**, **-hood**, **-ion**, **-ity**, **-ment**, **-ness**, **-our**, **-ure** and **-y**. Make any necessary spelling changes.

1 depart	6 attract	11 satisfy	16 theoretical
2 entertain	7 arrive	12 rude	17 deliver
3 betray	8 emancipate	13 please	18 widow
4 pious	9 dark	14 maintain	19 available
5 behave	10 patient	15 advertise	20 tolerant

H Make verbs from these adjectives and nouns by using the suffixes **-en**, **-ify** and **-ise**.

1 horror	5 category	9 ideal	13 peace
2 wide	6 long	10 short	14 false
3 straight	7 high	11 critical	15 computer
4 real	8 intense	12 red	

I Use the words in capitals to form longer words to fit the spaces.

GUILTY OR NOT GUILTY?

Yet another 1) _____ athlete has been branded a cheat.   NATION

A highly-qualified panel of experts has 2) _____ all the   VIEW

evidence in the case of Anna Morris, who was sent home in

3) _____ from the Olympics after a random drugs test   GRACE

proved positive. She continues to maintain her 4) _____,   INNOCENT

however. Her defence is based on the alleged 5) _____   LIKELY

that her urine sample was tampered with, although the

authorities claim that no 6) _____ occurred in the   REGULAR

handling of the sample.

Now Anna has been found guilty of taking an 7) _____   LEGAL

substance, and she is 8) _____ by the verdict. 'I find it   HORROR

9) _____,' she told our reporter outside her home. 'It   BELIEF

just isn't true! For me this verdict is simply 10) _____.   ACCEPT

And although I 11) _____ there is very little chance of   REAL

my 12) _____ in clearing my name, I'm still determined   SUCCESS

to appeal against the ruling.'

False friends and word pairs

> **A false friend** (from the French 'faux ami') is a word which looks very similar to a word in another language. Learners may mistakenly assume that both words have the same meaning and use.

A Choose the best synonym (A or B) for each word on the left.

1	particular	A	private	B	special
2	nervous	A	irritable	B	apprehensive
3	spiritual	A	witty	B	concerned with religion
4	gymnasium	A	sports hall	B	grammar school
5	extra	A	supplementary	B	best quality
6	control	A	regulate	B	check
7	process	A	trial	B	procedure
8	exact	A	precise	B	correct
9	mark	A	brand	B	stain
10	souvenir	A	memento	B	memory
11	notorious	A	famous	B	infamous
12	sympathetic	A	compassionate	B	likeable
13	chef	A	boss	B	cook
14	public school	A	state school	B	private school
15	actual	A	current	B	real
16	critic	A	reporter	B	review
17	saucy	A	with sauce	B	impolite
18	sensible	A	practical	B	sensitive

B Complete each sentence with the correct word from one of these pairs.

> waistcoats/vests   chips/crisps   insulated/isolated
> aerial/antenna   meaning/opinion   bank/bench
> birthday/anniversary   bargain/occasion

1 It's Andrew's _____ today! He's 25, I think.

2 Their television doesn't have very good reception. I think their outside _____ needs adjusting.

3 In order to retain heat in winter, a house should be properly _____.

4 Could I have a packet of cheese and onion _____, please, to eat with my packed lunch?

5 Snooker players on television always take their jackets off, and play in their _____ and trousers.

6 I've told you what I think about it. Now what's your _____?

7 I'm exhausted! Let's sit down on this _____ for a moment.

8 You only paid £9.95! That's a wonderful _____!

C Explain the difference between these pairs by giving a short definition for each word or phrase.

1 warehouse department store
2 recipe receipt
3 block notepad
4 smoking dinner jacket
5 costume suit
6 congealed frozen
7 salute *(verb)* wave to
8 pensioners boarders
9 deranged disturbed
10 prove test

> The words in certain **word pairs**, linked with **and**, have a fixed order. They may refer to two things which go together, e.g. *salt and pepper*, two opposites, e.g. *black and white*, or just one idea, e.g. *high and dry*.

D Put the pairs of words into the correct order to make expressions linked by *and*. EXAMPLE: *ladies and gentlemen*.

1 chips/fish
2 women/children
3 ink/pen
4 bed/breakfast
5 butter/bread
6 dead/buried
7 rules/regulations
8 socks/shoes
9 in/out
10 pros/cons
11 wrongs/rights
12 law/order

E Choose the correct word from the pair in brackets to complete each sentence.

1 Make sure you get your facts and _____ together in good time for the presentation. (figures/details)
2 Now that the property market is so unpredictable, it is not wise to invest all your savings in bricks and _____. (cement/mortar)
3 Connolly looked really emaciated after his hunger strike. He was just skin and _____. (skeleton/bone)
4 Simon rushed to and _____ in a panic, trying to collect what he needed. (away/fro)
5 Fortunately the potholers were rescued and brought back to base, safe and _____. (sound/unhurt)
6 Today the Prime Minister is out and _____ on the streets of the capital, meeting members of the public. (about/busy)
7 When we lost the kitten, we searched for her far and _____, but there was no trace of her anywhere. (near/wide)
8 As the tide went out, the remains of the wrecked ship were left high and _____ on the sand. (dry/tidy)
9 Miss Hunt didn't laugh at Antony's slightly risqué joke, did she? I think she's rather prim and _____. (proper/prudish)
10 We'll have to have a good clean-up before we go. We must leave the cottage spick and _____ for the next visitors. (shining/span)

F Complete the sentences with these expressions. They are used in a less literal, more idiomatic, way than those in Exercise E.

sick and tired	flesh and blood	hard and fast	odds and ends
song and dance	chalk and cheese	pins and needles	
head and shoulders	wear and tear	tooth and nail	
ins and outs	cut and dried	chop and change	
cock-and-bull	neck and neck		

1 For heaven's sake, losing your keys isn't the end of the world! Don't make such a _____ about it!

2 We can try claiming on our house contents insurance for _____ to the carpet, but I don't hold out much hope.

3 Penelope had been sleeping on her arm, and woke up with _____ in it.

4 The brothers aren't like each other at all. They're as different as _____.

5 You might find an elastic band in that box. I keep a few _____ in there.

6 Look, there's no point in trying to overturn the decision. It's all _____.

7 I'm surprised the old man didn't leave his fortune to his nephews. They were his own _____, after all!

8 I'm _____ of hearing the same old excuse, week after week. Use a bit of imagination and come up with a new one next time!

9 For thirty years the two next-door neighbours had fought each other _____ in the lawcourts.

10 There's no doubt that Glenda will win the competition. She's _____ above the other designers.

11 You weren't taken in by what he told you, I hope? It was a complete _____ story!

12 They're not so much rules as helpful guidelines. There's nothing _____ about them.

13 I thought you'd already decided on the Zanussi frost-free model. It's difficult to keep track when you _____ so much.

14 Let's meet for lunch tomorrow, and I'll explain the _____ of the proposal.

15 The horses were _____ in the final straight, but then the favourite pulled ahead and was first past the post.

Ways of walking, talking, looking and laughing

A Complete the sentences with these words, in the correct form. There is one more than you need.

wade	plod	march	limp	hop	shuffle	tiptoe
	ramble	stroll	toddle	stagger		

1 Today the whole family is going for a _____ over the hills, with a picnic.

2 We had to _____ into the water right up to our thighs in order to retrieve the beach ball.

3 Corinna proudly watched her one-year-old daughter _____ towards her across the sitting room.

4 The middle-aged woman _____ straight up to the duty officer's desk and demanded to see the head of CID.

5 Odette had polio when she was a child, and still walks with a slight _____.

6 The old man put his slippers on and _____ slowly out of the room.

7 The girls had all the time in the world. They decided to _____ along Regent Street to do a bit of window-shopping.

8 'Help!' cried the man, as he _____ into the shop clutching his chest. 'Get an ambulance! It's my heart!'

9 It was so late when Nina got home that she had to _____ upstairs, hoping Mr and Mrs Burdon wouldn't hear her.

10 Yawning, the security guard _____ round the premises for the tenth time that night. He was tired, his feet hurt, and he was looking forward to the end of his stint.

B Match these verbs of walking or moving with their definitions.

1 trudge	A move by jumping from one foot to the other
2 stumble	B stand idly or walk with frequent stops
3 skip	C move on hands and knees
4 stride	D walk unsteadily, stagger
5 saunter	E walk heavily or wearily
6 loiter	F walk lamely or awkwardly
7 totter	G run quickly and/or playfully
8 hobble	H walk with long steps
9 crawl	I almost trip or fall while walking
10 scamper	J walk in a leisurely way

C Choose the correct word for a way of talking from the pair in brackets to complete each sentence.

1 You'll have to _____ if you don't want the rest of the group to hear you. (mutter/whisper)

2 When the police managed to reach the potholer, he was barely conscious and _____ with pain. (sighing/moaning)

3 Ray feels frustrated when he goes to his Italian conversation class, as he can't _____ himself well enough. (talk/express)

4 Mr Mayhew has a lot on his plate at the moment. It's not surprising that he _____ at people sometimes. (snaps/retorts)

5 The official was so taken aback that he did not _____ a word, but just stared at us. (mention/utter)

6 My aunt always looks forward to a good _____ with her sisters whenever there's a family get-together. (gossip/argue)

7 The boys' parents _____ them for half an hour on the risks they had run. (lectured/warned)

8 There are several points of interest that the committee will be _____ at the meeting. (discussing/chatting)

9 Mrs Stephens _____ her son in from the garden. (called/shouted)

10 A colleague of mine had a childhood _____ which occasionally comes back if he gets nervous. (mumble/stammer)

D Complete the sentences with these words for ways of looking, in the correct form. Sometimes more than one word is possible.

spot   stare   gaze   recognise   glance   glimpse
scrutinise   watch   peep   observe   notice
peer   glare   examine

1 The Prime Minister's car went through the village so fast that the onlookers didn't even catch a _____ of him inside.

2 The lecturer had left his glasses at home, so he was _____ at his notes, trying to read his writing.

3 As he joined the main road, the motorcyclist _____ quickly to the right, but unfortunately did not see the pedestrian on his left.

4 Kelly looked so different when I saw her recently that I hardly _____ her.

5 The antiques expert _____ the silver vase very carefully, while its owner watched in suspense.

6 When the climbers reached the top of the mountain they were delighted to see the mist disperse and the sun _____ through the clouds.

7 The whole coachload of tourists _____ in wonder at the Pyramids, stark and black against the desert sand in the moonlight.

8 Silke recorded the last episode of her favourite television serial on video, but somehow never got round to _____ it.

9 Old Mrs Gudgeon fell and broke her hip last week. She lives alone, but luckily her neighbour _____ that she hadn't drawn the curtains, went round to check up on her and called the ambulance.

10 There's a competition in the local paper this week. If you can _____ the deliberate mistake in the editorial, you might win a brand new Ford Mondeo!

E Match these verbs of smiling or laughing with their definitions.

1	guffaw	A	laugh with pleasure or delight
2	giggle	B	laugh disrespectfully or furtively
3	grin	C	laugh softly or to yourself
4	chortle	D	smile broadly
5	sneer	E	scoff or mock
6	snigger	F	laugh nervously or foolishly
7	jeer	G	smile scornfully or contemptuously
8	chuckle	H	laugh crudely or noisily

F Complete the sentences with these expressions with *laugh*, in the correct form.

---

laugh all the way to the bank   Don't laugh   a laugh a minute
   no laughing matter   laugh someone out of it
laugh in someone's face   laughable   Don't make me laugh
laugh up your sleeve   laugh off   have the last laugh
         laugh on the other side of your face

---

1 Although the boxer looked quite badly cut and bruised, he staggered to his feet, _____ his injuries and insisted on continuing the fight.

2 You've decided to give up smoking? _____! You'll never be able to, not in a million years!

3 Have you seen the late-night comedy show on at the Festival Theatre? It's really funny, _____.

4 I thought I'd been so clever, getting myself an invitation to dinner at Linda and Pete's, but they _____ when they made me do all the washing-up!

5 Mark's married a wealthy heiress now, has he? He must be _____!

6 You can't possibly sell your house for so little. Really, what your buyer's offering you is _____.

7 The Minister went on with his speech. Meanwhile I was _____, waiting for him to make another embarrassing mistake.

8 You may think being in love is something to laugh at now, but you'll _____ when it happens to you one day!

9 When the probation officer tried to help Charlie, the youth just _____, saying he didn't want any help.

10 _____, but I've decided to sell up and move to a Greek island.

11 Take that smile off your face, Matthew! Bullying is _____ and will not be tolerated.

12 For some reason Pauline was in a foul mood, and it was impossible to _____.

Ways of holding and pulling
Words for light, water and fire

A Complete the sentences with these words, in the correct form. Use each word only once.

draw	tow	lug	haul	jerk	drag	tug	wrench

1 The breakdown lorry was called to the motorway to _____ away the Range Rover which had been involved in the pile-up.

2 The toddler _____ insistently at his mother's hand. 'Please can I have an ice cream?' he whined.

3 Paula felt too ill to go to work, but she managed to _____ herself out of bed to make some breakfast.

4 Jeremy gave the blind a sudden _____, and sunshine flooded into the room.

5 The plumber had some difficulty removing the bath tap, but finally, using all his strength, he managed to _____ it off.

6 Here's your homework file. I've been _____ it around with me all day. Quite heavy, isn't it?

7 The authorities had to use a crane to _____ the submerged wreck out of the water.

8 When he heard the shot, the bodyguard turned in a flash and _____ his own gun.

B Match these expressions with *drag*, *draw*, *pull* and *tug* with their definitions.

1	drag your feet or heels	A	disgrace someone
2	pull your weight	B	something boring
3	drag someone's name through the mud	C	very hostile towards someone
4	pull strings	D	get control of your feelings
5	draw a blank	E	deceive or delude someone
6	a drag	F	act with deliberate slowness
7	pull the wool over someone's eyes	G	be unsuccessful in finding something
8	pull apart or to pieces	H	come to an end
9	pull your socks up	I	appeal to someone's emotions
10	tug at someone's heartstrings	J	do everything you can to achieve something
11	pull yourself together	K	unnecessarily lengthy
12	long-drawn-out	L	improve your behaviour
13	a tug of love	M	criticise harshly
14	draw to a close	N	do your fair share of work
15	at daggers drawn with someone	O	a dispute over the child of separated or divorced parents
16	pull out all the stops	P	use influential friends or connections

C Make correct collocations by using these words and phrases after the verbs below. Some of the verbs have more than one collocation, and some of the phrases can be used more than once.

> your fists   forty winks   a concept   at straws   a flower
> the enemy soldiers   up courage   someone's brains   your eyebrows
> the nettle   your teeth   power   an audience
> his long-lost brother to his heart   your passport nervously
> a bag from an old lady   someone's imagination

1 grasp _____
2 pluck _____
3 clench _____
4 grip _____
5 snatch _____
6 seize _____
7 clutch _____
8 clasp _____
9 capture _____
10 pick _____

D Choose the correct word connected with light from the pair in brackets to complete each sentence.

1 As we came out of the cinema, we were _____ by the bright afternoon sunshine.   (dazzled/glared)
2 In the garden the wet leaves _____ in the sunlight. (glimmered/glistened)
3 Anneka's eyes were _____ with rage as she tore up the contract. (glittering/flickering)
4 Some distance across the moors the traveller could just make out a faint _____ of light through the fog.   (glimmer/sparkle)
5 The studio guests began to feel very hot under the _____ of the powerful television lights.   (glare/flare)
6 The children saw another _____ of lightning light up the dark sky, and heard the clap of thunder a few seconds later.   (flash/beam)
7 The surface of the lake _____ in the moonlight. (shimmered/dazzled)
8 When Frank opened the window, the candle on the table _____ briefly and then went out.   (flashed/flickered)
9 The large diamond on Sophie's finger _____ as it caught the light.   (shimmered/sparkled)
10 As the two men crept round the front of the house, they were suddenly caught in the _____ of a security light.   (beam/glitter)

E Match these words connected with water with their definitions.

1 downpour (*noun*)   A   fine rain
2 trickle (*verb*)   B   a man-made waterway
3 drip (*verb*)   C   to pour out suddenly and profusely
4 shower (*noun*)   D   to fall in drops
5 torrent (*noun*)   E   a small river
6 drizzle (*noun*)   F   a brief period of rain, snow or hail
7 canal (*noun*)   G   a small pool of water on the road or pavement
8 stream (*noun*)   H   to run or flow slowly and thinly
9 puddle (*noun*)   I   a heavy, sudden fall of rain
10 gush (*verb*)   J   a fast, violent flow of water

F Complete the sentences with these words connected with fire. Sometimes more than one word is possible.

	glow	smoke	embers	scald	swelter	flame
blaze	spark	burn	ashes	steam	scorch	sizzle	boil

1 In the darkness Michelle saw the red _____ of a cigarette and knew that Rod wasn't far away.

2 As the evening wore on and the fire died down, we put potatoes to bake in the _____, and ate them in our fingers.

3 Although police have not yet established the cause of the fire, it seems likely it was started accidentally by a _____ from a dropped match.

4 When the scouts put more dry wood on the bonfire, it began to _____ merrily, and the _____s leapt high into the sky.

5 Unfortunately my sister wasn't careful enough when ironing those trousers, so now there's a very noticeable _____ mark on the seat.

6 Benedict, be careful not to _____ yourself with all that boiling water.

7 Jason carefully _____ed open the letter while his mother was out shopping.

8 You'll _____ in that heavy jacket. Why don't you wear your linen one?

9 All that remained of their home after the fire was extinguished was a pile of sodden _____.

10 'There's no _____ without fire.'   (proverb)

G Think of **one** word only which can be used appropriately in all three sentences in each group.

1 The taxi _____ up smartly in front of the Savoy Hotel.
The chairman _____ our attention to the third item on the agenda.
The child _____ a picture of the farmhouse where she used to live.

2 Whenever Maria wins a race, her parents simply _____ with pride.
He lay beside the fire's dying embers, watching them _____ in the dark.
People say that horses sweat, men perspire, and ladies gently _____!

3 I spent the first two golf lessons learning how to improve my _____.
Don't panic, Kylie! Get a _____ on yourself!
Several countries in the region are in the _____ of the worst recession for a hundred years.

4 Her long hair was _____ out behind her in the wind as she rowed towards the shore.
Refugees were _____ across the border, carrying their few possessions.
The little boy was calling for his mother, with tears _____ down his face.

5 Fighting _____ up again last night in areas of unrest.
The horse's nostrils _____ as he sensed imminent danger.
The flames from the burning building _____ into the night sky.

Recycling

A Fill in the boxes with a suitable word to complete each sentence. In some cases, a letter is given to help you.

1 I know you told me it was expensive, but could you tell me what the ☐☐☐☐☐☐ price was?

2 I had to haggle, but in the end I only paid £10 for the set. It was a real ☐☐☐☐☐☐☐☐ .

3 There's a wooden ☐☐☐☐☐☐ by the pond, where I often sit and eat my sandwiches.

4 Have you read the wonderful ☐☐☐☐☐☐ in *The Guardian* of Barker's new play?

5 Surely you've heard of Spike Magee? He's the ☐☐T☐☐☐☐☐ bank robber who's on the run!

6 Try to use your ☐☐☐☐I☐☐☐☐☐☐ to make your composition as interesting as possible. Think up some new ideas!

7 Tell me more about your new ☐☐☐☐☐ . Has he given you a pay rise yet?

8 As Chantal's parents are working abroad, she's a ☐☐☐☐☐☐☐ at a well-known girls' public school, and only sees her family during the holidays.

9 The doctor asked his patient to step on to the ☐☐☐☐☐☐ to be weighed.

10 Daphne collected all the traditional ☐☐☐☐☐☐☐ used by the village women in their cooking, and managed to get them published.

11 If you are tolerant, you accept that other people have different ☐☐☐☐☐☐☐ from you on all sorts of subjects.

12 This is a ☐☐☐☐☐☐ beach, which belongs to a hotel. Only the hotel guests are allowed to use it, not the general public.

B Complete the word pairs with words from the box, then give a definition for each pair.

wide	ends	dried	buried	neck	mortar	dry	nail
blood	bull	tear	needles	cheese	cons	dance	

1 dead and _____

2 a song and _____

3 bricks and _____

4 pros and _____

5 flesh and _____

6 cock-and-_____

7 far and _____

8 neck and _____

9 wear and _____

10 odds and _____

11 high and _____

12 chalk and _____

13 cut and _____

14 pins and _____

15 tooth and _____

C Read the passage, then decide which word from A, B, C or D is most appropriate for each space.

HIDDEN DEPTHS

'I'll get soaked if I go out now,' said Hector. 'It's simply 1) _____!' Jane threw him a 2) _____ of contempt. Is he a man or a mouse? she thought. Outside the teashop the wet cobblestones in the village square 3) _____ in the light from the streetlamps.

'Oh dear!' said Hector. 'I've spilt my tea!' Some children at a table near them 4) _____ quietly to themselves, as the ancient waitress 5) _____ slowly over to wipe the table. Jane looked down at her engagement ring, and the very small diamond 6) _____ back at her. She took a deep breath. I'll have to tell him, she thought.

'Er ... Hector,' she started. But was he even listening to her? He seemed to be 7) _____ to himself about something – just when she'd 8) _____ up the courage to tackle him. It really was *too* much!

Suddenly she realised that Hector had got up and 9) _____ casually over to the cash desk.

'OK, babe, hand over the takings!' he barked to the shocked waitress. '10) _____ the door, Jane,' he added. In a few moments they were out in the square with £57 in small change in a plastic bag. It had stopped raining, but Jane was so stunned she didn't even notice.

	A	B	C	D
1	drizzling	showering	pouring	dripping
2	stare	gaze	glimpse	glance
3	glistened	glimmered	glared	glittered
4	guffawed	sniggered	jeered	sneered
5	waded	sauntered	scampered	shuffled
6	sparkled	shimmered	beamed	dazzled
7	snapping	uttering	muttering	stammering
8	seized	plucked	gripped	snatched
9	marched	strolled	rambled	staggered
10	Stare	Examine	Peer	Watch

D Use the words in capitals to make longer words that fit the spaces in the text. (Tasks of this type always include at least one word with a prefix.)

A POPULAR PAINTER

The American painter George Wesley Bellows (1882–1925) was the only son of an elderly couple who 1) _____ the Midwestern values of honest business practice and strict morality. From earliest 2) _____ he seemed determined to become an artist. Before graduating from Ohio State University, and in the face of stiff parental 3) _____, he moved to New York to study art. There he was strongly influenced by 'The Eight', or American Ashcan School. For the 4) _____ of his life, his work was characterised by

EXAMPLE

CHILD

OPPOSE

REMAIN

realist subject matter, 5) _____ which was a traditional   LIE

approach to composition. He was also fascinated by the

various systems of colour 6) _____ that painters were   RELATE

using at the time, and studied them in detail. The truly

7) _____ work that he produced in these early days   STAND

8) _____ and contributed to much of his later painting.   SHADOW

   Despite his 9) _____ with common, even low-life   IDENTITY

themes, he was elected an associate of the 10) _____   PRESTIGE

National Academy at the exceptionally early age of 27. One

of the reasons the Academy honoured Bellows, while

11) _____ approval from many of the other members of   HOLD

'The Eight', was the fact that there were 12) _____   MISTAKE

references to the old masters in Bellows' work. He was one of

the few artists who 13) _____ combined a modern verve   INSTINCT

and energy with an appreciation of artistic tradition, and his

almost 14) _____ appeal was therefore not surprising.   UNIVERSE

E Think of **one** word only which can be used appropriately in all three sentences in each group.

1 This is only a _____ estimate of the likely costs.
The truck bumped along the _____ mountain track.
I'm not taking the ferry if the weather's _____!

2 With a flourish the waiter _____ some pepper over the pasta.
The sisters were _____ down by their years of exhausting work.
The lorry _____ to a halt outside the factory gates.

3 All my worldly possessions are in three _____, due to arrive from Canada in a few days' time.
Take your _____ with you, lads, in case you're offered a dip in the pool.
Birds often like to nest in hollow tree _____.

4 Denise arrived home as the clock _____ midnight.
Something _____ me the other day. I need a new job!
Most people were still filing into the concert hall as the orchestra _____ up.

5 They're planning to dig over the vegetable plot in the _____.
Nigel's had a _____ in his step ever since he started going out with Lynne.
Luckily, the hikers were able to fill their water bottles from a _____, before continuing on their way.

6 The principal will have to _____ a decision soon.
However busy Geraldine is, she's always careful to _____ time for her family.
As the coffee was being served, the bridegroom rose to his feet to _____ what he promised would be a short speech.

Formal letters

It is important to use the correct layout for **formal letters**, as shown here.

Your address (but not your name):
house number/name and street,
the town, the county (if included),
the postcode, the country (if necessary).

The date: day, month and year
23rd June, 2001

Your correspondent's title and
name and/or position
e.g. Mr Robert Smith
Sales Manager
or, if you do not know the name, simply
The Sales Manager
plus the company name and address

Dear Sir/Dear Madam,
(if you do not know his/her name)
or **Dear Mr/Mrs/Miss/Ms/Dr Smith,**

Begin your letter under the word Sir/Madam or the person's title.
Use new paragraphs where appropriate.

Yours faithfully,
(if you have written Sir/Madam) or
Yours sincerely,
(if you have written the person's name)

Your signature
Your name legibly written, with your title
e.g. Miss Amanda White

The correct **register** is crucial in a formal letter. You should:
a use correct, formal language, complete sentences, no slang, contractions or
exclamations.
b use formal vocabulary and linking words.
c keep strictly to the point.

A Choose the correct word or phrase for a formal letter from these pairs of phrases or clauses.

1 a) I was wondering how things are going at the moment.
  b) I am writing to enquire whether satisfactory progress is being made.

2 a) We can lend you another two grand.
  b) Your credit facility can be extended to a ceiling of two thousand pounds.

3 a) At your earliest convenience

   b) As soon as you like.

4 a) We look forward to receiving your prompt reply.

   b) Hoping to hear from you soon.

5 a) Sorry I haven't written lately.

   b) I apologise for the delay in writing.

6 a) Please don't breathe a word to a soul!

   b) I would greatly appreciate your co-operation in keeping this matter confidential.

7 a) Please give my regards to your parents.

   b) All the best to your mum and dad.

8 a) I'll have to ask my solicitor.

   b) I shall have no option but to take legal advice.

9 a) Getting married! That's wonderful!

   b) May I offer my warmest congratulations on your forthcoming marriage.

10 a) I am extremely grateful to you.

    b) Thanks a lot.

B Unscramble this jumbled letter, from a customer in Brighton to her bank in Exeter.

a Yours faithfully,

b Cathedral Place

c statement monthly instead of quarterly, with effect from today.

d Dear Sir or Madam,

e Mrs S. Marsh

f 26 November 2000

g I would be grateful if you would send me a

h Thank you for your attention.

i Brighton

j Sylvia Marsh

k The Manager

l Seaview Cottage, Back Lane

m Lloyds Bank

n BN2 3GA

o Exeter

p My account number is 0553119.

q EX3 7BS

Here is some useful formal language for particular situations.

Apology I am writing to apologise for the omission/for omitting to send the order.

I am extremely sorry to cause you this inconvenience.

I assure you nothing like this will ever happen again.

Request for information I would be most grateful if you could send me an up-to-date brochure.

I would like further information about the services you offer.

I should be grateful if you would send me full details of your package.

Application I am interested in applying for the post of bilingual secretary, which was advertised in *The Daily Herald* on 30th May.

I would like to apply for the post of Head of Science, which was advertised recently. My qualifications and experience, as you will see from my curriculum vitae, make me a particularly suitable applicant for this post.

> **Complaint** I am writing to express my concern about the lack of facilities for disabled people.
>
> With reference to your letter of 24 April, I would like to point out that my car was not parked in contravention of parking regulations when I was given a parking ticket. I must insist that you look into the matter further.

C Read this letter, and make any changes necessary to improve its style and layout as a formal letter.

Bracknell
28 Woolston Drive
RG12 3JB

Randalls Ltd
75 Tenter Park
Northampton NN4 1SW

Dear Mr Randall,

 We haven't met but I like the look of your ad in one of those computer mags I was reading recently. It might have been PC Direct. Or perhaps it was PC Plus. The thing is, as you may have guessed by now, I really need a word processor. I'm writing a novel, you see, and it's getting a bit much for my wife to type it up every night on my old typewriter. And then she gets fed up when I make changes and she has to retype it. So I think I should get a PC, probably something like your 386SX – 'now even better value than ever' according to your ad! What do you think? Could you write back as soon as possible, telling me a bit more about the PCs you offer? Do you deliver? Our car's being repaired at the moment (my son had a little accident in it the other day). And by the way, Merry Christmas!

 All the best,

 Jerome Walsh

D Now write one or more of these letters.

1 Write a short letter to Professor Jane Barker of Oxford University, to thank her for leading the workshop you organised on self and peer assessment in the workplace. Mention that you hope to invite her back next year to talk on another aspect of staff development. (about 75 words)

2 Write to the Grand Hotel in Manchester, confirming your booking of their conference facilities for your company's annual planning meeting in June. Explain how many of your colleagues will be attending the two-day meeting, and what accommodation, meals and special diets will be required. Ask for audio-visual or computer facilities to be available in the conference room. (about 100 words)

3 You are going to attend university in Mexico City for a year, as an exchange student. Your father has an ex-colleague there, a Dr Juan Mendoza, who may be able to help you with accommodation and language problems. Write to Dr Mendoza, explaining your situation and asking for his help. (about 150 words)

4 Write a letter to an international company applying for a job in the Personnel Department. Give details of your qualifications, experience and suitability for the post. (about 200 words)

(There is a model answer to 1 in **Section 11** of the Appendix.)

Informal letters

The usual layout for **informal letters** is as follows.

1 Your address (not your name), although this may be shortened or omitted
2 The date
3 Dear + the name of the person you are writing to
4 Your letter
5 Yours/Regards/Best wishes/All the best/Love/Lots of love
6 Your signature

In an informal letter, you know the person you are writing to, and it is therefore quite correct to use slang, contractions, exclamations, direct questions and incomplete sentences. Do not use formal language.

A Match the formal expressions on the left with their informal equivalents.

1 furthermore		A	but
2 therefore		B	then/next
3 however		C	and another thing
4 in addition to		D	in spite of
5 notwithstanding		E	by the way
6 currently		F	I think
7 subsequently		G	as well as
8 incidentally		H	about
9 in my view		I	at the moment
10 approximately		J	so

Here is some useful informal language for particular situations.

Apology I'm really sorry I haven't written lately.
I just haven't been able to get round/down to writing recently.
I've been so busy at work/with the move/with the children.

Reassurance I'm sure everything will be all right, just you wait and see.
Don't worry about them. They're old enough to take care of themselves now.
It wasn't dangerous at all. I followed the instructions very carefully.

Advice If I were you, I'd go in for engineering.
Have you ever thought of voluntary work?
What about moving into a bungalow rather than a flat?
I think you should consult an expert before deciding.

Polite refusal I'd love to, but I'm afraid I won't be able to make it this time.
I really don't think there's much chance of my boss changing his mind, so I'll have to miss the party.
It's nice of you to offer, but I don't think we'll need any more help. Thanks anyway.

B In **most** lines of this letter there is one unnecessary word. It is either grammatically wrong or does not make sense. Write the unnecessary words next to the numbers on the right. Tick any lines that are correct.

Dear Susie,

Thanks very much for making babysitting last week. Rosie — 1 _____
and Steven really enjoyed it, and it gave me the chance to — 2 _____
get on with my work with very fewer interruptions than — 3 _____
usual. I've just started an interesting new project on — 4 _____
attitudes to recycling, of which the council are paying me for. — 5 _____
All very useful income by now that Paul's working part-time. — 6 _____

I may have to ask you to look after them again. It could — 7 _____
be next week, but even the one after is more likely. I'll — 8 _____
let you know soon. It's lucky for me than you're a friend and — 9 _____
can be such flexible. What would I do without you?! — 10 _____

By the way, I had spoke to Ivor about that tax problem. — 11 _____
Apparently I just add a note on my declaration, to make it — 12 _____
clear to the taxman. Now why didn't I think of that? — 13 _____

I hope your things are going well for you. — 14 _____

The best wishes, — 15 _____

Laura

C Rewrite this letter as if the Chairman of the Town Planning Committee were a friend of yours. Try to persuade him/her to take action on your behalf.

The Chairman
Rugley Council Planning Committee
St Anne's Hall
Rugley   CV21 2ZF

Dear Sir or Madam,

I am writing to protest in the strongest terms about Rugley Council's consent to the planning application submitted on 13 February 2002 by the developers, Haslers. Their proposal is a purely commercial one, with no thought given to the requirements or rights of residents in the Oxley Park area. We, the Friends of Oxley Park, are determined to resist any development of this beautiful and historic park, which has offered incomparable leisure activities to generations of Rugley residents. We are not only apprehensive about the disruption to our lives during the actual construction of the proposed blocks of flats, but we are also extremely angry that the town will be losing a public amenity which it will be impossible to replace.

We call upon you to reconsider your decision in the light of my remarks, bearing in mind the considerable public support for our stand. The petition handed in to the Council offices last Monday was signed by approximately five thousand people, as you are no doubt aware.

The Friends of Oxley Park are considering what legal action may be taken, in the event of your refusal to consult the wishes of residents. I can only reiterate that we are bent on opposing this ill-considered, blatantly profit-seeking proposal, and will fight tooth and nail for our voice to be heard.

I look forward to receiving your prompt reply.

Yours faithfully,

Gerald Portland
Secretary, Friends of Oxley Park

D Now do one or more of tasks 5–9 on **page 231**.

Notes, messages and postcards

Important points to remember when writing **notes and messages:**

a Make sure the message is clearly communicated.
b Make sure the tone is right (e.g. apologetic, friendly, business-like, etc).
c Always bear in mind the person whom you are writing to.
d Include all the relevant points.
e Sign a personal note or message, in most cases.
f Make sure you have chosen the correct register.

A Seven of these people have received a note. Match each note with the person for whom it was written.

flatmate	employer	postman	colleague
babysitter	mechanic	landlady	husband

1 Doug – Sorry, I've had to nip out to buy a sandwich. Help yourself to coffee from the machine. The file's on my desk. Back in 10 mins. *Roger*

2 Full service needed. Rear nearside brake light gone. Keys under sun shield. Any chance of it being ready by 3 pm?

3 Mrs Davenport – Will be late home today because our exam doesn't start till 4 pm. Could I please have my dinner at about 7.30? Very sorry to cause you this bother. *Juan Antonio*

4 Trevor – Your supper's in the oven. I've had to give the kids a lift to the youth club. Can you empty the dishwasher? *Pat*

5 Zoë – Girls are asleep, so hope you'll have a quiet evening! We're at my sister's (772166) so do ring if they wake up and make a fuss. Help yourself to anything you fancy in the fridge. Back by midnight. *Liz*

6 Anna – Axel rang. Can't make it tonight. Can you ring him at home when you get in? *Hazel*

7 Please don't leave parcels in porch. Next door (no. 30) will take them in.

When writing short notes and messages, you do not need to write complete sentences. As well as using abbreviations, you can often leave out personal pronouns (**I, he** etc.), articles (**a, the**), and sometimes even verbs:
• *Wants to see you a.s.a.p.*
• *Must dash – meeting has started.*
• *Gone to dentist. Home by 2.30.*

B Write a short message for each of these situations.

1 You are planning to go to lunch but will be back by 2.30 pm. Write the note that you leave for your secretary. (up to 10 words)

2 The photocopier at work keeps jamming. Leave a note for the caretaker, asking him to arrange for it to be repaired. (up to 15 words)

3 You are a doctor's receptionist. Dr Forbes' wife has just rung to ask her husband to collect their children from the tennis club on the way home. Write a note for the doctor. (up to 20 words)

4 You borrowed a dictionary from a fellow student's room while he was out. Your landlady tells you he was looking for it when he came back. Write a note to accompany the dictionary when you take it back, in case he is out again and you can't apologise to him in person. (up to 25 words)

5 You were alone in the house when your landlady's daughter rang this afternoon. She would like her mother to babysit for her on Saturday night. Write a suitable note to your landlady. (up to 25 words)

C Now write a longer note, paying special attention to the register required, for each of these situations. Use 50 to 100 words.

1 Write a note to the Chairman of a forthcoming council meeting, apologising in advance for your absence and giving your reasons.

2 A friend recently recommended a holiday company for a particular destination. You took his advice and had a wonderful holiday. Write a note to thank him for his recommendation, and describe one or two highlights of the holiday.

3 Write a note inviting a friend to stay for the weekend, and suggesting some places you might visit together.

(There is a model answer to 1 in **Section 13** of the Appendix.)

When writing **postcards**, remember that you do not need to write **Dear** …
It is not usual to put your address, but some people write the place and date:
• *Acapulco, 28.12.01*

Use the correct register. Most postcards are informal, so you can use colloquial language, contractions and exclamations. Keep formal postcards very brief and to the point. Use the same endings as for formal/informal letters.

You should sign a postcard. Make sure the name and address you are writing to are correctly laid out in the space provided. Note that when you already know someone, it's quite common to omit *Mr/Mrs* etc. from in front of their name.

D Put these parts of addresses in the correct order.

1 41/Surrey/Reigate/Valerie Burfield/Orchard Road/RG1 3BA

2 OX3 7MH/Princes Avenue/Dr J.B. Dodsworth/22 /Oxford

3 London/Mrs Ann Gilliatt/Court Close/SE10 8WX/79

4 Major K. Hennings/RH16 2HQ/High Street/Lindfield/4 /West Sussex

5 Campbell Street/Hexham Library/NE46 4RA/Hexham

E Rewrite these postcards. They contain mistakes in register, grammar and spelling.

1 My dear dentist,

I am having a wunderful holliday here. I am not writting to tell you this, but because I have just reminded that I won't can come for my apointment. I'll still be here in Hawaii! I apollogise most deeply for that. I'll ring you to do a new apointment when I get back. See you then!

Peter Greenaway

2 Dear my friend,

I am hoping all goes well with you and your family. How strange was it that I did not heer from you at christmas! Please will you phone me and come to lunch, if it isn't far enough to drive?

Lots of love and kisses,

Bettina

3 Dears Keith and Felicity,

Accept my warm thanks for the honnour you have done me in invitting me to yore home. However I am obbliged to point out that I shall be otherwise engaged on the partickler date you mention. Therefore, regretfully, I must decline.

Yours faithfully,

Roderick Marston

F Now write one or more of these postcards, in 50 to 100 words.

1 Write to thank some friends for a wonderful couple of days you spent recently in their country farmhouse. Say what you most enjoyed about your stay.

2 Write to wish a friend Happy Birthday and to let him know you are thinking of him, although you are living in different countries.

3 Write to a friend from a holiday resort, where your holiday is not going all that well. You regret going on your own, and next time you would like to go with him or her.

4 Write to a local sports club, where you are a member, informing them of your change of address.

5 You are sending a competition entry to a television station. Your answer to the competition is 'Look before you leap'. Write the postcard you send, stating your choice of prize (you would like the trip to Australia if you win) and your name, address and phone number.

(There is a model answer to 1 in **Section 14** of the Appendix.)

Instructions and directions

Some useful points to remember when writing instructions:

a Keep your points brief and clear.

b A numbered list of points may be appropriate.

c If your points are in paragraphs, a heading for each paragraph may help to focus the reader's attention.

d Use linking words to connect your points, if possible.

e You may use the imperative, for a more forceful style.

f Use the correct register: this depends on whom your instructions are aimed at.

Here are some useful phrases for use in instructions.

Whatever you do, don't ...	It's a good idea to ...
Try to avoid ..., otherwise ...	Don't forget to ...
Make sure you ...	You will need to ...
Be careful (not) to ...	This is especially important if/when ...

A Unscramble the instructions in this recipe.

A Mix in the milk to make a soft but not sticky dough.

B Roll out to 1 cm thickness.

C Turn the mixture on to a floured board.

D Sift the flour, baking powder and salt into a large bowl.

E Cut out 10 scones, using a 6 cm fluted cutter.

F Then knead the dough lightly till smooth.

G Rub the butter into the flour mixture.

H Bake for 10 minutes at 230°C.

I Place the scones on a greased baking tray and brush with a little milk.

J Finally, cool on a wire rack, before placing in an airtight container.

B The guidelines below are intended for students about to leave home and start their university course in another town. Decide which points should go under these five paragraph headings.

A WHERE TO LIVE   B THINGS TO AVOID   C STUDY SKILLS
D TIME OFF   E HELP!

1 Remember that there are trained people who can help you if you are worried or unhappy.

2 It is important to use your leisure time wisely.

3 If you apply early enough, you may be allocated a place in a hall of residence.

4 Try not to miss lectures or seminars if possible.

5 Make an appointment to see your personal tutor, or one of the university's student counsellors, to discuss your problems.

6 Make sure that you know what work is required of you.

7 Join one or two of the university clubs or societies, which are great places for meeting people.

8 However, you may prefer to share a flat with other students, or rent a room in a family house.

9 Don't be tempted to use drugs or alcohol to relieve stress.

10 Remember that some exercise is good for you, and that relaxation is also important. Try to incorporate both of these into your spare time activities.

11 Living with strangers can take some getting used to!

12 It is advisable to make a plan of the term's projects, reading, compositions etc., and to tick each one off as you complete it.

13 Don't run up bills if you can avoid it, and don't go into the red.

14 Try to find an angle of your studies that especially motivates you. This may provide an area of specialisation later.

C Write one or more of these sets of instructions, in about 150 words.

1 A cousin is going to have your two young children to stay for a night at her house. Write instructions about their evening routine, with any tips you can think of that will make their stay go smoothly.

2 You are lending your steam iron to a neighbour. As she hasn't used one before, write out some instructions for her.

3 You are a keen supporter of 'green' policies. Write guidelines for a colleague who asks what she and a group of friends can do to make a practical contribution to the environmental campaign.

(There is a model answer to 2 in **Section 15** of the Appendix.)

Here are some useful words and phrases for use in directions.

Watch/Look (out) for ...	roundabout
Turn/Bear right at ...	bypass
Go on past/over/across ...	pedestrian crossing
Drive/Go straight on ...	crossroads
Follow the signs to/for ...	junction
Take the left-hand turn ...	lane
You can park ...	track

D Complete the passage with words and phrases from the box above. Use each word or phrase only once.

Well, you come off the Birmingham 1) _____ at the exit marked Solihull. 2) _____ a signpost almost immediately, indicating Kindersley. Turn left, as it tells you to. Now 3) _____ the village of Kindersley. Slow down as you enter the village. There's always somebody on the 4) _____, so don't knock them over! Soon you come to a 5) _____. 6) _____, and follow signs to the church. It's just a narrow country 7) _____. 8) _____ a hump-backed bridge, then 9) _____ at the fork. Now 10) _____ till you reach the church, and just opposite there's a farm 11) _____. It's pretty muddy, because the tractors use it. Our house is twenty metres up the track, on the left. 12) _____ in the drive if there's room.

E Now do one or both of tasks 10 and 11 on **page 231**.

Articles, reports and proposals

> **An article** is a piece of writing for a newspaper, journal or magazine. It may aim to interest and entertain as well as to inform. It should have an eye-catching heading, which will make the reader want to read on. Its style will depend on the topic and on the type of publication. It will often include some description and narrative.

A Match each heading with the appropriate topic.

1 GREEN CARS	A Places of architectural interest
2 BUILDING SIGHTS	B Children's electrical design competition
3 UNDER THE SKIN	C Armed forces head is resigning
4 BRIGHT SPARKS	D Environmentally friendly vehicles
5 THE ANSWER'S A LEMON	E Survey of the effects of cosmetics
6 ONE MAN AND HIS DOG	F Benefits of cooking with citrus fruit
7 LOVE AT FIRST SIGHT	G Local man's relative has left him a fortune
8 MILITARY CHIEF STEPS DOWN	H Dead bodies discovered at bungalow
9 HOUSE OF HORROR	I A shepherd and his highly-trained collie
10 BOB'S YOUR UNCLE	J Romance between two film stars

B Put these sentences in suitable order to make a newspaper article.

A The most famous picture of Nessie, the Loch Ness Monster, is one of the greatest hoaxes of the century, according to its perpetrator.

B 'I'll go on looking for as long as it takes,' said a determined Rory McGrath from his motor-home parked overlooking the loch.

C But now it appears that Colonel Wilson was one of a group of conspirators, who succeeded in hoodwinking Fleet Street and the gullible British public.

D However, true Nessie fans say that this disappointing discovery will not stop them from searching for the lovable monster.

E It was revealed today that Scotland's best-loved tourist attraction is definitely a sham.

F The photograph spawned the flourishing Nessie tourist industry, which grew up around the shores of the loch.

G The picture was taken in 1934 by a respectable medical expert, Colonel Robert Wilson, and appears to show the long neck of a sea serpent rising out of the loch.

H Another of the group confessed, just before his death last November, that the 'Nessie' in the picture was, in fact, a model made of wood and plastic.

C Write an article on one of these topics, in about 250 words. Invent a suitable title for the article.

1 A student magazine has asked for views on the positive and negative aspects of living in a foreign country.

2 A quality newspaper has organised a competition for the best article on why reading books is more enjoyable than listening to the radio or watching television.

3 A local newspaper wants to hear what experiences visitors to its town have had.

4 A weekly international magazine has asked its readers to suggest alternative sources of energy which might replace oil or coal.

5 A quality newspaper is running a debate in its education section on the pros and cons of nursery education for pre-school children, and is asking for readers' opinions.

(There is a model answer to 2 in **Section 17** of the Appendix.)

A report is usually longer and more detailed than an article, and is generally aimed at people with some knowledge of the topic. It is a factual description of events or situations, and may include recommendations for further action. It may be written by one person or by a group, to be read by a sponsor, employer or colleagues, for example, or it may be published. A report should be written in a formal style, with a clear, business-like heading or title, and may have appropriate section headings.

A proposal has a similar layout to a report, but whereas a report describes past or present events, a proposal focuses on the future. It must be clearly structured, and must offer recommendations for action.

Here are some useful phrases for use in writing reports and proposals.

This report is intended to ...	It is based on ...
It appears that ...	It was felt that ...
According to ...	It is interesting to note that ...
It is recommended that ...	In short/On balance/To summarise, ...

D Your company recently sent you to a trade fair/exhibition. You have been asked to write a short report about it, which will be circulated to your colleagues.

Ask yourself questions before you begin to write.

Your answers to these questions should give you the raw material with which to write your report.

1 When was the fair/exhibition?

2 Where was it?

3 What was the name of the event?

4 Why did you go? What were your expectations, and were they fulfilled or not?

5 Were any companies sponsoring it?

6 What were the highlights? And the low points?

7 What lasting impression were you left with? Was there a 'message' for you in it?

8 Can you recommend it to other people? Why, or why not?

9 How long is the fair/exhibition on for?

10 How much does it cost to attend?

E Rewrite this short proposal where necessary, to produce a more appropriate formal style.

Changes to the office timetable

I've asked everybody, and they all agree that flexitime would be a good idea. Well, Molly at Reception doesn't want it, but then she'll probably have to be here from 9 to 5 anyway, won't she? Carrie and Mike in Design think the core time should be from 10 to 2. As you know, they always arrive and leave together, because he gives her a lift. They're neighbours, you see. They say they'd most likely do 8 to 4. It'd give Mike more daylight hours in his garden. But June, Rachel and Steve in Accounts want a longer core time. They think we should all be here between 9.30 and 3 p.m. And they want to know who will be answering the phone in each department if *everybody* decides to start at 9.30! Phil and Ted in Marketing are the only ones who're not sure about the plan. They say what about the poor customer? Shouldn't everybody be here from 9 to 5? But they like the idea for themselves. You know Phil likes the occasional game of squash – it's cheaper before 5 pm. And Ted sometimes has to collect his daughter from school. So, all in all, people seem well-disposed towards the scheme. I think we should now fix a core time and try it out for a month, then review it.

(There is a model answer in **Section 18** of the Appendix.)

F Write one or more of these reports or proposals, in 300–350 words.

1 You are studying English abroad. Write a report for a multinational class of students describing the languages and dialects spoken in your country.

2 Write a proposal for your local council on ways of improving the leisure and entertainment facilities available in your town or village. Make as many recommendations as possible.

3 Write a proposal for your employer on the feasibility of restructuring the working timetable for the workforce of twenty people at the factory (on the edge of a large town). Take into account factors like public transport and childcare arrangements.

4 Write a report on an international work camp you went on last summer. Include comments on the facilities, accommodation, food, work, other participants and the value or otherwise of the experience. The report will be submitted to the work camp organisers, and may be sent to future participants.

5 Write a report on a product (e.g. a car, a gadget, a cosmetic product, a new type of food) which a company asked you to try out. The report will be published in a consumer magazine.

6 You are a member of a group campaigning to reduce the use of cars and encourage people to walk, cycle or use public transport. Write a proposal to send to your MP (or other representative in government), suggesting what legislation should be introduced.

UNIT 85

Descriptive and narrative writing

Remember that it is important to describe details, to convey your own attitude and to include a human touch in any **descriptions** you write. Some useful vocabulary:

physical characteristics

freckles	bald	olive-skinned	tattooed
moustache	receding hair	ruddy-cheeked	pasty-faced
beard	greying	weather-beaten	spotty
dimple(s)	tousled	(sun)tanned	beetle-browed

size

plump	well-built	fat	minute	slender
stout	chubby	huge	tiny	thin
portly	tubby	enormous	petite	skinny

character

pushy	energetic	bubbly	caring
bossy	enthusiastic	bouncy	dependable
mischievous	sensitive	impulsive	down-to-earth
naughty	passionate	easy-going	witty

A In advanced writing, abstract nouns are often used to describe a feeling, a state or behaviour. Make nouns from these adjectives.

1 lazy	5 assertive	9 angry	
2 intelligent	6 strong	10 wrathful	
3 chubby	7 exhausted	11 resentful	
4 beautiful	8 embarrassed	12 sorrowful	

B Look at these notes and, including as many points as you can, write a description of Picasso's life in about 200 words.

Born in Malaga, Spain, in 1881.

Artistic training began in Barcelona in 1895.

Visited Paris in 1900, where he assimilated many different influences.

Painted Blue Period pictures, followed by Rose Period.

His painting was spontaneous and personal until 1906, when he converted to primitivism.

His Cubist period, with Braque, from 1907 to 1914.

After WW1 he returned to realism, producing elegant and precise drawings.

Married middle-class Olga Kokhlova.

Now a successful artist.

Began surrealist painting in 1925, producing disturbing and monstrous images.

Mainly sculpture from 1930 to 1934.

Visited Spain in 1933 and 1934.

Political comment in his famous painting *Guernica*, painted in 1937, expressing his horror of war and fascism.

Settled in the South of France in 1948.

Remarried in 1958.

Continued to paint, draw and sculpt until his death in Mougins, France, in 1973.

C Using these notes about a village called Chancton, write a description of it for someone who has never been there, in about 200 words.

Pros

Set in beautiful countryside. Farmland all around.

Good walking. Footpaths in all directions.

Friendly community. Everybody knows each other, and will help if anyone has a problem.

Useful small shops. Shopkeepers will order anything you want.

Relaxed lifestyle. Pleasantly slow pace of life.

Cons

No large supermarket, so range of foods not very wide.

No department store.

Shopping takes a long time in the small shops.

No cinema or theatre. Have to drive to next town 20 km away.

No railway station. Bus service links Chancton with nearest town, Broadmarket, but only once a week.

Few jobs available, so have to commute to towns in the area.

D Complete the sentences with these linking words and phrases.

as a result   moreover   otherwise   as though   all the same
as long as   as soon as   contrary to   as
even though   no matter   because of

1 There was a heavy snowfall, and _____ the flight was delayed.

2 I don't mind your driving _____ you don't go too fast.

3 She behaved _____ nothing had happened.

4 _____ the accident, the road was blocked.

5 We'll leave the country _____ we possibly can.

6 _____ I felt ill, I decided to go home early.

7 She knew he couldn't come, but she invited him _____.

8 _____ the doctor's orders, he was playing football again the next day.

9 _____ he's my friend, I wouldn't want to share a house with him!

10 _____ what they say, you shouldn't believe them.

11 They knew the money was stolen. _____, they knew who had stolen it.

12 You should work harder, _____ you won't get promotion.

E Now do one or more of tasks 12–16 on **page 231**.

Notices and leaflets

A **notice or sign** should attract the reader's attention and convey a message in just a few words. It may be effective to use different sizes of writing or type, or to put the heading in colour. Above all, the notice or sign must be easy to understand.

A Match the notice or sign (on the left) with the place where you might find it. Use each letter/number only once.

1	Please do not disturb	A	in an office
2	Out of order	B	on a bus
3	This is a hard-hat area	C	on a hotel bedroom door
4	No smoking	D	at the entrance to a park
5	Queue here	E	on a fence around a garden
6	Please have correct fare ready	F	on a public phone box
7	Shoplifters will be prosecuted	G	outside a building site
8	Please keep dogs on a lead	H	at a hotel reception desk
9	Ring for attention	I	outside a cinema
10	Private property	J	in a department store

B Put the items in these scrambled notices in the correct order, starting with the heading in capitals.

1.

Toni Sept 25 Holiday
AWAYDAYS
Andrew Sept 19 Leave of absence
Penny Sept 5 & 6 Holiday
Thanks – GBS 30.3.02
Julia Sept 28 Conference
Will all staff please note the following:

2.

Short walk to beach, shops and restaurants
Tel: 422066 for details   Sleeps 2/4
Beautifully appointed holiday apartment
PLAYA DE FORNELLS, MENORCA

3.

Classes as normal tomorrow   QUIET PLEASE
Architecture students to Room 42   External exams in progress

4.

my tan leather wallet?   Contact Dave in Room 10, Block G.
Last seen in the snack bar.   HAS ANYONE SEEN
It had £50, driving licence and credit card in it.

5.

Thanks – Anne   It's getting iced up.
We need them for reference.   CLEANERS
And please don't throw away newspapers.   Please defrost fridge.

C These are headings for notices which might be seen on a university students' noticeboard. Complete the notices with appropriate information in up to 30 words each. Remember to give a contact name and telephone number.

1 FOR SALE

2 LOST

3 LIFT WANTED

4 HELP!

5 FOURTH GIRL WANTED

6 SPANISH CONVERSATION LESSONS

> Notices are usually very short and snappy. To achieve this, you can use short sentences, contractions, initials and abbreviations.
> If the meaning is clear, you can also omit pronouns and, in certain cases, auxiliary verbs:
> • *Driving to London next weekend.* (= I am driving to London ...)

D Delete the words which are unnecessary in these notices, and make any other changes you consider appropriate.

1 **Country cottage in Scotland**
We have an exceptionally beautiful cottage to rent just outside the picturesque village of Auchencairn in Galloway. There are three bedrooms (one with a double bed, two with twin beds), a kitchen, a bathroom and a comfortable living room with a large fireplace. We have a big walled garden with views of the sea. We offer all modern conveniences including central heating. The rent is £400 a week. Write to Mrs S. Halday, Bay View, Auchencairn, Galloway.

2 **Drinks machine**
The soup has run out. For tea and coffee, the machine is only accepting 10p and 50p coins. The technician has been called and the machine will be repaired soon.

3 **Franking machine**
This is not to be used by any unauthorised personnel. Private letters may be franked, but payment must be made immediately, and a receipt issued by the receptionist.

E Write one of these notices, in up to 50 words.

1 You want to sell your car. Write an advertisement for the Cars For Sale column of your local newspaper.

2 You are a doctor's receptionist. Write a notice to display in the waiting-room, explaining how patients can get help if they are taken ill at night or at weekends.

3 You are the head of a large secondary school. Write a notice to be put up in every classroom, telling staff and pupils what they should do if fire breaks out.

4 You are organising a new Mothers and Toddlers group, which will be meeting in your local village hall. Write a notice to put on the noticeboard, giving details and the starting date and time.

5 You have a large garden, where you grow fruit, vegetables and flowers. You sell the surplus to passers-by. Write a notice to put on your gatepost, stating what you are offering, with prices and times when you are available to sell produce.

(There is a model answer to 4 in **Section 20** of the Appendix.)

> **Leaflets and information sheets** are usually produced and distributed by a group publicising its activities, a commercial organisation trying to widen its market, or a government or administrative body aiming to inform or warn the general public. As with notices, the heading should be eye-catching, and the details clear.

F Change this text so that its message is more striking. You can alter the layout as well as the words.

In only two hours the Heartbeat course will show you how to deal with someone who's choking, or with someone who's unconscious, how to control serious bleeding, how to check if the person is breathing, how to recognise a heart attack, and how to check if the heart has stopped and then take the appropriate action. A public training session is being held in August. Phone 676444 to book places.

(There is a model answer in **Section 21** of the Appendix.)

G Look at these headings of leaflets and say what kind of organisation produced them. Explain what you think the message of each leaflet is.

1 Dream Holiday Giveaway!
2 Save up to £100 on CDs!
3 Enter the £50,000 race to riches!
4 Pick up the phone
5 Annual Report 2000–2001

H Now do one or more of these tasks.

1 You are starting up a new restaurant in your area. Write a leaflet which you will deliver door to door, informing potential customers of the restaurant's whereabouts and what it offers. (about 100 words)

2 Write a leaflet to be issued by the local tourist office, giving advice to tourists on keeping valuables safe and avoiding attack or injury while on holiday. (about 200 words)

3 You are the secretary of a college environmental group. You would like to increase your membership. Write a leaflet explaining your group's aims and activities, to be circulated to students. (about 200 words)

4 Some foreign students are coming on an exchange visit to your school. Your teacher has asked you to write an information sheet for them, outlining the differences they will find in eating habits, daily timetable, social language and customs (you can choose their nationality). (about 250 words)

5 You are organising a language conversation group in your town. Write a leaflet, which will be delivered to as many houses as possible, explaining your ideas and asking people who are interested to contact you and/or attend the group's first meeting. (about 100 words)

Discursive essays

In **discursive essays**, an abstract topic is discussed, using neutral, or, more often, formal language. It is crucial to read the question or title carefully, in order to decide on the correct approach. You may be asked to write an essay on a theme, a quotation or a set text. For the CPE compulsory writing task, you will be asked to write discursively in the form of an article, an essay, a letter or a proposal, so your writing style needs to be suited to the format. (See **Unit 80** for formal letters and **Unit 84** for articles and proposals.)

Discursive essays, in whatever format, need to be carefully planned. The completed task should show a logical sequence of ideas and a clear structure: introduction, main section and conclusion.

A Match these informal remarks with their more formal equivalents.

1 Look, I'm absolutely sure that ...
2 Loads of people say ...
3 People have got it all wrong when they say ...
4 I just can't stand ...
5 I think ... is a brilliant idea.

6 Don't you think that ...?

A I am strongly opposed to ...
B I am totally in favour of ...
C I am convinced that ...

D I would suggest that ...
E Contrary to popular belief, there is no evidence that ...
F Many people maintain that ...

B Read this extract from a magazine article about whether famous people are entitled to keep their personal lives private. Then answer the questions.

Celebrities claim to be hounded by the paparazzi, who apparently allow them no privacy or space to 'be themselves'. But isn't it *their* fault, for seeking the limelight? Surely they must accept the consequences of fame along with its many rewards. Aren't we entitled to know the details of their personal lives? After all, we pay to watch them act or play football or present TV programmes – without us, they would not *be* celebrities!

1 What are the writer's main arguments?
2 What opposing views can you think of?
3 What is your personal opinion?
4 How would you organise the ideas you have written down, if you were asked to write an essay on this topic?

C Read this paragraph from a newspaper article on urban living. The editor has asked readers to contribute their opinions, so you want to write a letter expressing your own views. After reading the text, answer the questions that follow.

Large cities hold a strong fascination. For many of us they act like a magnet, drawing us irresistibly to them. They offer amazing opportunities for work and play, but there is a price to pay, in terms of expensive housing, greater exposure to crime, and reduced space for leisure activities. So, is urban living now an outdated concept? Or is it the way forward? If so, how can we make our cities more attractive places to live in?

1 What are the main ideas expressed in the text?

2 Which of these ideas do you agree with?

3 Which of them do you disagree with?

4 What further points could you make, either agreeing or disagreeing with the writer?

5 How could you answer the writer's questions?

6 What would your conclusion be, including your personal view?

7 How would you organise the answers to these questions, in your letter of reply?

D You have been asked to write an article for a health magazine on ways in which people can improve their general health and fitness. First, choose from statements a–m the ones you wish to include in your article. Then re-order them to make three paragraphs.

FITNESS FACTORS

a) Stress, at work and at home, can contribute to heart disease and stress-related illnesses, such as migraine.

b) More fibre in the diet makes for better digestion and helps to prevent bowel cancer.

c) Excessive alcohol consumption can cause liver disease.

d) It is important to cut salt and fat intake, in order to reduce the likelihood of heart disease and circulatory problems.

e) Cigarette smoking can cause bronchial disease and lung cancer.

f) Eating fewer sugary foods will result in less tooth decay and better weight control.

g) Recent tests have shown that even passive smoking can cause lung cancer.

h) It is essential to maintain a well-balanced, varied diet, in order to provide the body with all its needs, and to control weight.

i) Alcohol is also addictive: it is better to limit oneself to a 'safe' number of units per week.

j) Exercise can be both enjoyable and healthy, as it controls the appetite, gives a feeling of well-being, reduces susceptibility to many diseases, and helps to eliminate stress.

k) Vitamins taken in fruit and vegetables help to give resistance to infection.

l) A person may have to change his or her lifestyle, if it is producing excessive stress.

m) Habits which are harmful to health should be controlled.

Now write the complete article in 300–350 words, using any of sentences a–m and any of these linking words and phrases. Write your own introduction and conclusion. You should have five paragraphs altogether.

> To start with, ...   For some, ...   For others, ...
> Not only... but (also) ...   In today's health-conscious society ...
> While/Whereas ...   In addition, ...
> Another point to remember is that ...
> A further factor to consider is ...   However, ...
> In conclusion, ...   On balance, ...   To sum up, ...

(There is a model answer in **Section 22** of the Appendix.)

E Rewrite this sentence five times, using the following linking words and phrases: *In spite of, nevertheless, yet, however, although.*

Many experts believe that energy consumption in developed countries should be reduced, but governments are having difficulty in achieving this.

F Complete the sentences correctly, choosing from these jumbled endings and putting the words in the correct order.

> street still available the on addicts to readily are supplies
>
> excellent qualifications his
>
> this go planning the are authorities to ahead with
>
> expensive extremely are they
>
> impersonal is rather service the
>
> eye eye he always to with hadn't them seen

1 Rolls Royce cars have a legendary track record for quality and reliability.
   However, _____

2 Buying food from a supermarket is convenient and saves money. On the other hand, _____

3 Unfortunately Robin failed to get the job, in spite of _____
   _____

4 Malcolm was sad to leave the colleagues he had worked with for so long, although _____

5 Customs officials have been very successful in discovering massive drug hauls, yet _____

6 A fierce campaign is being waged against the introduction of higher prescription charges. Nevertheless, _____
   _____

G Plan and write these essays, in 300–350 words, using introductory and linking expressions from this unit.

1 'To travel hopefully is a better thing than to arrive.' (Robert Louis Stevenson)
   Do you agree? Explain your ideas.

2 'The greatest of evils and the worst of crimes is poverty.' (George Bernard Shaw)

   Do you agree? Suggest some practical ways of reducing poverty in countries with high unemployment.

3 'The hand that rocks the cradle is the hand that rules the world.' (William Ross Wallace)

   Do you agree? Should both parents play an equal role in bringing up a child? And how important is a child's upbringing in determining his or her future impact on society?

4 'Politics and sport should always be kept separate.'

   Do you agree, or can you think of situations where they might complement each other?

5 'The achievements of advanced technology have made our lives more complicated, not simpler.'

   Do you agree? Explain your ideas.

Reviews and short stories

A review may be of a film, play or book, but it may also be of a restaurant, hotel or exhibition. It should include an overview of the subject, with all the relevant facts, a description or presentation of its good and bad points, and a conclusion or personal recommendation. It may include narrative as well as descriptive language, and the style may vary according to the intended readership.

Here are some useful phrases for use in reviews.

The book/film/programme/exhibition deals with/tells the story of/ focuses on/includes ...

The story/plot is based on ...   The hotel/restaurant/café provides ...

I found the photography/acting/ending ...

The staff/whole cast are incredibly ...

It conveys a sense of ...   It exudes an atmosphere of ...

Grant's acting/performance/portrayal of ... was ...

Each chapter/scene is devoted to/involves ...

I was bowled over by ...   I was most impressed by ...

A Match these nouns, related to the cinema, theatre or radio/television, with their definitions.

1	cast	A	part of a television series
2	stage	B	where a film/programme is made
3	screen	C	actors in a play/film
4	studio	D	person financially responsible
5	broadcast	E	part of a play/film
6	plot	F	part of a theatre
7	stunt	G	radio/TV programme
8	scenery	H	clothes worn by an actor
9	producer	I	part of a cinema
10	costume	J	moveable background for a play
11	scene	K	dangerous action
12	episode	L	events or storyline

B Match these adjectives and nouns to make phrases used to describe hotels. Then decide which are positive and which are negative.

1	inventive	A	staff
2	comfortable	B	atmosphere
3	obsequious	C	prices
4	cosy	D	brochure
5	complimentary	E	beds
6	misleading	F	corridors
7	astronomical	G	newspapers
8	draughty	H	cuisine

C These are adjectives you might use to describe a play, film etc. Divide them into two lists: positive and negative.

boring	unusual	awful	informative	brilliant
successful	fantastic	amateurish	stunning	original
conventional	unimaginative	witty	fine	outstanding
hopeless	predictable	thrilling	amazing	superb
dreadful	horrible	great	pathetic	dull

D Choose the correct word or phrase from the pair in brackets to complete each sentence.

1 Barry Thomas wrote a stinging _____ of your friend's book in *The Times*. (critic/review)

2 Fellini is one of Italy's best-known film _____. (directors/managers)

3 The actors had to learn their lines from the _____. (book/script)

4 It's a long play but fortunately there's a twenty-minute _____ after Act Two. (pause/interval)

5 Spielberg's films are famous for their _____. (special effects/ particular tricks)

E Choose from the list A–J the best phrase to fill each gap. Use each correct phrase only once. There are more answers than you need.

HOT STUFF FOR CURRY FANS

The Pride of Bengal Tel: 244224

This popular restaurant has become one of the jewels of Indian cuisine in Northwick, constantly drawing a regular stream of customers, 1) _____ and beyond. Since taking over from the previous incumbent last May, Ahmed Uddin and his family have spent a small fortune transforming 2) _____ and building up a faithful clientele. Ahmed's management and his uncle Malik's considerable culinary talents combine to ensure the smooth running of the restaurant, 3) _____. All food is freshly prepared to order on the premises, and vegetarians are well catered for. Takeaways are available at a 10% discount, 4) _____ at a very reasonable price in the comfort of your own home.

With its spacious new layout, the Pride of Bengal has capacity for 70 diners, with large smoking and non-smoking areas, 5) _____. It is well situated at the corner of Newmarket Road and Stoneygate, 6) _____, and it is open for lunch and dinner seven days a week.

Each time I've eaten there, I've been impressed by the inventiveness of the cooking and the exceptionally charming and efficient staff. I strongly recommend the Pride of Bengal for those of you 7) _____ in stylish and comfortable surroundings.

A who have an excellent track record

B who come from within the area

C who want a memorable meal

D where he had established his business

E which means you can eat quality food

F what most customers really want

G where ample free parking is available

H what was a fairly run-down property

I both of which are air-conditioned

J which offers an extensive selection of exotic dishes

When writing a **short story**, make a plan, bearing in mind the word limit. Create interest at the beginning, to keep the reader's attention. Add colour by using carefully chosen vocabulary. Make every word count, by selecting exactly the right word or phrase to communicate a feeling, manner or behaviour.

Remember that characters must be believable. Do not just tell the reader about your characters: show them in action. Dialogue can be useful for this.

F Put these story plans into the following order: Introduction, Development, Suspense, Ending.

1 a) Peter goes abroad to find a job, and Lucy is lonely.
  b) Just in time Peter returns (his death was only a rumour) and marries Lucy.
  c) A young girl, Lucy, grows up with her childhood sweetheart, Peter.
  d) Lucy hears of Peter's death, and decides to marry his cousin, Bob.

2 a) A girl from one family and a boy from the other fall in love.
  b) There is a long-standing feud between two important gangster families.
  c) When their families find out, the young couple die accidentally in a shoot-out.
  d) They marry in secret, knowing their parents will never agree.

3 a) They hatch a clever plot to kill their rich uncle.
  b) They succeed in killing him and inheriting his fortune.
  c) A man and his wife are desperately poor but have a good relationship.
  d) They both feel guilty and conscience-stricken: their relationship is ruined and they now hate and fear each other.

Here is an example of using dialogue to give the reader a better understanding of a character in a story:
• *Her boss was a short-tempered, impatient man, who chain-smoked and had no sense of humour.*
  'It's not funny, I tell you!' Mr Sinclair snapped. 'Take that dog away at once!' He stubbed out his cigarette and picked up the packet on his desk.

G Now do the same with these descriptions of character.

1 My grandmother was worried about my diet, and always tried to make me eat more.

2 The Prime Minister was quick-thinking and decisive, especially in an emergency.

3 The Chief Inspector was really more interested in jazz than pop music, but he did not want to hurt his assistant's feelings.

4 Jane was very careful with money, and never bought anything without comparing prices in various shops first. She was always delighted with a bargain.

H *'You'll never win!'* said Tom. *Said* conveys nothing of Tom's feelings. Match the verbs on the left with the impression of Tom's feelings that they convey.

1	bellowed	A	He was pleased or triumphant.
2	whispered	B	He was angry or rude.
3	gasped	C	He was dismissive or mocking.
4	sighed	D	He wanted to keep it a secret.
5	exclaimed	E	He was sad or depressed.
6	sneered	F	He was frightened, shocked or out of breath.

I In **most** lines of this story there is a spelling or punctuation mistake. Write the correct spelling or punctuation next to the number on the right. Tick any lines that are correct.

The little boy walked down the tree-lined street, kicking   1 _____

a can aimlessly alone the pavement. He had his hands deep   2 _____

in his pockets, and a wurried expression on his face.   3 _____

Sureley his mother should be home soon! She was always   4 _____

their when he came home from school. She would be in the   5 _____

kitchen, with her apron on, ironing or peeling potatos.   6 _____

He would rush in dump his sports bag on the table, and   7 _____

give her a big hug. Than he would tell her all about his day.   8 _____

But today the big house was empty. He had his own key,   9 _____

so hed been able to get in, but now he just didn't know   10 _____

what to do. Were could she be? She never went anywhere,   11 _____

even when Dad was live, and since his death she had not   12 _____

wanted to leave the house except for shoping and the   13 _____

occasional visit to her sister.   14 _____

'Auntie Josie! Perhaps that's it!' he thought. 'Perhaps   15 _____

Auntie Josie's ill and, Mum's gone to look after her.'   16 _____

He started walking purposefuly towards the station. He   17 _____

was the man in the family now, and he would have to   18 _____

collect his mother from Auntie Josies.   19 _____

J Do one or more of these tasks, in 300–350 words.

1 Write a short story beginning or ending with the words *Smiling, he picked up the receiver and started dialling.*

2 Write a review of a book you have read recently, for the cultural section of a national newspaper.

3 Describe and compare two different types of television programme you have seen recently, as part of a letter to a friend who did not see them.

4 Write a review, for the leisure and travel section of your local newspaper, of a country hotel in your area.

(There are model answers to 1 and 3 in **Sections 23 and 24** of the Appendix.)

UNIT 89

Help with writing tasks

1 The most important thing is to **read the question carefully** and make sure that you answer every part of it.

2 Make **notes** on what you are planning to include in your writing, and work out a clear and logical **plan**.

3 Think about the **register** you should write in. Is it formal or informal? If you are writing a note, letter, article or report, who is it for?

4 To make your plan clear, write in clearly-defined **paragraphs**, which should be indented, or separated by a line space. Each paragraph should represent a step forward in your thinking, or a new topic, but paragraphs should be connected to each other with linking words.

5 Check how much **time** you are allowed (2 long tasks in 2 hours for CPE, 1 composition and (usually) 2 short tasks in 2 hours for CAE).

 Allow enough time for planning, and keep an eye on the clock as you write. You will lose marks if you do not finish answering the question.

6 Get used to writing straight on to the paper in **ink**, as there may not be time to write a rough draft in pencil first.

7 When doing writing tasks at home, keep a check list of your **common mistakes**, and check your work for these before handing them in.

8 Do not become too reliant on your **dictionary**. You will not be allowed to use one in the exam.

9 **Mistakes** should be neatly crossed out with one pen stroke. Try to present your work as tidily as possible. If your handwriting is difficult to read, make sure it is at least legible.

10 Get used to **counting your words**. You can do this roughly by counting words in several lines, and finding your average line count, then multiplying by the number of lines on the page. You will soon be able to estimate how many words you have written, just by looking at your work on the page.

 Try to keep close to the required number of words. You will not be penalised specifically for writing over the word limit, but the part of your work that is over the limit will not be marked, which may mean that you lose marks for not fully answering the question.

Additional writing tasks

1 You are a member of Coltsfoot Cycling Club. The local newspaper recently published a letter criticising the behaviour of cyclists in the town. At the same time, your club asked members to complete a questionnaire on cycling in Coltsfoot. The results of this survey were published in the club's newsletter.

The club's chairman has asked you to write to the newspaper on behalf of your fellow cyclists, in order to give the public a more balanced view. You also decide to write a personal note to the chairman, telling him what you have done, and commenting briefly on the results of the survey.

Read the letter below, to which you have added your comments, and the results of the survey. Then, selecting the information carefully, write an appropriate **letter** to the newspaper (about 150 words) and a **personal note** to the chairman (about 100 words).

On the warpath

Dear Sir,

I'm glad to see that wayward cyclists are being <u>targeted by police</u> and can only say that it's not before time.

Is this fair?

As a pedestrian I have had many close encounters or even confrontations with <u>pavement cyclists</u> or those riding straight <u>through red lights on pedestrian crossings.</u> I have on occasion stood my ground in the face of a cyclist heading for me at breakneck speed on the pavement. Usually these <u>offenders</u> expect pedestrians to move out of the way, but on ever busier pavements this is not always possible.

Of course this is irresponsible

Sometimes roads are too dangerous for us!

That's why we need cycle lanes!

There are very few like this

I think it's high time that these cyclists are reminded that they are the ones who are breaking the law and are in the wrong – not the pedestrians. The pavement is for pedestrians and the <u>road is for cyclists!</u>

But we have to share it with motorists!

Yours faithfully,

Bradley Wood

Coltsfoot

WHAT YOU THINK
Results of our survey carried out in March

• *Are you dissatisfied with Coltsfoot's traffic management system?*	YES 94%	NO 6%
• *Are you in favour of a complete network of cycle lanes in Coltsfoot?*	YES 100%	
• *Should cycle lanes be separated from the road by a barrier or safe distance?*	YES 98%	NO 2%
• *Should cyclists be allowed by law to share pavements with pedestrians?*	YES 10%	NO 90%

Thanks to all of you who sent back your questionnaires. Your views matter!

(See Appendix, **Sections 25 and 26**, for model answers.)

2 'The punishment should fit the crime.' Do you agree? State your opinion. (about 350 words)

3 Write a review of your school's production of a musical, for your local newspaper. (about 250 words)

4 Write a note to your boss, telling him about a problem you have had recently with a colleague, and asking him/her to help solve it. (about 100 words)

5 Write a letter, giving advice to a friend who is determined to leave home and marry her boyfriend. They are both eighteen. (about 250 words)

6 You are settling into a new job in a new town. Write to your family, giving details of your living arrangements and daily routine, and saying whether you are happy or not. (about 250 words)

7 A friend of yours has written to you, asking for some advice. He wants to visit your country for three weeks this summer, and would like to know which places to visit, where to stay, what sights to see, and what clothes to bring. Write to him, giving as many practical suggestions as you can, and mentioning any national customs that may seem strange to him. (about 250 words)

8 An acquaintance of yours has offered to help out in your office, in a temporary part-time capacity, while your receptionist is on maternity leave. You feel she would not be suitable for the job, as she gets easily flustered, and is not very organised. Write to her, thanking her for her offer, but refusing politely. (about 100 words)

(See Appendix, **Section 12**, for model answer.)

9 You have let one of your friends down rather badly. Now you have to write to him or her to apologise and explain why it happened. Describe your feelings as well as the train of events leading up to the incident. (about 200 words)

10 Write careful instructions for a friend who is going to stay in your house while you're away. Include instructions on keys and locking up, feeding pets, watering plants, using your hi-fi equipment, and what to do in an emergency. (about 150 words)

11 You have a second home which you rent out to summer visitors. It is just outside a small village, and rather difficult to find. Write the directions that you send to any visitors who book the cottage. (150–200 words)

(See Appendix, **Section 16**, for model answer.)

12 Describe your favourite hobby or sport to someone who has never tried it, and say why you like it. (about 350 words)

13 Describe your childhood, and say how it has affected your life. (about 350 words)

(See Appendix, **Section 19**, for model answer.)

14 Describe the town or village where you were born or brought up, indicating its advantages and disadvantages from your point of view. (about 350 words)

15 Describe the most interesting person you have ever met, including his or her physical characteristics. (about 350 words)

16 Describe the most embarrassing or frightening experience you have ever had. (about 350 words)

1 Verbs which do not usually take the continuous form

dislike, like, hate, love, wish, prefer, want, hear, sound, understand, suppose, remember, recognise, realise, mean, know, imagine, guess, doubt, believe, astonish, satisfy, surprise, please, impress, belong, concern, consist, contain, possess, own, owe, matter, need, depend, deserve, fit, include, involve, lack, appear, resemble, seem

(See Unit 2, Present tenses)

2 Verbs which can be used in simple or continuous tenses, with different meanings

look, see, smell, taste, feel, think, measure, weigh

(See Unit 2, Present tenses)

3 Verbs which are usually followed by a gerund (-*ing* form)

admit, appreciate, avoid, consider, contemplate, delay, deny, detest, dislike, dread, endure, enjoy, escape, excuse, face, fancy, feel like, finish, forgive, give up, can't help, imagine, involve, leave off, mention, mind, miss, postpone, practise, put off, recollect, resent, resist, risk, can't face, can't stand, suggest, understand

(See Unit 7, Gerund and infinitive)

4 Verbs which are usually followed by the infinitive with *to*

want, would like, would prefer, ought, have, be able, appear, seem, decide, attempt, intend, plan, hope, expect, arrange, manage, fail, pretend, dare, afford, tend, teach

(See Unit 7, Gerund and infinitive)

5 Verbs and expressions which can be used with either a gerund or an infinitive, with different meanings

remember, forget, regret doing: a past action or state
• *I'll never forget seeing the World Cup final.*

remember, forget, regret to do: information to be remembered or passed on
• *I regret to inform you ...*

stop/go on doing: stop or continue doing the same action

• *He decided to stop smoking.*

stop/go on to do: the current activity is stopped, and a new one started
• *He stopped to light his cigarette.*
• *She went on to explain how it had happened.*

be interested in doing: keen on (a hobby or an interest)

be interested to do: would like to do
• *I'm interested to know what you thought of the film.*

try doing: use a technique in order to achieve something
• *Try soaking it in salt water to loosen the stain.*

try to do: attempt something, usually unsuccessfully
• *He tried to persuade her to go with him.*

need doing: an object (usually) needs something done to it
• *The house needs painting.*

need to do: a person (usually) needs to do something
• *Gregory needs to find a job.*

be/get used to doing: be or become accustomed to certain actions or situations

used to do: habitual actions in the past, but not now

like/enjoy/love/hate/prefer doing: any action generally liked/enjoyed/hated etc.

would like/enjoy/love/hate/prefer to do: an activity chosen or rejected for a particular occasion

allow/advise/forbid/permit doing: general permission/advice etc.
• *The doctor advises giving up smoking.*

allow/advise/forbid/permit someone to do: permission/advice etc. for a particular person
• *I forbid you to climb that wall.*

mean doing: involve/entail/signify something
• *Love means being able to forgive.*

mean to do: plan/intend an action
• *I didn't mean to hurt you.*

(See Unit 7, Gerund and infinitive)

6 Structures used after reporting verbs

1 verb + *(not)* to do:
• *We refused to have anything to do with the plan.*
• *He threatened not to come.*
promise, agree, refuse, threaten, offer

2 verb + someone + *(not)* to do:

• *He advised her to say nothing about it.*
warn, beg, remind, recommend, tell, persuade, advise, encourage, instruct, order, invite

3 verb + *that* + verb clause:
• *She pointed out that she had been there first.*
claim, state, explain, add, report, boast, complain, point out, agree, confirm, estimate, promise, insist, admit, deny

4 verb + preposition + doing:
• *He insisted on seeing the manager.*
apologise (to someone) for, accuse someone of, insist on, object to someone, congratulate someone on, blame someone for, thank someone for, charge someone with

5 verb + someone *(that)* + verb clause:
• *They assured me that there was nothing to worry about.*
assure, inform, tell

6 verb + doing:
• *He admitted having sent the letter.*
admit, deny, regret

7 *suggest* + doing/*suggest that* someone should do something
(See Unit 11, Reported speech)

7 Adverbs and adjectives used adverbially
(All meanings given below refer to adverbial usage only.)

close (to): near
• *We live very close to the hospital.*
closely: intimately
• *She's closely related to the archbishop.*

direct: without stopping or making a detour
• *We're going direct to Paris.*
directly: a) immediately
• *He'll do the shopping directly.*
b) frankly
• *The producer spoke honestly and directly to the cast about the play's future.*

easy: in a relaxed way
• *Take it easy!*
easily: with no difficulty
• *You can easily go in for that competition.*

fair: according to the rules
• *Play fair!*
fairly: a) justly, honestly, correctly
• *He was fairly judged and punished.*
b) quite, not very
• *It was fairly good weather, but not as good as last week.*

fine: well
• *She's feeling fine now.*
finely: in tiny pieces, in meticulous detail
• *Chop the onions finely.*
• *The lines of the pen-and-ink sketch were finely drawn.*

flat: a) completely, outright
• *They turned me down flat.*
b) lower than the correct musical note
• *She always sings flat.*
c) in an exact or short time
• *He arrived in four minutes flat.*
flatly: a) completely
• *He flatly refused to help me.*
b) in a dull, lifeless way
• *'What's the point?' she asked flatly.*

free: a) without paying
• *He was allowed in free*
b) at liberty
• *They let the dog roam free.*
freely: willingly, as much as desired
• *They partook freely of their hosts' generous hospitality.*

hard: with great energy
• *His father has always worked hard.*
hardly: scarcely, only just
• *You'll hardly have time to get to the bank.*

high: at or to a height
• *She jumped high over the bar.*
highly: to a high degree
• *The professor's work is highly respected at Oxford.*

late: opposite of early
• *They arrived at the meeting very late.*
lately: recently
• *The neighbours have been making a lot of noise lately.*

near: close to
• *Does your boss live anywhere near us?*
nearly: almost
• *They nearly had an accident this morning.*

pretty: quite, fairly
• *They're pretty good at carpentry.*
prettily: nicely, charmingly
• *The little girls were prettily dressed for the party.*

right: correctly (normal adverbial use)
• *Do it right, for heaven's sake!*
rightly: correctly (referring to a whole clause)
• *He had assumed, rightly, that no food would be provided.*

sharp: punctually, on the dot
• *They turned up at ten sharp.*
sharply: brusquely, crossly
• *'Don't do that!' she said sharply.*

short: suddenly, just before the end
• *He stopped short.*
• *She cut him short.* (= she interrupted him)
shortly: soon
• *News of the takeover will be released to the press shortly.*

sound: deeply (with *asleep*)
• *He was sound asleep.*
soundly: deeply, thoroughly
• *He was sleeping soundly.*
• *They were soundly punished.*

tight: in a close, firm way
• *Sit tight.* • *Hold tight.*
tightly: firmly and securely
• *The mast was tightly lashed to the deck.*

wide: a) a long way away, far from the target
• *The parents searched far and wide.*
• *The arrow fell wide of the target.*
b) fully open
• *Open (your mouth) wide!*
c) completely (with *awake*)
• *The children were wide awake.*
widely: in many places, all over the world
• *Those theories are widely accepted.*

(See Unit 14, Adverbs)

8 Prepositional phrases

above
all, average (size/height), -mentioned, suspicion, freezing(-point), zero

over
a cup of tea/coffee/a meal, all ~ the world, and above the call of duty, pull the wool ~ someone's eyes, the odds

beneath
contempt, marry ~ you

below
sea-level, the belt, freezing(-point), zero

under
age, contract, control, guarantee, his/her etc breath, pressure, stress, suspicion, the circumstances

at
all costs, a loose end, a loss, a profit, any rate, best, first, first sight, hand, heart, high speed, large, last, once, peace, present, random, risk, sea,

short notice, the beginning, the end, times, war, worst, someone's disposal

by
accident, all means, chance, cheque, day, degrees, far, force, hand, heart, mistake, night, oneself etc, plane/taxi/train etc, post, return, rights, sight, surprise, the way, your own admission

between (usually two people or objects)
you and me, jobs

among (more than two people or objects)
the bushes/trees, themselves, others

in
advance, all likelihood, any case, bed, cash, conclusion, control, danger, debt, detail, doubt, due course, fact, full, future, general, good/bad condition, hand, ink, pain, particular, person, public, reply, retrospect, short, tears, the end, the long run/term, time, trouble

on
a diet, approval, a visit, behalf of, business, call, duty, earth, fire, foot, guard, holiday, horseback, land, offer, your way home, paper, purpose, second thoughts, the contrary, the mend, the other hand, the whole, time, your own, your own admission

out of
breath, control, danger, date, doors, focus, hand, luck, reach, order, pocket, practice, sight, stock, the question, work

(See Unit 21, Prepositions)

9 Adjectives/nouns with dependent prepositions

admiration for
advance on
advantage in/over/to
angry about/at/with
appeal to
attack on
attitude towards
aware of

benefit to

chance of
change in/from
concerned about/in/with
confidence in
confident of
confined to
conscious of
contrary to

convinced of
critical of
crowded with
curious about

damage to
danger of/to
dealings with
death from
delay in
deprived of
deterioration in
developments in
devoted to
difficulty in doing
disappointed at/in/with
disposed towards
doubt about

eligible for
envious of
essential for/to
exception to
expert in/on

faith in
familiar with
famous for
fed up with
foreign to
free from/of
friendly towards

good at/for/with
greedy for
guilty of

habit of
honest with
hope for/of
hungry for

ignorant of
ill (in bed) with
important for/to
impression on
improvement in/on
incapable of
increase in
independent of
indifferent to
indignant at
influence on/over/with
intention of
interested in
involved in

jealous of

keen on
key to

lacking in
likelihood of
limit to

missing from

need for
(be) news to
noted for

obstacle to

occupied with
opinion about/of/on
opportunity of/for doing
opposed to

particular about
patient with
peculiar to
pleasure in
point in
poor in/at
popular with
possibility of
preferable to
pride in

qualified for
question of

reason for
relationship between/
    with
relief from
reputation for
responsible for/to
restricted to
restrictions on/to
result of
revenge for/on
rich in
rise in

safe from
satisfied with
self-sufficient in
sensitive to
solution to
strict about/with
substitute for
success with
superior to
surprised at
suspicious of
sympathetic towards
sympathy for/with

threat of/to
typical of

victory over
views on

(See Unit 24, Dependent prepositions)

10 Verbs with dependent prepositions

accuse someone of
agree on/to/with
allow for
amount to
apologise for
appeal for/to
apply for/to
approve of
attend to

bargain for/with
beat someone at
benefit from
blame someone for, something on
boast about/of

care for
change into
charge someone for/with
cheat someone out of
compete against/with/for/in
compliment someone on
concentrate on
condemn someone to
confess to
confide in
conform to
congratulate someone on
consent to
contribute to(wards)
convince someone of
cure someone of

deal with
decide between/on
declare war on
depend on
deprive someone of
die for/from/of
differ from
disapprove of
discourage someone from

end in/with
enter into (an agreement etc)
equip someone with
excuse someone for/from

feed someone/sth. on
fish for
fit someone/sth. with
fool someone into
force someone into
forgive someone for

grow in/into
guard against

have pity on
have sympathy for
help oneself to
hint at
hold sth. against someone

impress on someone
impress someone with
inform someone of/about
insist on
insure against
interfere in/with
invest in
involve someone/yourself in

keep something to yourself
know of

listen (out) for
live by/for/on/up to

make someone/sth. into
make up your mind about
mean something by
mistake someone/sth. for

object to

part with
plead guilty to
prevent someone/sth. from
profit from
provide for/with
puzzle over

reason with someone
reduce something by, someone/sth. to
resort to
restrict something to
result from/in
rob someone of

sacrifice someone/sth. for/to
seethe with
share something with
show mercy to(wards)
speak of
specialise in
struggle against/with
succeed in
suffer for/from
supply someone with
surrender to
suspect someone of

take advantage of
think about/of
threaten someone with
trust someone with
turn someone/sth. into

warn someone about/against
wait on
watch (out) for
work at a job etc/on a project etc
worry about

(See Unit 24, Dependent prepositions)

11 Formal letter (Unit 80, D1)

Wick Hall School
Simonstone
Burnley
Lancs. BB12 8HL

20th March 2002

Professor J. Barker
Somerville College
Oxford OX1 2AP

Dear Professor Barker,

I would like to thank you for leading the Self and Peer Assessment workshop so efficiently and enthusiastically. Your preliminary talk was quite an eye-opener for most of the staff, but several of them have told me how much they enjoyed it and the workshop activities that followed. Thank you for a most successful session.

I hope you will find time to lead another staff development workshop for us next year.

Yours sincerely,

Edward Prendergast (Headmaster)

12 Informal letter   (Unit 90, 8)

Dear Lucy,

      Thank you very much for your kind offer. I do appreciate it, especially as I know how busy you are at the moment. But I've discussed it with Jo Smith, my partner, and she agrees with me that we really need a full-time replacement for Jackie. It's a pretty tough job at Reception, what with the phone going all the time and customers needing constant attention. I think we'll advertise in the local press, and until then Jo's secretary will be responsible for the switchboard.

      Anyway, we're very grateful to you for wanting to help. I hope you're not too disappointed.

          Best wishes,

          Caroline

13 Long note   (Unit 82, C1)

Dear Toby,

Unfortunately I won't be able to make the next meeting, as I've got to go abroad on business for a couple of weeks. Please pass on my apologies. I'm sure you'll be able to manage without me! I'll be at the one after, of course.

Kind regards,
Mark Toller

14 Postcard   (Unit 82, F1)

Had a wonderful time with you both last weekend. Really enjoyed the trip on the river, and that gorgeous walk over the moors. Nice being able to have a good long talk about life, just as we used to. Hope to see you up here soon. Let me know if you feel like coming any time. Thanks again, and have a good summer!

Love,
Babs

15 Instructions   (Unit 83, C2)

First, stand the iron upright and set the dial to 0. Then pour water in. Remember to use distilled water only, as this is a hard water area. Don't fill the iron higher than the MAX line.

Next, plug the iron into the socket. You have to choose the correct temperature setting, depending on the material. They're clearly marked on the dial. Setting number 4 is for steam. When the iron has heated to the correct temperature, the little red light goes out, so you can then start ironing. You can push the spray button if you want to dampen something – a difficult crease, for example.

When you've finished, unplug the iron and pour away the rest of the water. Turn the dial back to 0, and let the iron cool down, standing upright.

It's very simple really.

16 Directions   (Unit 90, 11)

Make sure you take the Malaga bypass (it's called la Ronda de Malaga). You get a good view of the city and the sea as the road sweeps round the back of Malaga. Follow signs to Almeria. The bypass comes to an end at Rincon de la Victoria, where you join the main road. There's a fork at this point. Bear left and follow the coast road eastwards until you reach Torre del Mar.

As you pass Muebles Garcia (a large furniture store on your right), you will see a signpost to Algarrobo on your left. Take this narrow road which winds steeply uphill. Watch out for some fairly sharp bends!

About 17 kilometres from the coast, you will see our village, Competa, straight ahead of you. Don't take the road into the village, but turn sharp right on the Torrox road, past the Villa Chile.

After another 4 kilometres, take a dirt track to the left which passes a white stone shrine. Fork right round two more bends, and our house is the second on the left, up a steep drive. It's called Casa Juliana, and the name's painted on the wall.

17 Article (Unit 84, C2)
Speaking volumes

My idea of heaven is reading *Far From the Madding Crowd* in a hayfield in summer, with rolling wooded downs around me. Or it might be *A Christmas Carol* in front of an open fire, with the curtains tightly drawn to keep out the cold. You can take a book anywhere with you, to read on the train on the way to work, or at the airport while waiting for your flight, or to sunbathe with on the beach. It is the most portable form of entertainment, and comes in all shapes and sizes. And because you do not have to concentrate all your senses on reading (there is no flickering screen to watch, or disembodied voice to listen to), your surroundings can add to the reading experience. You are almost unconsciously aware of the jolting of the train, or the scent of wild flowers, or the warmth of the sun on your skin. This gives an extra dimension to your reading, and you may in future associate butterflies with *Nineteen Eighty-Four*, or the smell of Ambre Solaire with *War and Peace*, or freshly ground coffee with *The Hound of the Baskervilles*.

Radio and television have their place as purveyors of current affairs, international events, educational information and light entertainment, but for me books are simply a source of endless delight. Who can read of the deaths of famous literary characters such as Sydney Carton, Piggy, Lord Jim and Heathcliff without emotion? Only the written word has the power to inspire as well as to move.

18 Proposal (Unit 84, E)
Changes to the office timetable

The proposed scheme The proposal for a flexitime working timetable has been considered by the entire staff, and approved by almost all personnel. Only the receptionist (MW) is not in favour, but this may not affect the success of the scheme, as she will almost certainly have to maintain her normal 9 to 5 working day in any case.

Core time The Design Department (CA and MS) suggest a core time of 10 to 2. They envisage working from 8 to 4 if the scheme is introduced. However, the Accounts Department (JG, RN and SB) propose a longer core time of 9.30 to 3. They also point out that it is essential for cover to be provided in each department for the whole working day.

Negative feedback The Marketing Department (PH and TV) have reservations about the scheme because of the impact it may have on customers.

Nevertheless, they are personally in favour of flexitime.

Recommendations As there are few objections, I recommend that a core time should be fixed, and the scheme tried out on an experimental basis for one month, to be reviewed after that time.

19 Description (Unit 90, 13)

I was brought up in a large house in a medium-sized town, with a younger brother and sister. When we were young I had my own bedroom, and I still love having my own space. I was allowed to read for hours at night, because I wasn't disturbing anybody. But when we all got a bit older, my brother had to have his own room, and I had to share with my sister. I resented it at the time, and I think I still hold it against him a bit, even now.

My mother managed brilliantly on a schoolmaster's small salary, producing the most delicious meals out of scraps and leftovers. But we could never afford large joints of meat, and to this day I cannot eat a lot of meat. I am much happier eating vegetables, eggs, rice and so on. We were all made aware of the value of money at an early stage, and because of that I am careful with money, even now.

I went to the local girls' grammar school. Everyone agreed it was the best school for miles. I certainly thought it was, at the time. I loved everything about it: the bottle-green uniform, the currant buns at break, the rules, the teachers, the damp smell in the basement, the hockey field, the school song ... I was intensely proud to be part of it, and studied my way eagerly up the school, becoming a House Captain and Prefect, and doing in every way what was expected of me.

It was only when I went to university that I began to challenge some of the doctrines I had been taught at school, and to realise that learning to think for yourself is more important than learning what someone in the past thought. These days I do not conform to the rules of society quite so slavishly, and am prepared to question a decision or stand up for a principle.

It was, all in all, an extremely happy childhood, which I think has given me a pretty balanced and positive outlook on life.

20 Notice (Unit 86, E4)

Mothers and Toddlers

New group starting Monday May 10th in village hall. All mothers and toddlers (0-5 years) very welcome. Mon, Wed and Fri 9.30-11.30 a.m. £3.50 per session for church funds. Please bring unwanted books and toys for children to use. For further details ring Sue Jones on 810350.

21 Leaflet (Unit 86, F)

HEARTBEAT

In only 2 hours the Heartbeat course will show you how to

- deal with someone who's choking
- deal with someone who's unconscious
- control serious bleeding
- check if the person's breathing
- recognise a heart attack
- check if the heart has stopped
- take appropriate action

A public training session is being held in August. Phone 676444 **NOW** to book your place!

22 Discursive essay (Unit 87, D)

In today's health-conscious society, more and more attention is being paid to the benefits of exercise, a balanced diet and a healthy lifestyle. People want to maintain their fitness throughout their lives and into a healthy retirement. For some, a radical change to the habits of a lifetime is needed; others will merely continue their present healthy lifestyle.

To start with, habits which are harmful to health should be controlled. Not only can cigarette smoking cause bronchial disease and lung cancer, but recent tests have shown that even passive smoking can cause lung cancer. Excessive alcohol consumption can cause liver disease, and alcohol is also addictive: it is better to limit oneself to a 'safe' number of units per week. Help in controlling these habits is available at NHS and private clinics, or alternative treatments such as acupuncture and hypnosis may be useful.

'We are what we eat', and therefore it is essential to maintain a well-balanced, varied diet, in order to provide the body with all its needs, and to control weight. Vitamins taken in fruit and vegetables help to give resistance to infection, while more fibre in the diet makes for better digestion and helps to avoid bowel cancer. In addition, it is important to cut salt and fat intake, in order to reduce the likelihood of heart disease and circulatory problems. Another point to remember is that eating fewer sugary foods will result in less tooth decay and better weight control.

A further factor to consider is stress, at work and at home, which can contribute to heart disease and stress-related illnesses, such as migraine. A person may have to change his or her lifestyle, if it is producing excessive stress. However, there is a partial solution in the form of physical exercise and relaxation therapy. Exercise can be both enjoyable and healthy, as it controls the appetite, gives a feeling of well-being, reduces susceptibility to disease, and helps to eliminate stress. Yoga, meditation, massage and listening to music are all types of relaxation therapy which are popular and often very effective.

In conclusion, no matter how fit we imagine ourselves to be, there is always room for improvement. Reducing nicotine and alcohol intake, establishing a balanced diet, and incorporating both exercise and relaxation into the daily routine would certainly be beneficial for most people.

23 Short story (Unit 88, J1)

Smiling, he picked up the receiver and started dialling. 'Ready, Benson?' he asked quietly. 'Check on your men, will you? I want this to go without a hitch, you understand?' He put the phone down, and, still smiling, looked at himself in the mirror. A good-looking, grey-haired man stared back at him, with piercing cold blue eyes and an air of authority. The smile did not seem to connect with the eyes, and soon it faded. Cosgrove sat there for a while, looking out over the roofs of the city, and drumming his fingers impatiently on his desk. This was his most ambitious project so far. Failure would spell disaster for him. But could he pull it off, where so many others had tried and failed?

Meanwhile, George Benson had stationed his men at pre-arranged positions along the route. He was confident they would play their part well when the moment came. They had all been carefully selected for their military background and physical fitness, and all the details of the ambush had been practised over and over again. Cosgrove had seen to that. George Benson shivered when he thought of his chief's cold smile. He had a feeling that an unpleasant fate would be in store for him if he let Cosgrove down.

From his window, Cosgrove watched the cavalcade of black limousines leave the gates of the President's mansion, and start their slow, deliberate progress down the wide avenue. Now the cars were approaching the corner, where the road narrowed and the police motorcyclists could not ride close to the Mercedes, which was flying the presidential flag. 'Now!' said Cosgrove. 'Where the hell is Benson?'

Benson was, in fact, in the back of a police van, where Cosgrove was soon to join him. The police had been alerted by one of Benson's own men. So there was no ambush that day. To the great relief of the authorities, Cosgrove and Benson were given life sentences for the assassination attempt. But when, a year later, Benson was found dead in his cell, in suspicious circumstances, those who knew Cosgrove had no doubt what had really happened. Cosgrove himself just smiled when he heard the coroner's verdict of accidental death.

24 Review   (Unit 88, J3)

I can't understand why you haven't been watching *The Boys in Blue*. It's on on Saturdays, starting at 10 pm on BBC2. It's one of the best police series I've ever seen. I know you're not all that keen on thrillers, but really, this is excellent. The hero (good-looking, blue eyes etc!) and his team are detectives who work for the C.I.B., whose job is to investigate complaints made about the police. So they're checking up on their colleagues, in a way. The main plot develops over ten or twelve episodes, with a new character or twist or sub-plot every Saturday. I have to concentrate really hard on it! The script is very realistic – it sounds just like policemen talking. Of course there's a bit of violence, but also very interesting character development. I almost think of the C.I.B. team as real people now!

The other programme I usually watch is *Food for Friends* on Tuesdays at 8.30 on BBC1. Last week two top chefs were competing to produce a starter in two minutes. It was quite thrilling to watch as they beat eggs and chopped parsley and squeezed lemons, talking all the time, as the clock on the screen ticked inexorably away! They do wine-tasting as well. It's quite different from *The Boys in Blue*, of course, as it's informative and amusing, and very relaxing to watch.

But *The Boys in Blue* is so well done and so gripping that I really think you should watch it. Give *Food for Friends* a miss, maybe, but make a date for 10 p.m. on Saturday!

25 Letter to a newspaper   (Unit 90, 1)

Dear Sir or Madam,

As a member of the Coltsfoot Cycling Club, I was interested to read Bradley Wood's letter last week about problems experienced with what he calls 'wayward cyclists'.

Naturally, it is extremely irresponsible of cyclists to ride on pavements or cross red lights, and fortunately there are very few cyclists who behave like this. However, they only do it because, when traffic is heavy, roads become too dangerous for them. It may be true in a legal sense that 'the pavement is for pedestrians and the road is for cyclists', but it does not work in practice, because cyclists have to share the road with motorists. It is also unfair for cyclists to be 'targeted by police', as other road users (motorists in particular) are frequent offenders.

Cyclists need their own space, and this means giving them a network of wide cycle lanes, separated from the road, if possible, by a barrier or safe distance.

Yours faithfully,

Adele Lloyd

26 Personal note   (Unit 90, 1)

Dear Morgan,

I've written a letter to *The Coltsfoot Herald*, as you asked me to. (Copy attached.) Let's hope they publish it, and then perhaps there can be a more balanced discussion of the issues.

The survey results show pretty clearly that hardly any cyclists are happy with the way things are. It's time for pedestrians and motorists to consider *us* for a change! Interesting, though, that very few of us want to be allowed to ride on pavements. Decent cycle lanes are definitely the way forward.

Anyway, see you at the next meeting.

Regards,

Adele

Unit 1

A 1 The, –
  2 –, –, the
  3 the, the, a
  4 the, a, a, –, a
  5 –, –, –, a, the, –
  6 –, –, a, a, the
  7 a, an
  8 a, –
  9 –, –, –
  10 a

B 1 the Himalayas
  2 ✓
  3 the Lake District
  4 ✓
  5 to Kathmandu
  6 the Annapurna region, the Nepalese
  7 ✓
  8 The group leader, the River Trisuli
  9 the world's, of Mount Everest
  10 the group, simple village rooms, the Nepalese
  11 the group, the Himalayas
  12 the most exciting, to Nepal, the very first

C 1C 2U 3U 4C 5U 6U, C 7C 8U

D 1D 2E 3B 4G 5F 6I 7A 8H 9J 10C

Unit 2

A 1i 2g 3h 4a 5d 6c 7b 8e 9d 10f 11i 12c 13a 14d 15g 16f

B 1 ✓
  2 ✓
  3 ✓
  4 Do you understand what the lecturer said?
  5 I think that they made a mistake.
  6 ✓
  7 The police don't know why he came here.

  8 ✓
  9 ✓
  10 He's commuting to Paris every day this week.

C 1 You look very worried. What are you thinking about?
  2 Listen, he's climbing the stairs! What's he doing now? He's ringing the bell!
  3 Thank goodness Barbara is taking more exercise these days! She seems much fitter, don't you think?
  4 When water boils, it gives off steam.
  5 Alex never breaks a promise or lets down a friend.
  6 The house stands on its own, on a hill that overlooks the park.
  7 I know her husband is looking for a new job at the moment, but I don't suppose he will find one quickly.
  8 When you heat the pan, the fat begins to sizzle.
  9 The Foreign Ministers of several EU countries are currently meeting in Luxembourg, where they are attempting to negotiate a solution.
  10 He's always spilling coffee on his shirt! It makes me furious!
  11 At weekends she frequently drives up to her mother's in Liverpool, and spends an evening with her sister on the way back.
  12 I'm a bit worried about Greg. He's working too hard in his present job. He really needs a holiday.

D 1 I have been studying English here since August.
  2 ✓
  3 We met several fascinating people at the conference last week.

  4 Once upon a time a beautiful princess lived in a castle ...
  5 ✓
  6 I've owned this answerphone for three years.
  7 They haven't sold all the tickets for the Cup Final yet.
  8 My friends have been married for a long time now.
  9 ✓
  10 A light plane has crashed in the French Alps.
  11 I've already spoken to the delegates three times.
  12 ✓

E 1 I haven't had time to do any typing since Monday.
  2 Nobody has heard from Amanda since she went to the Seychelles.
  3 She's worn/been wearing the same old clothes for a week.
  4 He hasn't ridden a bike since 1970.
  5 I don't think I've seen you since the sales conference.
  6 It hasn't snowed here for ages.
  7 They've lived/been living in that house since it was built.
  8 My neighbour hasn't spoken to me for more than two years.
  9 I haven't bought a new battery since last year.
  10 She's been waiting for you for an hour and a half.

Unit 3

A 1 dare   5 be able
  2 should   6 have
  3 used   7 ought
  4 May   8 will

B 1 Did you have to ...?
  2 ... ought to have given you ...

3 The President can't be re-elected for a fourth term.

4 ✓

5 I might have returned the book.

6 Will you be able to help me ...?

7 They couldn't have a picnic because of ...

8 ✓

C 1 needn't
2 has to
3 must
4 have to
5 had to
6 didn't need to
7 needn't have bothered
8 mustn't

D 1d 2e 3d 4f 5c 6a 7d 8f

E 1D 2G 3A 4C 5H 6E 7B 8F

F 1 couldn't   5 couldn't
2 would   6 were able to
3 could   7 could
4 used to

G 1 can we?
2 oughtn't I?
3 will/won't you?
4 wouldn't you?
5 mustn't he?
6 mightn't it?
7 didn't they?
8 will you?
9 shall we?
10 don't you?
11 had I?
12 couldn't we?

Unit 4

A 1B 2A 3C 4E 5F 6D

B 1 won't
2 'll/will, ✓
3 Shall
4 will, ✓
5 will

6 Shall
7 won't
8 ✓, ✓
9 ✓, 'll

C 1 ✔
2 'What are you doing/going to do tonight?' 'Oh, we're having a barbecue.'
3 By this time next week I'll have filled in my tax forms.
4 I promise I'll support you whenever you need me.
5 You won't see him this summer. He'll be doing his military service then.
6 I'm going to be an architect when I finish my studies.
7 ✓
8 Will you come/Are you coming to dinner with me tonight?
9 I think he'll/he will probably marry the girl next door.
10 What will you be doing at 3 o'clock next Sunday afternoon?

D 1 If you don't object, we'll ask the committee to approve the proposal.
2 By the time Juan finishes/has finished his maths project next week, he'll be exhausted!
3 What will our world be like in the year 2050?
4 Anne won't be happy until she sees/has seen the doctor this afternoon.
5 This time next year I'll probably be living on the other side of the world.
6 I'm not going to watch the horror film that's on tonight. I know it will give me nightmares.
7 By the end of this week we'll have raised over £800 for the children's charity.
8 I swear I'll do my best from now on. Things will be different, you'll see.

Unit 5

A 1b 2a 3d 4b 5d 6a 7b 8d 9c 10a 11a 12b 13d 14a 15b 16c 17d 18b 19a 20c 21d 22b 23c

B 1 taste   5 article
2 touch   6 turned
3 dare   7 pressed
4 heavy   8 hold

C 1 has
2 been
3 the
4 as
5 to
6 an
7 the
8 its/a
9 will/may
10 has
11 a
12 the
13 is
14 may/could
15 in
16 which/that
17 If
18 surround
19 continuing
20 have

D 1 can   6 to   11 are
2 a   7 the   12 ✔
3 do   8 being   13 be
4 from   9 should   14 are
5 ✔   10 ✔   15 ✔

Unit 6

A 1 had received/had been receiving, told
2 made, had been
3 had tried, met, fell in love
4 found, wanted, had graduated
5 (had) asked, was not, had gone
6 arrived, realised, was still breathing

7 spent, had finished

8 hit, were playing, were having

9 was raining, beginning, set out

10 was, wanted

11 recognised, had been

12 opened, felt, had been ringing

13 went back, were still quarrelling

14 did not answer, was trying

15 did you get

16 (had) worked, moved

B 1 My aunt (had) worked in London before she moved to Norwich.

2 ✓

3 ✓

4 The judge brought the trial to an end yesterday.

5 ✓

6 Pierre owned a sailing boat for several years.

7 The company were thinking of giving ...

8 ✓

9 ... just before the British team arrived.

10 A police car almost knocked me over as I crossed/was crossing the road.

11 ✓

12 'Oh, a group of students who arrived in Oxford a week ago.'

13 ✓

14 ✓

15 The mountain seemed very high ...

C 1 'So-called villain of the piece' and 'merely circumstantial' evidence.

Suggested answers:

2 He desperately wanted to be king/He was prepared to take other drastic action to gain or keep the crown/The princes, Elizabeth and their cousin were all dangerous rivals, with a better claim to the crown than he had.

3 They came to an end when Henry Tudor, leader of the house of Lancaster, conquered King Richard III, leader of the House of York, at Bosworth in 1485.

4 To establish his power, and to bring lasting peace by ending the conflict between the Houses of Lancaster and York.

5 The removal of the princes cleared the way for Richard to become king. He had the opportunity to kill them, because he was their uncle, living close to them and seeing them regularly. After his death he was presented to the public as a wicked assassin by Tudor propaganda. A final point is that he never denied the rumours that circulated at the time, naming him as the murderer.

Unit 7

A 1 Taking regular exercise ...

2 I don't mind being interviewed ...

3 ✓

4 ✓

5 ✓

6 You can go sightseeing ...

7 In addition to losing all my money ...

8 ✓

9 It's no use telling me ...

10 ✓

11 Most cats enjoy being stroked.

12 I'm afraid I just can't face going into the witness box and telling ...

B 1 They didn't ask me to leave early.

2 The army made him complete his training course.

3 ✓

4 Try not to keep interrupting the speaker this time.

5 ✓

6 ✓

7 ✓

8 In my view parents should not let their children watch too much television.

9 He enrolled at a language school in Pisa to learn basic Italian.

10 ✓

11 She didn't want you to go to all this trouble for her.

12 ✓

C 1 being

2 to enter

3 to know

4 seeing

5 to reduce

6 reviewing

7 to stir up

8 being, going

D 1C 2B 3C 4D 5A 6A 7A 8B 9D 10D 11A 12A 13A

Unit 8

A 1 make

2 hadn't eaten

3 have

4 had been

5 is

6 take

7 leave

8 asked

9 had dropped

10 were

11 would have been/would be

12 are

13 Were

14 happens

15 broke down

16 like

B 1 ... go on defying instructions, there will be/we will take ...

2 ... to change your mind, we would be ...

3 ... turn out to be true, I'll hand ...

4 ... passes the final examination, he'll be ...

5 ... had been muzzled, it wouldn't/couldn't have bitten ...

6 ... been presented, the prisoner might/would have been ...

C 1D 2E 3B 4A 5C 6G 7F 8H

D 1 come
2 had just landed
3 didn't agree
4 are
5 end up
6 had spotted
7 receive
8 hadn't gone
9 hadn't come
10 weren't
11 hadn't heard
12 find

E 1 I wish he weren't/wasn't so boring.
2 I wish I hadn't accepted that job.
3 I wish they hadn't all heard about it.
4 I wish I had shares in the company.
5 I wish he would contribute his opinions more tactfully.
6 I wish I had gone to the conference.
7 I wish I could remember Myra's address.
8 I wish it would stop snowing.

Unit 9

A 1 was originally used
2 being put
3 is known
4 was/has been successfully deployed
5 is involved
6 be laid out
7 was ended
8 were punctured
9 is hoped
10 be caught

B 1 had been found
2 were discovered

3 were/have been pronounced
4 were not made
5 be carried out
6 was thrown
7 were made
8 was published
9 are handed over
10 be regarded

C 1 ✓
2 The whole community was/were told the news.
3 ✓
4 ✓
5 I have been given a lucky mascot ...
6 She will be awarded a postgraduate diploma ...
7 He is being refused a chance to participate ...
8 ✓
9 ✓
10 The officials in charge of the institution at the time seem to have been offered a bribe.

D 1 ... are expected to be announced ...
2 ... are understood to be going up ...
3 ... is said to have had ...
4 ... are feared (to have been) lost ...
5 ... was considered/thought/ judged to be ...
6 ... cannot be denied/is true/ is undeniable that certain mistakes were ...
7 ... was reported to have been helping ...
8 ... was alleged that the accused had ...

E 1 put away
2 slept in
3 ✓
4 put off
5 ✓
6 brought up
7 made out
8 taken down

Unit 10

A 1a 2c 3b 4c 5d 6b 7c 8a 9c 10b 11d 12c 13b 14d 15a 16c 17b 18c 19b 20a 21d 22c

B 1 rather 5 catch
2 see 6 form
3 free 7 threw
4 reach

C 1 the
2 were
3 order
4 being
5 was/became
6 should
7 to
8 did (were/was)
9 succeed (successful)
10 would
11 A
12 with/involving
13 one
14 The/This
15 solved/resolved
16 would/could
17 were
18 for
19 All
20 towards

D 1 one 9 own
2 still 10 in
3 of 11 quite
4 ✓ 12 ✓
5 was 13 being
6 the 14 so
7 to 15 But
8 very 16 ✓

Unit 11

A 1D 2B 3A 4H 5C 6E 7G 8I 9J 10F

B 1 She boasted (that) she had had better marks than anyone else all term.
2 She accused me of stealing her watch.

3 She threatened to hit me if I didn't give her my money.

4 She apologised for not getting round/not having got round to writing earlier.

5 She suggested (that) we should all go for a drive in the country/going for a drive in the country.

6 She insisted on seeing the manager at once.

7 She begged me not to tell anyone I had/I'd seen her.

8 She confirmed (that) my flight was taking off at midnight.

9 She reminded me to bring the binoculars.

10 She estimated that Mexico City had about 20 million inhabitants.

C 1I 2L 3A 4K 5J 6H 7C 8F 9D 10G 11B 12E

D 1 He pointed out that it was already five o'clock.

2 He agreed to help.

3 He assured me (that) there would be no difficulty.

4 He thanked me for bringing the flowers.

5 He advised me to keep it under my hat.

6 He added (that) there would be a 2% surcharge.

7 He denied robbing/having robbed the old lady.

8 He refused to make a speech.

9 He warned me to be careful when I crossed the road.

10 He congratulated me on passing the test first time.

11 He blamed Charlotte for letting them down.

12 He admitted causing/having caused/(that) he had caused the accident.

E 1 She said that if she had known, she would have come earlier.

2 He said that unless John told the truth, somebody

would get hurt.

3 She said (that) she really thought (that) I should join the tennis club that summer.

4 Her teacher said that if she practised more, she might be able to make a career out of music.

5 He said that he wouldn't have had the accident if the brakes had been repaired properly.

6 The magistrate said (that) he would be sent to prison if he committed a further offence.

7 He said (that) I could stay there as long as I liked.

8 Maggie said (that) she wished Bob would buy himself a new suit.

F 1 I asked how far it was to the station.

2 ✓

3 She asked me if I could do the shopping for her.

4 Her father asked if what she had told him was true.

5 ✓

6 The traffic warden asked why I had parked there.

7 I asked the old man what his recipe for long life was.

8 We wondered how our neighbours managed to keep their garden so neat.

9 The officials asked him what he wanted.

10 ✓

G 1A 2C 3E 4H 5B 6D 7F 8G

H 1 ... congratulated me on passing ...

2 ... apologised for forgetting to ...

3 ... (that) Jim should put off his marketing trip ...

4 ... me to put/enclose a cheque in ...

5 ... me to run through my speech ...

Unit 12

A 1 In spite of revising/having revised/ In spite of the fact that he (had) revised hard for his exams, he didn't pass.

2 ✓

3 All the same, he doesn't know what he's talking about.

4 ✓

5 ✓

6 ✓

7 ✓

8 Quiet though this spot seems now, ...

9 'Try a bit harder!' 'But I don't want to!'

10 ✓

11 In spite of/Despite your lack of agreement, ...

12 Even though his creditors are baying for satisfaction, ...

B 1 aware

2 Deprived

3 Alone

4 Because

5 Sad

6 for

7 Surprised

8 Told

9 Horrified

10 Due

11 Embarrassed

12 Disgusted

C 1 The matter is important enough for you to deal with yourself.

2 She didn't study enough to pass the end-of-term test.

3 The door was too narrow for us to squeeze through/ wasn't wide enough for us to squeeze through.

4 She had too little energy/ She didn't have enough energy to keep going all day.

5 The leisure centre is too inaccessible/isn't accessible enough for tourists to find.

D 1 They had so little money (that) they couldn't afford to run a car.

2 There was such a lot of food (that) we could have fed ten hungry men with it!

3 You're such an experienced worker (that) you should know what to do.

4 He has had so little acting experience that we can't give him the part.

5 I draw so badly that I can't do a very good sketch map.

E 1 ever needed/should ever need

2 see

3 is

4 has got lost

5 spots, tries

6 was selected

7 don't get

F 1 the undersigned

2 are as follows

3 respectively

4 The former

5 The latter

6 In terms

7 aforementioned

8 hitherto

9 the above address

10 twice

11 Gourlays

12 Merryford

13 a complaint about the closure of a village bank and a request for the bank to reconsider its decision

14 the undersigned, the former, the latter, the aforementioned, hitherto

Unit 13

A 1 There's the woman who sold me the oranges.

2 This is my brother, whose wife's French.

3 ✓

4 I don't like people who talk too loudly.

5 ✓

6 I know a little taverna where you can get a wonderful meal.

7 ✓

8 I suppose that's the house where we'll have to stay.

9 ✓

10 ✓

11 What I can't stand is queuing in the rain.

12 Have you any idea who I'll be speaking to?

13 Is that the school where/at which you studied/which you studied at?

14 Deirdre will show the new students what to do.

15 You'd better tell me the reason why he didn't turn up.

16 That's the old chap (who) ...

17 ✓

18 ✓

B 1a She was only interested in going to Strasbourg, and let other trains pass until the Strasbourg train arrived.

1b She took the first train to arrive. It happened to be going to Strasbourg.

2a Everybody was caught unawares because they hadn't seen the forecast.

2b Only some people (the ones who hadn't seen the forecast) were caught unawares.

3a All the food was bad, so we couldn't eat it.

3b Some of the food was bad, so we couldn't eat that part.

4a I only have one cousin. He/She happens to live in New Zealand.

4b I have several cousins. One of them lives in New Zealand.

5a They only picked some of the fruit – the fruit that had ripened.

5b They picked all the fruit. By the way, it had all ripened.

C 1 The bus that goes up Edward Avenue doesn't stop at the railway station.

2 The debate the backbenchers had demanded went on all night.

3 The escaped convicts stashed away the gold bars they had stolen in an earlier bank raid.

4 It was the dream cottage she had always wanted.

5 They booked into the hotel where they had stayed on their honeymoon.

6 The bodyguards who were flanking the King had revolvers concealed inside their jackets.

7 It wasn't their dog but their cat I was taking care of.

8 They cut down the tree that had died.

9 That's the cruise I've always wanted to go on.

10 I think it was the manager I was speaking to.

D 1 It's the tallest building I've ever seen.

2 ✓

3 ✓

4 ✓

5 He'll be playing with the same racquet he always plays with.

6 Next Tuesday I'll have to visit the dentist again, which I detest.

E 1 She had invited a hundred guests, none of whom I knew.

2 Growling in the corner were two big dogs, both of which looked extremely dangerous.

3 The manager called in my new colleagues, one or two of whom I had met already.

4 There were several large holes in the road, three of which had to be repaired urgently.

5 There were some vegetables left over, a few of which I was able to use in some soup for supper.

6 The talk was attended by over two hundred delegates, most of whom took notes.

7 The researchers reported back on the questionnaires, the most interesting of which showed a marked change in leisure habits among older people.

8 He comes from a large family, all of whom now live in Australia.

Unit 14

A 1 gracefully
2 well
3 importantly
4 fully
5 straight
6 hard
7 heavily
8 cruelly
9 timidly
10 illegally
11 inevitably
12 fast
13 noisily
14 in a jolly way
15 increasingly

B 1 Tomorrow the boss is having a day off/The boss is having a day off tomorrow.
2 She likes watching videos at home very much/She very much likes ...
3 ✓
4 ✓
5 Yesterday they mowed their lawn/They mowed their lawn yesterday.
6 ✓
7 Suddenly he slammed the book down on the table.
8 Alma stamped out of the office angrily/Alma stamped angrily out of the office.
9 I always make sure I do my homework every day.

10 We frequently go for a picnic in the forest.
11 The foreman always gives the workmen a ticking off.
12 ✓

C 1 With hindsight/In retrospect
2 in the wake of
3 by ... %
4 in monthly instalments
5 Without more/further ado
6 at the expense of
7 With reference to
8 by no means

D 1 at the end
2 eventually
3 at the beginning
4 actually
5 at last
6 finally

E 1 close
2 easy
3 finely
4 pretty
5 shortly
6 tight
7 highly
8 hard
9 widely
10 sharp
11 free
12 fair
13 flat
14 direct
15 late
16 flatly
17 sound
18 short
19 nearly
20 right

Unit 15

A 1a 2b 3c 4a 5c 6d 7b 8c 9c 10d 11c 12d 13b 14a 15c 16c 17a 18b

B c, e, a, d, b

C 1 ... being blamed for ...
2 ... causing/having caused harm to ...
3 ... a shortage of ammunition, the battle was won ...
4 ... your scheme is, it is doomed to ...

5 ... enjoy/like her company, I find her/I think she's ...
6 ... is rumoured to be planning ...
7 ... were awarded without more ...
8 ... cut me short/cut in halfway ...

D 1 by
2 may/might/could
3 which
4 have
5 which/that
6 they
7 Recently/Newly
8 to
9 order/detail
10 could
11 producing
12 could
13 which/that
14 spreading/transmitting
15 wake/light
16 is
17 will/may

E 1H 2C 3B 4F 5A 6D 7J

Unit 16

A 1 Seldom had they participated in such a fascinating ceremony.
2 In vain did I plead with him. He was adamant.
3 Under no circumstances will Miss Weaver be offered the job.
4 Should the film be a box-office success, there may be a sequel.
5 So surprised was he to be addressed by the Queen that he didn't answer at once.
6 Had they confirmed by phone, the airline could have warned them.
7 Hardly had he entered the house when the police arrested him.

8 Never for one moment did I think the consequences would be so far-reaching.

9 Rarely has she travelled more than fifty miles from her village.

10 On no account must you lift heavy weights like that again.

11 Scarcely had I put the phone down when it rang again.

12 In no way did the defendant express his misgivings.

13 So difficult was the task that expert assistance was required.

14 Had they accepted our offer, we would have moved house by now.

B 1C 2E 3B 4A 5D

C 1 Over I fell, and broke my leg.

2 'So would I.'

3 Not only did she twist her ankle, but she also dropped her purse.

4 ✓

5 ✓

6 ✓

7 Up the stairs puffed the plump old housekeeper.

8 ✓

9 Right through the underwater tunnel she swam.

10 ✓

11 ✓

12 There stands the famous statue of Admiral Lord Nelson.

13 Only last week did I find the information I'd been looking for.

14 Here come the police! Someone must have called them.

D 1 ... is it worth giving his suggestion any ...

2 ... was his disgust at her behaviour that ...

3 ... hard Adele tries, she gets ...

4 ... did the volunteers attempt to ...

5 ... was I ever shown how to make ...

6 ... before had such a lavish celebration/such lavish celebrations been ...

7 ... did the minister admit to an error ...

8 ... you wish to accept the offer, put a ...

9 ... may have to be turned ...

10 ... had the date been chosen when/before the ...

11 ... than four helpers are needed to enable ...

12 ... been for his father's advice, he might be ...

13 ... a full bonus would satisfy ...

14 ... should/must this computer data be revealed ...

Unit 17

A 1 like

2 As

3 As

4 as

5 like

6 as

7 as

8 as

9 as

10 As

11 as

12 like

13 Like

14 like

15 Like

B 1 She's nothing like as good at tennis as her friend.

2 ✓

3 Have as many potatoes as you like.

4 His hand is as steady as a rock.

5 ✓

6 ✓

7 ✓

8 ✓

9 The dictionary wasn't nearly as helpful as I had hoped.

10 ✓

11 Laurie drank half as much beer as Hugo.

12 Their offer is every bit as acceptable as yours.

C 1 That's the same formula (that) ...

2 ✓

3 ✓

4 That's the same man that ...

5 ✓

6 The rules are the same (as) in my country.

7 ✓

8 Did you pay the same as I did?

D 1 The more you work, the more money you earn.

2 The more difficult it is, the harder he tries.

3 He's been working longer than you.

4 This meat's tougher than yesterday's.

5 ✓

6 You're the most infuriating person I've ever met.

7 He's by far the best boxer in the world.

8 ✓

9 My cousin is much/far/a lot taller than me.

10 ✓

11 I think the driver is a bit tireder/more tired than me.

12 ✓

13 The more, the merrier.

14 ✓

15 It was the dreariest hotel I'd ever had the misfortune to stay in.

16 That one's the slowest train.

17 ✓

18 Your work's more impressive than anyone else's.

19 ✓

20 ✓

Unit 18

A 1 Having

2 annoyed/shocked

3 exciting/interesting/gripping

4 broken

5 Supposing

6 Feeling/Being
7 asking/enquiring
8 Having
9 Taking
10 bored
11 carrying/bearing/bringing
12 Being/Feeling
13 Coming
14 Judging
15 looking/feeling, smoking

B 1 close   5 standing
2 repairing   6 well
3 cooking   7 throw
4 bang   8 open, take

C 1 Once   4 After
2 since   5 On
3 When   6 as

D 1 When I booked a room for myself and my wife ...
2 Looking at my diary, I saw (that) there were several double-booked appointments.
3 ✓
4 I hope you've mentioned this to the people concerned in the matter.
5 As I had not written about the required topic ...
6 ✓
7 While I was working in California ...
8 As it was such a sunny day ...
9 ✓
10 Do you know anyone who's been to the Canary Islands?
11 ✓
12 ✓
13 ✓
14 Once he was ensconced in his comfortable armchair ...

Unit 19

A 1 asleep   6 burning
2 alone   7 live
3 frightened   8 open
4 blazing   9 afloat
5 awake

B 1 pale   6 angry
2 ✓   7 ✓
3 ✓   8 ✓
4 ✓   9 ✓
5 ✓   10 unconscious

C 1 for the disabled.
2 a two-hour lecture.
3 for the blind.
4 ✓
5 ✓
6 The French negotiated with the Spanish ...

D 1 I saw a sweet little green silk scarf.
2 There was a huge mediaeval stone castle on the hill.
3 A beautiful white sailing ship was moored at the quay.
4 There is a battered old leather suitcase on the table.
5 They live in an ancient fisherman's cottage by the sea.
6 She was carrying a heavy striped canvas shopping bag full of vegetables on her arm.
7 She was introduced to a remarkably handsome young executive.
8 He was wearing a smart grey business suit with a jazzy waistcoat.
9 She only makes cakes with the best unsalted Danish butter.
10 He has just bought an extremely exotic oriental carpet.

E 1H 2O 3B 4J 5A 6D 7K 8F 9L 10E 11G 12M 13N 14C 15I

F 1 blatant
2 insatiable
3 abortive
4 fierce
5 mere
6 gruelling

7 innovative
8 heinous
9 burgeoning
10 sworn
11 dire
12 lucrative
13 contemporary
14 primary
15 first-hand

Unit 20

A 1b 2b 3b 4a 5c 6d 7c 8c 9a 10c 11c 12c 13a 14d 15a 16b 17a 18b 19d 20c

B 1C 2K 3J 4A 5H 6E 7G 8F

C 1 until/before
2 directives/laws
3 another
4 who
5 as
6 provided
7 have
8 which
9 By
10 chance/opportunity
11 such
12 without
13 increasingly/extremely/very/too
14 focus/area

D 1 in touch
2 salary
3 lower than/less than
4 withdraw
5 forward
6 any information
7 vacancy/post/position
8 an interview
9 available
10 except (for)
11 (most/very) grateful
12 appreciate
13 behalf

Unit 21

A 1 under age
2 above suspicion

3 under guarantee

4 under control

5 above-average height

6 Above all

7 below the belt

8 under contract

9 under his breath

10 beneath contempt

11 above-mentioned

12 below zero/below freezing (-point)

13 over a (cup of) coffee

14 over the world

15 below sea level

16 under stress/pressure

17 over my eyes

18 over the odds

B 1H 2E 3N 4P 5A 6G 7C 8J 9M 10O 11F 12D 13K 14I 15L 16B

C
1	out of	11	out of
2	Between	12	over
3	out of	13	out of
4	between	14	among
5	among	15	out of
6	out of	16	out of
7	over	17	among
8	out of	18	out of
9	among	19	out of
10	between	20	out of

D
1	On	7	by
2	by	8	on
3	in	9	in
4	by	10	on
5	on	11	by
6	In		

E
1	On	9	with
2	By	10	by
3	in	11	with
4	in	12	by
5	in	13	of
6	in/during	14	In
7	at	15	in
8	on		

Unit 22

A
1	doing	11	do
2	makes	12	make
3	make	13	making
4	done	14	do
5	make	15	making
6	do	16	does
7	do	17	do
8	makes	18	making
9	made	19	make
10	doing	20	do

B
1	told	9	speaking
2	talked	10	said
3	said	11	tell
4	tell	12	say
5	speak	13	told
6	Tell, say	14	tell
7	tells	15	say
8	talking	16	speak

C
1	rise	6	✓
2	✓	7	✓
3	risen	8	arise
4	✓	9	rise
5	✓	10	✓

D
1	laid	8	lay
2	lain	9	lay
3	laid	10	laying
4	laying	11	lies
5	lying	12	laid
6	lying	13	lies
7	laid	14	lies

Unit 23

A 1E 2I 3J 4H 5A 6B 7D 8C 9G 10F

B 1 The prisoner gave an honest answer to the question/was honest in answering the question.

2 He is reputed to have been born in Segovia.

3 We were about to finish/We had just about finished when Isabel arrived.

4 Their recent behaviour has been very strange.

5 His medical treatment appears to have seriously affected his mental state.

6 On his arrival at the stage door, the star was (immediately) surrounded by screaming fans.

7 The staff have always held the headmaster in very high esteem.

8 The electrician's advice (to me) was to have the wiring checked.

9 The guided tour takes place at hourly intervals.

10 By/On her own admission, she is rather selfish.

C 1F 2J 3I 4A 5D 6B 7C 8E 9H 10G

D 1 She is by no means a good cook.

2 I was unaware (that) it was a breach of protocol.

3 The store should definitely refund (you) your money/give you a refund.

4 The castle made a great/a big/the greatest/the biggest impact on the tourists.

5 Building societies will not be able to rest on their laurels.

6 They're on the horns of a dilemma.

7 Taxpayers had to foot the bill for the privatisation plan.

8 I did my utmost to expedite the matter.

9 Juliet could only long for his return.

10 By the time we all sat down to dinner, there was still no sign of the Morrises.

11 I think you've got the wrong end of the stick.

12 Thanks to Gerry's advice, the firm didn't go bankrupt.

13 A relaxing break would do you good/It would do you good to have a relaxing break.

14 With the advent of the assembly line, five hundred workers were dismissed.

15 It came as a shock to his colleagues to hear of Ahmed's illness/The news of Ahmed's illness came as a shock to his colleagues.

16 Alan does nothing but complain (all the time).

17 She stands a good chance of winning first prize.

18 The policeman drew our attention to the speed limit sign.

E 1 exclusive   6 grain
   2 household   7 shed
   3 lacked   8 justice
   4 quandary   9 economical
   5 deadlock   10 tendency

Unit 24

A 1 for   14 in
   2 in   15 in
   3 of   16 of
   4 to   17 in
   5 from   18 for
   6 about   19 of
   7 in   20 for
   8 of   21 in
   9 in   22 of
   10 with   23 of
   11 to   24 of
   12 of   25 in
   13 of

B 1 apologise   9 applied
   2 worry   10 hold
   3 to   11 for
   4 on   12 in
   5 keep   13 to
   6 depends   14 in
   7 insist   15 with
   8 for

C 1G 2H 3J 4I 5F 6B 7C 8A 9E 10D

D 1 about
   2 doubt
   3 for
   4 in
   5 for

6 responsible
7 in
8 in
9 working/concentrating
10 in
11 with
12 of
13 suspected/accused/guilty
14 damage

Unit 25

A 1a 2b 3c 4b 5b 6d 7c 8b 9a 10d 11b 12d 13a 14d 15a 16b 17b 18a 19d 20b 21a 22c 23b 24a 25c

B 1 ... lacked in numbers, they made up for ...
   2 ... no difference of opinion between ...
   3 ... was left to foot ...
   4 ... own admission, he (has) ...
   5 ... point (in) shedding tears ...
   6 ... bore/took the brunt of ...
   7 ... nothing but sit in the office ...

C 1 of   11 has
   2 was   12 which
   3 the   13 as
   4 which   14 the
   5 by   15 that/the
   6 had   16 leading
   7 than   17 were
   8 For   18 so
   9 over   19 be
   10 to   20 lies/waits/is

D 1 Japanese
   2 gruelling
   3 marathons. He
   4 ✔
   5 committed
   6 sought
   7 ✔
   8 achieve
   9 monks who
   10 whose
   11 ✔

12 affected
13 there
14 resident
15 and
16 ✔

Unit 26

A 1 sat down
   2 closed down
   3 going/coming down
   4 broke down
   5 pouring/pelting down
   6 slammed the book down
   7 play down
   8 put down
   9 fell down
   10 got me down
   11 calmed down
   12 tore down the notice from/tore the notice down from

B 1 slow
   2 pull/tear
   3 squatted
   4 blew/tore
   5 tone
   6 marked
   7 narrowed
   8 tracked
   9 bring
   10 cut
   11 tumble
   12 noted

C 1 Family traditions have been handed down through the centuries.
   2 Jeremy is forever running down his wife's achievements.
   3 The man in a business suit flagged down a taxi.
   4 With two small children, she's rather tied down at the moment.
   5 The preservation order will prevent them from chopping down the tree.
   6 I listened to the lecture and jotted down the professor's points.

7 The authorities are cracking down on fraud everywhere.

8 After the interview I turned down the job they offered me.

9 When Steve wouldn't help, I felt badly let down by him.

10 The holiday gave us a chance to wind down properly.

Unit 27

A 1D 2J 3E 4I 5M 6N 7H 8O 9B 10F 11A 12C 13K 14G 15L

B
1 set about
2 call back
3 pay, back
4 go, back
5 look after
6 set about
7 turn/go back

8 went about
9 called, back
10 holding/ keeping back
11 get back
12 fall back

C 1 We are campaigning to bring about a change in the law.

2 You'll have to take back what you said about him.

3 A passer-by went after the pickpocket.

4 I'll ring you back when I get home.

5 How are you going to go about raising the money?

6 A severe frost could set my roses back by several weeks.

7 Sometimes a certain smell can bring back memories of a person or place.

8 For the children's sake he held back his anger.

Unit 28

A 1 F carefully aim at and shoot one of a group

2 F live with money or food provided by

3 T

4 F leave

5 T

6 T

7 F display boastfully, to draw people's attention to

8 T

9 T

10 T

B 1 put/turned
2 gone
3 telling
4 give
5 cordon
6 worn
7 wrote
8 send
9 fight/shake/throw
10 Come
11 be
12 come

C 1 She called it off (the party)

2 I'm sure he'll pull it off (his job/task)

3 –

4 Turn it off, please (the light)

5 –

6 I'll drop it off (a letter/parcel/present etc)

7 to scrape it all off (mud/paint etc)

8 –

9 I just laughed it off (their opinion)

10 Noel will shave it off (his beard or moustache)

11 the moment had come to break it off (her relationship)

12 –

D 1 The plane will be taking off in two hours' time.

2 Fortunately Zoë got off very lightly in the accident.

3 The factory will be laying off 500 workers until after the summer.

4 I don't think his gamble will pay off as he is hoping.

5 Her family cut her off without a penny.

6 The boys let off fireworks in their garden.

7 The rain kept off during the cricket match.

8 James refuses to be put off by what people say.

9 The effects of our holiday wore off all too quickly.

10 We'll have to set off before first light.

Unit 29

A 1I 2O 3F 4G 5J 6K 7E 8A 9L 10D 11M 12B 13N 14C 15H

B Across: 1 see   4 fish for
7 pull   8 check   10 by
11 account   12 get   13 look
Down: 2 ask   3 go   4 fall
through   5 fall   6 run
7 put   9 care   10 break

Unit 30

A 1b 2a 3c 4d 5c 6a 7b 8d 9c 10a 11c 12a 13c 14b 15d 16c 17a 18c

B get by: manage with little money

look for: try to find

sit down: take a seat

apply for: ask for

go about: approach, start, tackle

jot down: write down quickly

send off: post

see through: not be deceived by

turn down: reject

pull off: manage to do (something difficult)

C 1E 2A 3G 4D 5C 6B 7F

D 1 as
2 with
3 Unlike
4 enabling/allowing
5 by
6 While/Whereas/Although
7 feeding

8 most
9 seldom/rarely/never
10 another
11 Even/When
12 whose
13 makes
14 So
15 put
16 until/before
17 least
18 what
19 despite
20 no

Unit 31

A 1E 2H 3A 4B 5L 6C 7I 8D
9K 10F 11G 12J

B 1 cheered me up
2 tied the dog up/tied up the dog
3 ate her food up/ate up her food
4 bottle up his emotions/ bottle his emotions up
5 split/break up
6 give up
7 gets up
8 filled up
9 sealed up
10 went up
11 took up
12 pick you up

C 1 picked   7 held
2 build   8 blowing
3 shut   9 grew
4 keep   10 ended
5 fix   11 Hurry
6 cut   12 turned/showed

D 1 We should look Lorenzo up if we pass through Rome.
2 The taxi pulled up in front of the hotel.
3 The boy was told to clear up his room before doing his homework.
4 Tom's grandmother brought him up on her farm in Cornwall.

5 Prices simply shot up last month.
6 I didn't expect that topic to crop up at the meeting.
7 I can easily put you up if you need to stay overnight.
8 The story was obviously made up, if you ask me.

Unit 32

A 1 T
2 F make tired, make unfit or useless through wear
3 T
4 T
5 F separate from a larger group, find a solution to, organise
6 T
7 T
8 T
9 T
10 T
11 F exclude
12 F discover
13 T
14 T
15 F choose, identify
16 F extend your activities

B 1 eat   8 passed
2 taking   9 pulled
3 dropped   10 hand/give
4 turned/came   11 let
5 laid   12 come
6 lock   13 stick/put
7 point   14 throw

C 1 to try it out (a computer/ car/camera etc)
2 measure it out (food or drink)
3 get it out (the diary)
4 –
5 –
6 Rub it out (my name)
7 thought it out (your plan)
8 we can share it out (the work)
9 Could you check it out (the information etc)

10 I'll look it out for you (the Kingman family file)

D 1 ruled   6 coming
2 sort   7 sticking
3 drop   8 pick
4 try   9 handed
5 put   10 branch

Unit 33

A 1D 2H 3M 4E 5L 6F 7A
8K 9B 10G 11C 12N 13J
14I

B 1 part with
2 came apart
3 go/run over
4 boiled over
5 tell, apart
6 fighting with
7 look over
8 deal with

C 1 The engine finally turned over the fourth time I tried it.
2 The state airline took over the small private company.
3 My sister has always identified with the feminist cause.
4 Everyone was quite bowled over by the success of the plan.
5 I expect it will cloud over later on today.
6 The newly-weds could do with some financial assistance.
7 Sally could only toy with the food on her plate.
8 It was a long time before she got over her tragic loss.

D 1 boiled   5 dealing
2 taking   6 do
3 reason   7 toying
4 sided   8 blown

Unit 34

A 1F 2I 3D 4H 5G 6J 7C 8A
9E 10B

B 1 put on
2 hold/hang on
3 went/carried/kept on
4 switch/turn on
5 rambled on
6 let on
7 added on
8 having me on?

C 1 catch 7 getting
2 try 8 moved
3 touch 9 let
4 live 10 passed
5 count 11 call
6 Hang/Hold 12 put

D 1 For no apparent reason, the professor turned on his unsuspecting assistant.
2 The workers decided to soldier on without a pay rise.
3 Philippa is getting on well in her new job.
4 The new boy was picked on to clean the whiteboard.
5 Car manufacturers have carried on their business for 100 years now.
6 Dave's nervous breakdown was brought on by overwork.
7 Her mail is being sent on to the new address.
8 Be careful not to take on too much extra work.
9 We'll have to keep on advertising until we find someone suitable.
10 There was a loud party going on somewhere in the street.

Unit 35
A 1a 2c 3d 4b 5c 6a 7d 8c 9c 10a 11b 12b 13d 14c 15d 16c

B dress up: put on smart clothes
turn up: arrive
find out: discover
point out: indicate, draw attention to

go on: continue
get on: make progress
do with: find useful
think over: consider
apply for: ask for (a job)
let on: reveal information
cheer up: make someone feel happier

C 1 We haven't entirely ruled out the possibility of a cure.
2 The competition judges picked out the best display.
3 The little boy's ears stuck out from under his school cap.
4 Tracy's boyfriend took her out to the disco.
5 The steam train pulled slowly out of the station.
6 The royal servants laid out the banquet in the palace.
7 The farmer found it hard to keep foxes out of the chicken shed.
8 I can't quite make out Marcella's handwriting.
9 When my favourite sweater wore out, I bought another one just like it.
10 Just as we set out, there was a clap of thunder.

Unit 36
A 1 T
2 F donate or give as a gift, prize etc
3 T
4 T
5 F leave
6 T
7 T
8 T
9 T
10 F die
11 F act or play irresponsibly
12 T

B Across: 1 gamble 4 pass 6 hang 8 Take 10 die 11 throw 14 pull 15 come 16 send 17 look 18 break

Down: 1 give 2 blaze 3 clear 5 stow 7 get 9 crowd 12 scare 13 get 14 put 16 shop

Unit 37
A 1L 2H 3A 4J 5B 6C 7I 8E 9F 10G 11D 12K

B 1 ran/bumped
2 sank
3 tuned
4 sent
5 talk
6 taken
7 drop/pop/call
8 settle
9 turned
10 dig/break
11 barge/burst
12 show
13 phase
14 paid

C 1 plug it in (the hairdryer)
2 –
3 –
4 Hand it in (the report)
5 –
6 –
7 take it all in (the information/situation)
8 –
9 break it in (the horse)
10 –
11 –
12 fill it in (the form)

D 1 On her aunt's death Karin came into a fortune.
2 Burglars have broken into the isolated house.
3 Daisy burst into tears as she waved goodbye.
4 It's no good. You can't fool me into believing you!
5 Don't you think we should check in before we have dinner?
6 Is your sister moving in soon?

7 Think about it. Don't rush into anything.

Unit 38

A 1 T

2 T

3 T

4 F get rid of, abolish

5 T

6 F find time to

7 F consider another person inferior

8 F become too big for

9 T

10 T

11 F complete a course of action

12 T

B 1 looks up to

2 go ahead with/go on with/carry on with

3 go along with

4 cut down on

5 caught up with/kept up with

6 got out of doing

7 settled up with the hotel

8 walked out on

9 got rid of/done away with

10 keeping up with

C 1 put up

2 write off/send off/write away/send away

3 got on/along

4 feel up

5 get round

6 came up

7 come down

8 get down

9 live up

10 getting up

11 run out

12 faced up

D 1 Sarah was disappointed at missing out on such a good opportunity.

2 The boss always lets Fred get away with murder!

3 The President has come in for a great deal of criticism lately.

4 Many people would like to do away with the monarchy.

5 The baby's ill: she came out in spots yesterday.

6 You should hang on to those stamps. They're valuable.

7 Rachel decided she couldn't go through with the wedding.

Unit 39

A 1 comedown

2 lookout

3 handout

4 breakdown

5 breakup/breakdown

6 castaway

7 breakthrough

8 go-ahead

9 dropouts

10 grown-up

11 outlook, upbringing

12 let-up

13 outburst

14 getaway

15 lay-offs, cutbacks

16 stopover

17 turnout

18 onlookers

B Across: 3 standby 5 takeover

7 sell-out 10 in 11 on

12 stowaway 13 hold

14 layout 19 outbreak

20 setback 21 together

23 hangover

Down: 1 stand 2 let-down

4 break 6 knockout 8 lay-by

up 15 onset 16 check

17 goings 18 get 22 in

Unit 40

A 1c 2a 3b 4c 5d 6c 7a 8b 9d
10c 11a 12d 13b 14c 15a 16a

B rule out: exclude, consider ineligible

go on: continue

close down: cause to stop working

get over: recover from

look for: try to find

take on: employ

put up with: tolerate

take off: depart (a plane)

join in: take part in

lay off: dismiss

give up: stop

go back: return

C 1 There was an impressive turnout for the by-election.

2 Police investigated the goings-on at the student hostel.

3 The culprits made their getaway in a stolen car.

4 Please fasten your seatbelts ready for take-off.

5 The hospital closures are the result of government cutbacks.

6 Their ticket to Sydney allows them a stopover in Hong Kong.

7 The accused's antisocial behaviour was blamed on his upbringing.

D 1 The plain-clothes policeman hung around outside the star's home.

2 Josephine came across a rare coin among her loose change.

3 The fire blazed away, completely out of control.

4 Eventually he owned up to having started the rumour.

5 News of their affair will get around pretty fast.

6 She'll never talk him into giving up golf.

Unit 41

A 1 PC, phone line

2 search engine, newsgroup, chat room

3 crashed, back up

4 cursor, icon, double-click

5 attachment, virus

B 1B 2D 3B 4C 5A 6A 7B 8A
9D 10B 11A

C 1 inform
2 unhappy/disappointed/
dissatisfied
3 providing/supplying
4 get online/log on
5 problem/lengthy process
6 technicians
7 solve
8 unhelpful
9 target
10 unsolicited/junk/unwanted
11 Unless
12 cancel/suspend/end/
terminate
13 prompt/speedy/early

Unit 42

A 1 slogans/jingles
2 jingles/slogans
3 commercials
4 brand
5 subliminal
6 pressure groups
7 disseminate
8 posters
9 hoardings
10 press

B 1D 2B 3H 4A 5C 6E 7G 8F

C 1 critic
2 commentator
3 censorship
4 coverage
5 circulation
6 catchy

D 1 rehearsing
2 stage
3 series
4 characters
5 channel
6 on location
7 role
8 review

E 1 box-office success
2 standing ovation
3 soap opera
4 final curtain
5 subtitles
6 low-budget
7 prime-time
8 supporting roles

Unit 43

A 1 ambition
2 jet set
3 Rising
4 best-seller
5 Success
6 achieve
7 potential
8 expanding
9 rocketed
10 whizz-kid
11 reap
12 respected
13 market
14 public

B 1 prodigious
2 dedicated
3 ruthless
4 (un)skilled/skilful
5 notorious
6 (un)successful
7 ephemeral
8 stressful/stressed
9 celebrated
10 legendary
11 renowned
12 talented

C 1 prodigy
2 lights
3 stardom
4 infamous
5 champion
6 status
7 autograph
8 failure
9 invasion
10 reputation
11 posthumous

12 big break
13 posterity
14 gap
15 winnings
16 celebrities

Unit 44

A 1 experiments
2 animal rights
3 widespread
4 blood sports
5 activists
6 tested
7 consumers
8 vivisection
9 opposition
10 climate
11 entertainment
12 cruelty
13 free-range
14 battery hens
15 factory farming
16 livestock

B 1 H bookworm
2 D stag party
3 J dark horse
4 A puppy fat
5 B zebra crossing
6 C pigeon-hole
7 E crocodile tears
8 I dog collar
9 G wolf whistle
10 F cat's eyes

C 1 fly
2 frog
3 butterflies
4 bird's
5 parrot-
6 dog
7 wild goose
8 horse
9 wolf
10 rat
11 whale
12 sardines

D 1E 2A 3B 4F 5D 6C

Unit 45

A
1 authors
2 Translation
3 dialect
4 translators
5 allusions
6 nuances
7 original
8 colloquial
9 Evoking
10 literal

B 1F 2I 3J 4H 5A 6G 7C 8E 9D 10B

C
1 spoonerism
2 slang
3 alliteration
4 onomatopoeia
5 palindrome
6 jargon
7 malapropism
8 tongue-twister/alliteration
9 pidgin
10 limerick

D
1 lecture
2 sermon
3 quarrel
4 speech
5 accent
6 debate
7 pronunciation
8 anecdote
9 sentence
10 riddle

Unit 46

A
1 policy
2 bypass
3 consultants
4 collapses
5 emergency
6 cardiac
7 heavy smokers
8 surgery
9 interim
10 patient
11 medical
12 treatment
13 addicts
14 transplants
15 National Health Service

B
1 under the weather
2 disease
3 surgeon
4 side effects
5 ward
6 donor
7 surgery
8 clinic
9 first
10 diets
11 theatre
12 prescription
13 casualty
14 transfusion
15 sling

C
1 T
2 T
3 F cannot resist infection well
4 F specialises in children's illnesses
5 T
6 F means being excessively fat/overweight
7 F a means of inserting a drug with a needle
8 T
9 F treating patients with small amounts of drugs that would cause symptoms in a healthy person
10 T

Unit 47

A 1E 2H 3J 4L 5I 6A 7K 8C 9G 10F 11D 12B

B
1 narrow escape
2 run the risk
3 safe and sound
4 been swept overboard
5 sheer folly
6 peace of mind
7 bear a charmed life
8 take sensible precautions
9 risk life and limb
10 a false sense of security
11 raise the alarm
12 odds are heavily stacked against

C 1D 2A 3E 4B 5I 6L 7K 8C 9F 10G 11H 12J

D
1 hardships
2 foolhardy
3 funding
4 sponsors
5 provisions
6 survivors
7 hazardous
8 jeopardising
9 intrepid
10 determination
11 endurance
12 casualties

Unit 48

A
1 rugged
2 construction
3 irrigation
4 drought
5 source
6 developing
7 environmental
8 scale
9 damage
10 tribal
11 obliterated
12 environmentalists

B
1 world
2 land
3 countryside
4 pick
5 sky
6 coast
7 eradicate
8 lake
9 resources
10 fumes

C 1 tropical
2 global
3 urban
4 rural
5 (un)natural
6 scenic
7 mountainous
8 coastal
9 regional
10 protective/protected
11 congested
12 coniferous
13 polluted
14 climatic
15 disastrous
16 (ir)replaceable
17 disposable
18 biodegradable
19 (in)soluble
20 (un)productive
21 problematic
22 polar

D 1F 2D 3I 4H 5G 6E 7C 8J
9K 10A 11L 12B

Unit 49

A 1H 2F 3I 4B 5D 6J 7C 8G
9A 10E

B 1 rival
2 accused
3 hoodwinked
4 espionage
5 loyalty
6 devious
7 blame
8 integrity
9 traitor
10 reproached
11 disgrace
12 bribed
13 corrupt
14 conscience

C 1 integrity
2 traitor
3 loyalty
4 devious

5 reproached
6 hoodwinked

D 1 (dis)honourable
2 (un)ethical
3 suspicious
4 petty
5 bankrupt
6 scandalous
7 fraudulent
8 deceitful
9 vicious
10 sinful
11 sacrificial
12 treacherous

E 1 tax evasion
2 looted
3 offence
4 bribing
5 culprit
6 shortcomings
7 amoral
8 betrayed

Unit 50

A 1 wealth
2 poverty
3 increase
4 income
5 satisfaction
6 level
7 economists
8 material
9 expenditure
10 factors

B 1I 2E 3A 4B 5G 6C 7F 8J
9D 10H

C 1 T
2 F buys from the producer
and sells to the retailer,
who sells to the public
3 F before tax
4 F young professional people
who wish to improve
their standard of living
and social status (from
'young urban professional')

5 T
6 F *impecunious* means short
of money
7 T
8 T
9 T
10 F you are borrowing money
from someone
11 T
12 F an extra payment in
addition to your salary

D 1 direct debit
2 mortgage
3 will
4 in arrears
5 creditors
6 competition
7 profit
8 bounced
9 expense
10 cash
11 receipt
12 discount
13 fare
14 priceless
15 within their means
16 proceeds

Unit 51

1a 2d 3a 4b 5c 6a 7c 8b 9a
10d 11a 12b 13a 14b 15d
16a 17c 18d 19a 20b 21a
22c 23d 24a 25b 26c 27d
28c 29a 30d 31b 32d

Unit 52

A 1A 2D 3C 4B 5A 6D 7A 8C
9B 10C 11D 12B 13D 14A
15A

B 1G 2C 3E 4A 5I 6B 7D 8F
9H 10J

C 1 electorate, general election
2 candidate, constituency
3 MP
4 Opposition

Unit 53

A 1E 2F 3A 4L 5I 6J 7C 8G
9H 10D 11B 12K

B
1 feud
2 antagonise
3 motive
4 wreak
5 warfare
6 reconciliation
7 reprisal
8 vindictively
9 victims
10 rancour
11 retaliated
12 aggressive

C
A *8 down*
B *12 across*
C feud
D victims
E vindictiveness
F *5 across*
G motive
H *10 down*
I *1 across*
J *2 down*
K *13 down*
L reconcile
M wreak
N antagonise
O warfare
P rancour

Unit 54

A 1M 2D 3C 4F 5B 6L 7K 8I
9H 10N 11E 12G 13J 14A

B
1 revenues
2 system
3 PCs
4 integrated
5 compatible
6 rivals
7 monopoly
8 consumers
9 market
10 growth
11 investing

12 digital
13 encoded
14 lucrative
15 initiative

C
1 robot, remote control
2 electromagnetic field
3 anti-nuclear
4 solar
5 closed-circuit
6 security tags
7 streamline
8 white goods
9 microchip
10 optimum efficiency
11 central locking
12 programme

D
1 T
2 F a small piece of equipment, not necessarily electrical
3 T
4 F usually four-wheeled
5 T
6 T
7 F a device on a wall into which a plug can be inserted to make an electrical connection
8 T

Unit 55

A 1F 2I 3G 4B 5D 6E 7H 8J
9A 10C

B
1 overtime   5 redundant
2 candidates   6 living
3 benefit   7 loan
4 sabbatical   8 syllabus

C 1c 2a 3b 4a 5d 6a 7b 8c 9d
10a

D
1 on the dole
2 enter the labour market
3 on-the-job training
4 achieve his potential
5 wage dispute
6 picket line

Unit 56

A 1M 2C 3N 4I 5F 6J 7K 8L
9D 10H 11E 12A 13B 14G

B
1 renovation
2 cottage
3 habitation
4 belongs
5 bare necessities
6 evict
7 demolish
8 plight
9 polarised
10 support
11 sympathise
12 victimising
13 threats
14 brave

C
1 T
2 T
3 F someone who wants to acquire/possess many things
4 F Affluence is wealth.
5 T
6 T
7 T
8 T
9 F the first, most important things to think about
10 F a young person, usually a girl, who goes to a foreign country to learn the language while staying with a family and helping to look after their children
11 T
12 T

D
1 boom
2 beyond their means
3 suburbs
4 second-hand
5 rat race
6 investment
7 security
8 sophisticated
9 apart
10 image

11 entertaining

12 debt

Unit 57

A 1D 2J 3F 4I 5B 6K 7G 8L
9C 10E 11H 12A

B 1 F usually of an unwelcome event

2 T

3 T

4 T

5 F the study of the movements of the stars, interpreted in terms of their influence on human behaviour

6 T

7 T

8 F someone who can predict the future or see what is happening out of sight

9 T

10 T

11 T

12 T

13 T

14 F someone who believes there is no God

15 T

16 T

17 T

18 T

C 1 mirage

2 medium

3 mythical

4 monster

5 Magic

6 miracle

7 mesmerised

D 1b 2a 3c 4d 5a

Unit 58

A 1D 2E 3I 4A 5B 6F 7H 8C
9J 10G

B 1 reminisce

2 a total blank

3 lasting

4 souvenirs

5 prevaricated

6 nostalgia

7 absent-minded

8 haunted

9 historical

10 ancient

11 memorising

12 contemporary

13 sooner or later

14 on the dot

15 forecast

16 on time

17 at the end

18 refresh

19 recognise

20 elderly

C 1 tip

2 rack

3 sieve

4 Ages

5 predecessor

6 prehistoric

7 high

8 passage/passing

9 flies

10 documents

11 posterity

12 hindsight

Unit 59

A 1H 2F 3A 4J 5B 6C 7I 8E
9G 10L 11D 12K

B 1 F is an electronic device fitted to an aircraft for collecting and storing information about the flight

2 T

3 T

4 T

5 F is a bed or a bunk on a ship or train

6 T

7 F records a vehicle's speed on a journey, and how far it has travelled

8 F a plan for a journey to different places

C 1 brochure

2 range

3 resort

4 facilities

5 cruise

6 luxury

7 lounging

8 spectacular

9 self-catering

10 picturesque

11 cuisine

12 excursions

13 inclusive

14 accommodation

D A *7 across*

B bypass

C villa

D *10 down*

E roundabout

F cabin

G *8 across*

H package

I safari

J via

K *4 down*

L ticket

M brochure

N overland

O *17 across*

P journey

Q Tube

R *16 across*

S exhaustion

Unit 60

A 1 copyright

2 proofs

3 phrasebook

4 plot

5 browse

6 dust-jacket

7 edition

8 imagination

9 key

10 paragraphs
11 rhyme
12 literally
13 page
14 thrillers
15 library

B 1 hardback
2 translated
3 engrossed
4 best-seller
5 chapter
6 author
7 prose
8 biography
9 copy
10 illustrated

C 1F 2K 3A 4B 5J 6H 7C 8E
9D 10I 11L 12G

Unit 61

A 1E 2A 3J 4B 5C 6D 7I 8F
9G 10H

B 1 charged
2 offence
3 stand
4 plead
5 court
6 jury
7 evidence
8 witnesses
9 lawyers
10 sum up
11 reach a verdict
12 defendant
13 pass sentence
14 acquitted
15 committed
16 criminologists
17 offenders
18 deterrent

C A court
B wrists
C *6 across*
D excuse
E magistrate

F riot
G *13 down*
H *1 down*
I deterrent
J acquitted
K authorities
L *9 down*
M jail
N judge
O delinquent
P barrister
Q *7 across*
R *17 across*
S fine
T mug

Unit 62

A 1b 2c 3c 4c 5b 6c 7d 8a 9c
10a 11d 12b 13a 14b 15b
16c 17b 18c 19a 20b 21c
22a 23b 24c 25c 26d 27d
28a 29b 30c 31a 32a 33b

B 1D 2C 3A 4B 5A 6C 7B 8C
9D 10B 11D 12A 13B 14D

C 1 saved   4 stand
2 pose   5 backed
3 held

D 1C 2I 3G 4B 5E 6A

Unit 63

A 1 Refuse   7 dressing
2 pride   8 skate
3 crane   9 trunk
4 Hailing   10 spotted
5 branch   11 spirits
6 spring   12 scales

B *Possible answers:*
1 Why don't you have one then?
2 Only another few minutes, sir.
3 Flowers, perhaps, or chocolates?
4 Delicious, thank you.
5 When it's a French window.
6 They don't want people to get tangled up in them.

7 Mostly vegetables.
8 Oh, he was in Wellington's army, was he? (*At the Battle of Waterloo in 1815, Napoleon was defeated by the Duke of Wellington's and Field Marshal Blücher's armies. Waterloo is also a well-known railway station in London.*)
9 It is part of their migration pattern.
10 Certainly, sir, including lobster.
1G 2J 3E 4F 5A 6C 7D 8B 9H 10I

C 1 red/read
2 boar/bore
3 cheetahs/cheaters
4 crypt/script
5 tiers/tears
6 carrots/carats
7 moose/mousse
8 twirly/too early
9 ewe/you

D 1 Hair today, gone tomorrow!
2 an unidentified frying object
3 by Norse code
4 No time like the present!
5 drop him a line
6 to make ends meet
7 He wanted to make a clean getaway.
8 He took a very dim view of things.

E 1 unprovoked
2 wonderful
3 playwright
4 thoughtfully
5 enclosing
6 unfortunately
7 unable
8 updated
9 politician
10 long-term
11 sworn

12 apparently

13 whereupon

14 wittily

15 ahead

F 1F (*by Friday* could mean a time deadline, or it could refer to the person, Man Friday, who did the chores for Crusoe in Daniel Defoe's novel)

2E (*ham* is cooked pork, and *-let* can be used as a diminutive)

3A (a pun on the word *vessel*)

4G (a pun on the word *skeleton*)

5D (a pun on the word *wave*)

6B (sounds are transposed)

7C (a deliberate confusion of *meters* and *meteors*)

Unit 64

A 1 make a mountain out of a molehill

2 pulling my leg

3 out of the question

4 a bone to pick

5 down in the mouth

6 takes the biscuit

7 give them the slip

8 tongue in cheek

9 got her own back

10 on the tip of my tongue

11 watch your step

12 takes her/it for granted

B 1H 2A 3L 4F 5B 6D 7C 8K 9E 10G 11J 12I

C 1 bee in his bonnet

2 sort out the sheep from the goats

3 flogging a dead horse

4 get the lion's share

5 let the cat out of the bag

6 putting the cart before the horse

7 dark horse

8 lame duck

9 red herring

10 barking up the wrong tree

11 whale of a time

12 dog-eared

D 1D 2F 3J 4C 5A 6B 7I 8E 9H 10G

E 1 chain

2 Dutch

3 pitch

4 close

5 bone

6 song

7 tail

8 shop

9 house

10 bell

11 day

12 loggerheads

13 wall

14 cake

15 thoughts

Unit 65

A 1J Too many helpers cause confusion.

2A People have different tastes and interests.

3G The first one to apply often gets the job/prize/bargain etc.

4F Don't rely on something happening until it is certain.

5B Eat fruit to stay healthy.

6I Think carefully before you decide to marry.

7C Whoever is paying the bill has the right to choose.

8E It's better to be sure of having a little than only the possibility of having more.

9D Enjoy yourself while you can.

10H If you put off doing a necessary job or repair, it may take longer in the end.

B 1B 2D 3E 4C 5A

C 1 mouth

2 stone

3 dogs

4 dangerous

5 No

6 Rome

7 summer

8 spots

9 dog

10 milk

D 1I Office juniors/employees/pupils don't concentrate on their work if the boss/teacher is away.

2A Look at your own faults before criticising others.

3B Don't anticipate success, because many things can go wrong and prevent you from succeeding.

4C Even a setback or disaster has some good in it for somebody.

5H You have to take some risks to make progress.

6D If you do something too fast, you may do it badly and have to do it again, which will take more time.

7F There's a little truth in every rumour.

8J A tiny extra burden/annoyance can be the final factor causing breakdown/dispute etc.

9E People of the same type usually associate with each other.

10G A job is done faster if there are a lot of helpers.

E 1 unflappable

2 well-behaved

3 without shame

4 very pale

5 tough

6 defunct

7 extremely short-sighted

8 healthy

9 hard of hearing

10 crazy

11 obvious

12 ancient

F 1 as sound as a bell

2 as red as a beetroot

3 like a bull in a china shop

4 like a fish out of water

5 as thick as two short planks

6 as thin as a rake

7 as sober as a judge

8 as stubborn as a mule

G 1G 2A 3F 4B 5D 6E 7C

H 1C 2F 3B 4G 5J 6H 7A 8D 9I 10E

Unit 66

A
1	top	8	woo
2	wed	9	cut
3	rock	10	net
4	clash	11	clear
5	axe	12	dog
6	name	13	go
7	up	14	flee

B
1 Three people have been rescued from a dangerous cliff.
2 The number of people killed in a motorway crash has gone up.
3 The Prime Minister has promised to create more jobs.
4 The police have stated that long hair is not allowed.
5 There is still no explanation why an explosion happened in a fish shop.
6 Railway workers' attempt (to improve working conditions?) is expected to fail.
7 A large amount of drugs has been discovered at Heathrow Airport.
8 The Government's position has been weakened by a recent corruption case.
9 Help is being sent to victims of an earthquake.
10 A dangerous situation is likely to arise in a coal mine.

C
1 weapons
2 negotiations
3 employment
4 ambassador
5 disappointment
6 election
7 angry outburst
8 hurried visit

Unit 67

A
1 vice versa
2 coup d'état
3 bona fide
4 curriculum vitae
5 faux pas
6 persona non grata
7 post-mortem
8 blasé
9 non sequitur
10 contretemps
11 née
12 spiel
13 ad lib
14 alibi

B 1J 2H 3G 4I 5A 6K 7B 8E 9D 10L 11F 12C

C
1 carte blanche
2 ad infinitum
3 alfresco
4 tête-à-tête
5 in camera
6 aplomb
7 kamikaze
8 quid pro quo
9 entrepreneur
10 macho
11 incognito
12 verbatim

Unit 68

A
1	common	6	coach
2	initial	7	suit
3	surgery	8	trip
4	pound	9	plot
5	very	10	degree

B
1	coach	6	trip
2	common	7	plot
3	surgery	8	initial
4	pound	9	suit
5	very	10	degree

C
1	firm	4	club
2	arms	5	spell
3	letter	6	trunk

7	file	11	like
8	bill	12	book
9	plant	13	quite
10	novel	14	sole

D
1	serve	5	show
2	carry	6	broke
3	roll	7	concern
4	take		

Unit 69

A
1	judicious	8	illegible
2	continually	9	advise
3	gaol	10	suit
4	childish	11	corpse
5	humane	12	diary
6	effect	13	moral
7	economic	14	principal

B
1	classical	7	officious
2	practical	8	credulous
3	stationary	9	troop
4	respectively	10	dessert
5	✔	11	infer
6	Loath	12	✔

C
1	pare	17	core
2	ore	18	coarse
3	gilt	19	isle
4	gamble	20	fair
5	medal	21	suite
6	wave	22	pier
7	course	23	horse
8	corps	24	canvass
9	tears	25	gambol
10	canvas	26	oar
11	meddle	27	fare
12	peer	28	tiers
13	pair	29	waive
14	guilt	30	bier
15	beer	31	hoarse
16	aisle	32	sweet

Unit 70

A
1 hurries
2 ✔
3 wholly
4 installing

5 ✓
6 ✓
7 flapping
8 ✓
9 separating
10 ✓
11 ✓
12 ruining
13 ✓
14 played
15 ✓
16 bowing
17 comfortably
18 friendly
19 ✓
20 ✓

B 1 separate
2 dependent
3 interested
4 receive
5 lose
6 developed
7 responsibility
8 advertisements
9 any more
10 definite
11 than
12 embarrassing

C 1 their   7 whether
2 been   8 which
3 ✓   9 review
4 know   10 whole
5 too   11 reigned
6 ✓   12 ✓

D Plans for a spectacular pop concert in Falmer Park, just outside Portsmouth, have been submitted to Hampshire County Council. The open-air event, featuring the singer Neil Silver and his backing group The Raiders, is planned for Wednesday 6th July and Friday 8th July, to coincide with Portsmouth Arts Festival as well as the Tour de France. The organisers, Gigs Unlimited, say the show will have a French theme to fit in with the cycle race. The proposal will be considered at a special meeting on Thursday 12th May.

Local people are divided on the issue. While some welcome the influx of visitors and the increase in trade that the concert will bring to Portsmouth, others are predicting an invasion of New Age travellers. Hampshire's Chief Constable Edward Lang-Jones is, however, confident that he has adequate manpower to deal with any disturbance that may occur.

E 1 aunt's a
2 isn't a
3 Brown's b, teachers' b
4 1920's c
5 He's a, i's c, t's c
6 James's b
7 children's b
8 Celia's b, can't a
9 Bennets' b, Joneses' b
10 Tom's b, won't a, father's b

F 1b 2b 3a 4c 5c 6a 7b 8c

Unit 71

A 1 the lion's share
2 Many hands make light work.
3 Nothing venture, nothing gain.
4 the sheep from the goats
5 ✓
6 Waste not, want not.
7 A stitch in time saves nine.
8 ✓
9 The early bird catches the worm.
10 Make hay while the sun shines.
11 a close shave
12 before they're hatched
13 blow your own trumpet
14 Birds of a feather flock together.
15 down in the mouth
16 An apple a day keeps the doctor away.
17 out of the blue
18 Every cloud has a silver lining.
19 kicked the bucket
20 ✓

B 1 alfresco
2 rapport
3 ad infinitum
4 cuisine
5 eligible
6 aplomb
7 paparazzi
8 waive
9 siesta
10 cache

C 1 suit   8 coach
2 trip   9 very
3 plot   10 degree
4 initial   11 arms
5 surgery   12 sole
6 common   13 trunk
7 pound   14 race

D 1 as white as a sheet
2 ✓
3 as mad as a hatter
4 like a fish out of water
5 as like as two peas in a pod
6 as cool as a cucumber
7 ✓
8 as strong as an ox
9 as bold as brass
10 as old as the hills
11 ✓
12 like hot cakes
13 as red as a beetroot
14 ✓

E 1 its   8 ✓
2 ✓   9 shopping
3 closing   10 of
4 days, if   11 where
5 Cambridge   12 products.
6 which   Town
7 ✓   13 ✓

14 ✓   19 points
15 for   20 and
16 definitely 21 ✓
17 their   22 weeks
18 development

Unit 72

A 1 quits   6 day
   2 tune   7 a halt
   3 mind   8 names
   4 celebration 9 bluff
   5 question

B 1 first   6 make
   2 shed   7 face
   3 travelling 8 years
   4 let   9 In
   5 come   10 set

C 1 in the heat of the moment
   2 a heated discussion
   3 blowing hot and cold
   4 piping hot
   5 take the heat off you
   6 hotting up
   7 hot under the collar
   8 get into hot water
   9 a hot potato
   10 just so much hot air
   11 hot off the press

D 1D 2A 3C 4D 5B 6A 7B 8C
   9A 10B 11D 12A 13B 14C

Unit 73

A 1 cutting edge
   2 user-friendly
   3 keyhole surgery
   4 healthcare
   5 number cruncher
   6 dotcom
   7 biodiversity
   8 raves
   9 text messages
   10 asylum seeker
   11 counsellor
   12 sell-by dates
   13 grassroots
   14 proactive
   15 name of the game

B 1 PIN (personal identification number) *This is the true acronym.*
   2 TLC (tender loving care)
   3 RSI (repetitive strain injury)
   4 OTT (over the top)
   5 aka (also known as)
   6 asap (as soon as possible)
   7 PC (politically correct)
   8 BSE (bovine spongiform encephalopathy)

C 1 camcorder
   2 biopic
   3 docusoap
   4 psychobabble
   5 sitcom
   6 heliport
   7 guesstimate
   8 telebanking

D 1 a bad hair day
   2 big time
   3 cherry-picked
   4 been there, done that
   5 gobsmacked
   6 drop-dead gorgeous
   7 to die for
   8 the full monty
   9 a couch potato
   10 vegging out

E 1J 2H 3C 4E 5B 6G 7A

Unit 74

A 1 mosquitoes
   2 pianos
   3 avocados
   4 volcanoes
   5 mottoes
   6 casinos
   7 shampoos
   8 ghettos
   9 rodeos
   10 tomatoes
   11 echoes
   12 potatoes
   13 heroes
   14 studios
   15 concertos
   16 videos
   17 kangaroos
   18 radios
   19 biros
   20 solos

B 1 leaves   12 postmen
   2 geese   13 beliefs
   3 deer   14 halves
   4 feet   15 wolves
   5 wives   16 sheep
   6 children   17 lives
   7 houses   18 lice
   8 mice   19 knives
   9 roofs   20 selves
   10 teeth
   11 hooves/ hoofs

C 1 S/P   11 S
   2 S   12 P
   3 P   13 P
   4 S   14 S
   5 S   15 S
   6 S/P   16 S
   7 S   17 S/P
   8 P   18 S
   9 S   19 S
   10 S   20 S

D 1 bunch   7 swarm
   2 flight   8 herd
   3 pack   9 pack
   4 gang   10 flock
   5 flock   11 bunch
   6 shoal   12 swarm

E 1 nuclei
   2 formulae/formulas
   3 boyfriends
   4 press-ups
   5 take-offs
   6 aquaria/aquariums
   7 brothers-in-law
   8 bonuses
   9 stimuli
   10 criteria
   11 circuses

12 cacti/cactuses
13 breadwinners
14 operas
15 diagnoses
16 viruses
17 appendices
18 larvae
19 bacteria
20 automata

F 1 heiress
2 fiancée
3 masseuse
4 nun
5 niece
6 actress
7 sculptress
8 empress
9 heroine
10 widow
11 doctor
12 manageress
13 hostess
14 barmaid
15 bride
16 aunt
17 landlady
18 cousin
19 headmistress
20 stewardess

G 1D 2C 3I 4J 5G 6A 7E 8H
9F 10B

Unit 75

A 1 unattainable
2 non-existent
3 illegitimate
4 irresistible
5 inaccessible
6 unprepared
7 unaware
8 inexpensive
9 unconscious
10 intolerant
11 unlikely
12 improbable
13 dissatisfied

14 impatient
15 uncomplicated
16 unable
17 incapable
18 unenthusiastic
19 illegible
20 irrational
21 imperfect
22 non-resident

B 1 undo
2 disapprove
3 anticlockwise
4 misunderstand
5 dis/mis/unused
6 debriefing
7 miscast
8 unwrap
9 disembark
10 decentralise
11 anticlimax
12 disprove
13 declassify
14 disincentive
15 unconfirmed
16 dismount
17 undamaged
18 uncommon
19 unemployment
20 depersonalise
21 misfire
22 anticyclone

C 1 co-worker
2 over/counterbalance
3 co-pilot
4 counterclaim
5 co-author
6 overpriced
7 counterattack
8 overestimate
9 overreact
10 co-director
11 co-operate
12 overanxious
13 counter-espionage
14 overboard
15 oversimplify

16 coeducational
17 overdue
18 overdose

D 1 outpouring
2 ex-wife
3 outlast
4 outvote
5 redirect
6 undercooked
7 reorganise
8 ex-boyfriend
9 re-elect
10 undermine
11 outsize
12 redistribute
13 underexposure
14 outstay
15 reclaim
16 reunite
17 reassure
18 underclothes
19 underachiever
20 reintegrate

E 1 hyperactive
2 amoral
3 malnutrition
4 neo-Nazi
5 malformation
6 apolitical
7 hypersensitive
8 monosyllable
9 neoclassical
10 hypercritical
11 malfunction
12 asymmetrical
13 maladjusted
14 hypermarket
15 monotone

F 1 foggy
2 helpful/helpless
3 destructive
4 friendly/friendless
5 hateful
6 childish/childless/childproof
7 tragic

8 fireproof
9 humorous/humourless
10 magical
11 homely/homeless
12 washable
13 nostalgic
14 quarrelsome
15 graceful/gracious/graceless
16 hopeful/hopeless
17 imaginative
18 reliable
19 dramatic
20 realistic

G 1 departure
2 entertainment
3 betrayal
4 piety
5 behaviour
6 attraction
7 arrival
8 emancipation
9 darkness
10 patience
11 satisfaction
12 rudeness
13 pleasure
14 maintenance
15 advertisement
16 theory
17 delivery/deliverance
18 widowhood
19 availability
20 tolerance

H 1 horrify
2 widen
3 straighten
4 realise
5 categorise
6 lengthen
7 heighten
8 intensify
9 idealise
10 shorten
11 criticise
12 redden
13 pacify

14 falsify
15 computerise

I 1 international
2 reviewed
3 disgrace
4 innocence
5 likelihood
6 irregularity/-ies
7 illegal
8 horrified
9 unbelievable
10 unacceptable
11 realise/-ize
12 succeeding

Unit 76

A 1B 2B 3B 4A 5A 6A 7B 8A
9B 10A 11B 12A 13B 14B
15B 16A 17B 18A

B 1 birthday   5 waistcoats
2 aerial   6 opinion
3 insulated   7 bench
4 crisps   8 bargain

C 1 warehouse: large shed for storing goods
department store: large shop selling clothes, furniture etc.
2 recipe: method of cooking a dish
receipt: proof of purchase
3 block: large chunk of wood, stone etc, or building containing flats or offices
notepad: paper for taking notes, attached to a piece of thick card
4 smoking: action of consuming tobacco
dinner jacket: man's evening suit
5 costume: special clothes, e.g. traditional or national costume
suit: matching two or three-piece outfit
6 congealed: having become thick or solid (of blood, fat, cold food)

frozen: below 0°C, hard and solid like ice
7 salute: give a military greeting
wave to: raise the hand in casual greeting to a friend
8 pensioners: elderly people who do not work and who receive a state pension
boarders: pupils who live at their school
9 deranged: mentally unbalanced
disturbed: confused, bothered
10 prove: show that something is true
test: try out something

D 1 fish and chips
2 women and children
3 pen and ink
4 bed and breakfast
5 bread and butter
6 dead and buried
7 rules and regulations
8 shoes and socks
9 in and out
10 pros and cons
11 rights and wrongs
12 law and order

E 1 figures   6 about
2 mortar   7 wide
3 bone   8 dry
4 fro   9 proper
5 sound   10 span

F 1 song and dance
2 wear and tear
3 pins and needles
4 chalk and cheese
5 odds and ends
6 cut and dried
7 flesh and blood
8 sick and tired
9 tooth and nail
10 head and shoulders
11 cock-and-bull
12 hard and fast

13 chop and change
14 ins and outs
15 neck and neck

Unit 77

A 1 ramble
2 wade
3 toddle
4 marched
5 limp
6 shuffled
7 stroll
8 staggered
9 tiptoe
10 plodded

B 1E 2I 3A 4H 5J 6B 7D 8F 9C 10G

C 1 whisper
2 moaning
3 express
4 snaps
5 utter
6 gossip
7 lectured
8 discussing
9 called
10 stammer

D 1 glimpse
2 peering
3 glanced
4 recognised
5 examined/scrutinised
6 peep
7 gazed/stared
8 watching
9 noticed/observed
10 spot

E 1H 2F 3D 4A 5G 6B 7E 8C

F 1 laughed off
2 Don't make me laugh
3 a laugh a minute
4 had the last laugh
5 laughing all the way to the bank
6 laughable
7 laughing up my sleeve
8 laugh on the other side of your face
9 laughed in his face
10 Don't laugh
11 no laughing matter
12 laugh her out of it

Unit 78

A 1 tow   5 wrench
2 tugged   6 lugging
3 drag   7 haul
4 jerk   8 drew

B 1F 2N 3A 4P 5G 6B 7E 8M 9L 10I 11D 12K 13O 14H 15C 16J

C 1 a concept, the nettle, at straws
2 a flower, up courage, your eyebrows
3 your fists, your teeth
4 an audience, your passport nervously, someone's imagination
5 forty winks, a bag away from an old lady
6 power, someone's imagination
7 at straws, your passport nervously
8 his long-lost brother to his heart, your passport nervously
9 the enemy soldiers, someone's imagination
10 a flower, someone's brains, your teeth

D 1 dazzled
2 glistened
3 glittering
4 glimmer
5 glare
6 flash
7 shimmered
8 flickered
9 sparkled
10 beam

E 1I 2H 3D 4F 5J 6A 7B 8E 9G 10C

F 1 glow
2 embers/ashes
3 spark
4 blaze/burn, flames/sparks
5 scorch/burn
6 scald/burn
7 steam
8 swelter/boil
9 ashes
10 smoke

G 1 drew   4 streaming
2 glow   5 flared
3 grip

Unit 79

A 1 actual   7 boss
2 bargain   8 boarder
3 bench   9 scales
4 review   10 recipes
5 notorious   11 opinions
6 imagination   12 private

B 1 buried (completely over, past)
2 dance (a fuss)
3 mortar (property, buildings)
4 cons (advantages and disadvantages)
5 blood (family)
6 bull (improbable)
7 wide (over a wide area)
8 neck (absolutely even in a race)
9 tear (damage through use)
10 ends (miscellaneous items)
11 dry (stranded, abandoned)
12 cheese (two very different things or people)
13 dried (already decided)
14 needles (prickly feeling in cramped limbs)
15 nail (fiercely, violently)

C 1C 2D 3A 4B 5D 6A 7C 8B 9B 10D

D 1 exemplified
2 childhood
3 opposition
4 remainder
5 underlying
6 relationships
7 outstanding
8 foreshadowed
9 identification
10 prestigious
11 withholding
12 unmistakeable
13 instinctively
14 universal

E 1 rough   4 struck
2 ground   5 spring
3 trunks   6 make

Unit 80

A 1b 2b 3a 4a 5b 6b 7a 8b
9b 10a

B l, i, n, f, k, m, b, o, q, d, g, c, p,
h, a, j, e

C

28 Woolston Drive
Bracknell
RG12 3JB

20th November, 2001

The Manager
Randalls Ltd
75 Tenter Park
Northampton NN4 1SW

Dear Sir or Madam,

I saw your advertisement for the PC 386SX in last week's edition of PC Direct. Please send me further details of this model, as well as other PCs you are currently offering, with prices. Please confirm that you can deliver.

Thank you for your attention. I look forward to receiving your prompt reply.

Yours faithfully,
Jerome Walsh

Unit 81

A 1C 2J 3A 4G 5D 6I 7B 8E
9F 10H

B 1 making   9 than
2 ✓   10 such
3 very   11 had
4 ✓   12 ✓
5 of   13 ✓
6 by   14 your
7 ✓   15 The
8 even

C *Model answer:*

Dear Fred,

I thought I'd drop you a line, as this is really very important, and I'm not sure you people up at St Anne's Hall understand how the man in the street feels.

Oxley Park is the best park we've got in Rugley. You can go there any afternoon, and find people walking, playing tennis, football or cricket, having an ice cream or a coffee, sailing or rowing boats, paddling canoes ... Well, you know what it's like – a wonderful place we've all grown up with, and I for one want it to be there, unspoilt, for my kids too.

Now Haslers have come along and made their bid to build luxury flats at the south end. If you agree to that, you can say goodbye to the tennis, cricket and football, secretaries sunbathing in their lunch hour, and staff from the offices sitting on benches eating their sandwiches. For Heaven's sake, that's where you and I used to run when we were training for the marathon we were misguided enough to enter! I was eighteen and you were nineteen. Seems centuries ago now.

Anyway, people are getting very steamed up about it.

Please give the whole thing a bit of thought, and get your Planning Committee to look at the application again.

Let me know what you've decided.

All the best,
Gerald Portland

Unit 82

A 1 colleague
2 mechanic
3 landlady
4 husband
5 babysitter
6 flatmate
7 postman

B *Model answers:*

1 Diana – Gone to lunch, but back by 2.30. Andrew
2 Mr Brown – Photocopier keeps jamming. Please arrange for repair a.s.a.p. Stephanie Bingham
3 Dr Forbes – Your wife rang. Please collect children from tennis club on your way home. Brenda
4 Eduardo – I borrowed this yesterday when you were out. Very sorry if you needed it. Thought you wouldn't mind! Markus
5 Mrs Booker – Your daughter rang this afternoon. Can you babysit for her on Saturday night? Charlotte

D 1 Valerie Burfield, 41 Orchard Road, Reigate, Surrey RG1 3BA
2 Dr J.B. Dodsworth, 22 Princes Avenue, Oxford OX3 7MH
3 Mrs Ann Gilliatt, 79 Court Close, London SE10 8WX
4 Major K. Hennings, 4 High Street, Lindfield, West Sussex RH16 2HQ
5 Hexham Library, Campbell Street, Hexham NE46 4RA

E *Model answers:*

1 (Dear Mr Macintosh,)

I have just realised I shall still be away on holiday next week, when my appointment with you is due. Please cancel this appointment. I'll make a new one as soon as I get back.

Best wishes,
Peter Greenaway

2 (Dear Trish,)

Do hope all is well with you and your family. Was a bit surprised at not hearing from you at Christmas. Can you ring me sometime? You could come to lunch, if it isn't too far to drive.

Love, Bettina

3 (Dear Keith and Felicity,)

Thanks so much for your kind invitation to stay. Unfortunately I'll be at a conference that weekend, so I won't be able to come. What a pity! Thanks anyway.

Have a great time!

All the best,
Roderick Marston

Unit 83

A D, G, A, C, F, B, E, I, H, J

B A 3, 8, 11
B 4, 9, 13
C 6, 12, 14
D 2, 7, 10
E 1, 5

D 1 bypass
2 Watch/Look (out) for
3 follow the signs to/for
4 pedestrian crossing
5 crossroads/junction
6 Take the left-hand turn
7 lane
8 Go on over
9 bear right
10 drive/go straight on

11 track
12 You can park

Unit 84

A 1D 2A 3E 4B 5F 6I 7J 8C 9H 10G

B E, A, G/F, C, H, D, B

Unit 85

A 1 laziness
2 intelligence
3 chubbiness
4 beauty
5 assertiveness
6 strength
7 exhaustion
8 embarrassment
9 anger
10 wrath
11 resentment
12 sorrow

D 1 as a result
2 as long as
3 as though
4 Because of
5 as soon as
6 As
7 all the same
8 Contrary to
9 Even though
10 No matter
11 Moreover
12 otherwise

Unit 86

A 1C 2F 3G 4A 5I 6B 7J 8D 9H 10E

B 1 AWAYDAYS

Will all staff please note the following:
Penny Sept 5 & 6 Holiday
Andrew Sept 19 Leave of absence
Toni Sept 25 Holiday
Julia Sept 28 Conference
Thanks – GBS 30.3.02

2 PLAYA DE FORNELLS, MENORCA

Beautifully appointed holiday apartment

Sleeps 2/4

Short walk to beach, shops and restaurants

Tel: 422066 for details

3 QUIET PLEASE

External exams in progress

Architecture students to Room 42

Classes as normal tomorrow

4 HAS ANYONE SEEN

my tan leather wallet?

It had £50, driving licence and credit card in it.
Last seen in the snack bar.

Contact Dave in Room 10, Block G.

5 CLEANERS

Please defrost fridge.

It's getting iced up.

And please don't throw away newspapers.

We need them for reference.

Thanks – Anne

C *Model answers:*

1 FOR SALE

First-year civil engineering set books.

Price negotiable.

Ring Sean on 551732 evenings.

2 LOST

Gold chain with locket, picture inside. Sentimental value. Probably Western Road area, near cinema. Reward. Please contact Janie on 771888 any time.

3 LIFT WANTED

to Manchester next weekend. Share petrol. Leaving Friday evening, back Sunday evening if possible. Ring Allen 893406.

4 HELP!

Has anyone seen my large black ring-binder with stencilled patterns on cover? Inside are my Economics notes for the year! I'm desperate.
If found, ring Eve on 257381.

5 FOURTH GIRL WANTED

to share large student house in Pembroke Crescent from September. £80 a week plus bills. Preferably non-smoker. Own room.
Ring Liz or Maggie on 993417.

6 SPANISH CONVERSATION LESSONS

offered by native postgraduate. Free most afternoons. Language exchange also a possibility. Ring Dolores on 564039 (not weekends).

D *Model answers:*

1 **Country cottage in Scotland**
Exceptionally beautiful country cottage to rent near picturesque village of Auchencairn in Galloway. Sleeps 6 (1 dbl, 2 twin). Comfortable living room with large fireplace. Big walled garden, sea views. All mod cons incl. c.h. £400 p.w. Mrs S. Halday, Bay View, Auchencairn, Galloway.

2 **Drinks machine**
No soup. Tea and coffee, 10p and 50p coins only. Machine to be repaired soon.

3 **Franking machine**
Not to be used by unauthorised personnel. Private letters may be franked, but immediate payment required, with receipt issued by receptionist.

G 1 Travel company offering free holiday for publicity or competition.

2 Music company or retail chain offering cheap/free CDs to encourage larger orders/purchases.

3 Company offering competition prize.

4 Telecommunications company promoting use of phone.

5 Company giving formal summary of its business performance to the public/its shareholders.

Unit 87

A 1C 2F 3E 4A 5B 6D

B *Possible answers:*

1 Celebrities seek publicity, so they are to blame for their loss of privacy. The public has the right to know about their lives, as the public is paying (through match tickets, film tickets, etc) for their lifestyle.

2 Privacy is everybody's right. Celebrities just happen to be famous for doing their job, so that shouldn't affect their private lives.

3 Celebrities should be realistic and accept that fame brings disadvantages as well as advantages. Every individual is entitled to a certain degree of privacy, but famous people should expect the public to be interested in their lives.

4 Paragraph 1: Introduction – short statement of the central issue
Paragraph 2: Main section – points for and against
Paragraph 3: Conclusion – summary and personal view

D *Possible answer:*

Paragraph 1 Introduction
Paragraph 2 (bad habits): m, c, i, e, g
Paragraph 3 (food): b, d, f, h, k

Paragraph 4 (stress): a, l, j
Paragraphs 2–4 may be in any order, and the order of the items within them can vary.
Paragraph 5 Conclusion

E *In spite of* the fact that many experts believe that energy consumption in developed countries should be reduced, governments are having difficulty in achieving this.

Many experts believe that energy consumption in developed countries should be reduced. *Nevertheless*, governments are having difficulty in achieving this.

Many experts believe that energy consumption in developed countries should be reduced, *yet* governments are having difficulty in achieving this.

Many experts believe that energy consumption in developed countries should be reduced. *However*, governments are having difficulty in achieving this.

Although many experts believe that energy consumption in developed countries should be reduced, governments are having difficulty in achieving this.

F 1 they are extremely expensive.

2 the service is rather impersonal.

3 his excellent qualifications.

4 he hadn't always seen eye to eye with them.

5 supplies are still readily available to addicts on the street.

6 the authorities are planning to go ahead with this.

Unit 88

A 1C 2F 3I 4B 5G 6L 7K 8J 9D 10H 11E 12A

B 1H 2E 3A 4B 5G 6D 7C 8F

Positive: 1H 2E 4B 5G
Negative: 3A 6D 7C 8F

H 1B 2D 3F 4E 5A 6C

C *Positive:* unusual, informative, brilliant, successful, fantastic, stunning, original, witty, fine, outstanding, thrilling, amazing, superb, great

Negative: boring, awful, amateurish, conventional, unimaginative, hopeless, predictable, dreadful, horrible, pathetic, dull

I 1 ✓
2 along
3 worried
4 Surely
5 there
6 potatoes
7 in, dump
8 Then
9 ✓
10 he'd
11 Where
12 alive
13 shopping
14 ✓
15 ✓
16 and Mum's
17 purposefully
18 ✓
19 Josie's

D 1 review
2 directors
3 script
4 interval
5 special effects

E 1B 2H 3J 4E 5I 6G 7C

F 1 c, a, d, b
2 b, a, d, c
3 c, a, b, d

G *Possible answers:*
1 'You'll waste away if you don't eat properly, June,' my grandmother told me crossly. 'Have some of this roast chicken.'

2 'Put a commando team on immediate standby at the airport, Colonel,' rapped out the PM briskly. 'I may order them to attack at any moment.'

3 'All right, Gordon, we'll interview the singers together, but *you* can ask them the questions. Jazz is more my sort of thing, really.'

4 'I bought it in that little boutique in the arcade,' said Jane proudly. 'Do you know, it was £10 cheaper than the one we saw the other day, and it's much nicer!'